The Barcelona Pavilion by Mies van der Rohe

THE BARCELONA PAVILION BY MIES VAN DER ROHE ONE HUNDRED TEXTS SINCE 1929

Dietrich Neumann
with David Caralt

Photographs: Hassan Bagheri

Birkhäuser
Basel

CONTENTS

INTRODUCTION

Imagine, for a moment, that Mies's German Pavilion at the 1929 International Exposition in Barcelona had never been built—a realistic proposition, by the way, as it was canceled three months before the opening due to financial reasons, its site sitting idle for several weeks. It immediately becomes obvious how differently the history of the modern movement would have unfolded without one of its key form-givers and legitimizing reference points.

While it stood unnoticed by most visitors on the exhibition grounds, many contemporary critics enthusiastically hailed the pavilion as an essential summary of the modern movement and a confident signal for its future. After the temporary exhibition, it survived only in a small number of photographs. Despite—and also because of—the brevity of its existence, the pavilion became one of modern architecture's most influential structures—an archetype whose formal vocabulary provided a central strand of Mid-Century Modern's DNA from California to postwar Germany and still commands a powerful influence today. It became also the most written-about building of the modern movement. Soon featured in every history of modern architecture, it inspired many critical essays and several monographs[1] in the following decades and became an easily ref-

erenced shorthand and argumentative tool in broader debates—albeit with an astonishing range of contexts and
implications.

This volume presents 100 selected texts about the pavilion
from 1929 to 2019. They include documents such as speeches
at the opening, excerpts from private letters, newspaper accounts and voices of critics, scholars, architects, and artists.
These writings about the same building over time provide us
with a lens onto an evolving critical landscape with different
ways of looking at architecture. As the Argentinian critic and
historian Juan Pablo Bonta put it in 1975, "An anthology of
texts about Barcelona can teach us more about changes in
architectural ideals over the last thirty-five years than a series
of exhibition buildings designed during the same period."[2]
Bonta's *Anatomy of Architectural Interpretation* (1975) is an
extraordinarily important contribution to a history of architectural methodology—according to Charles Jencks "the most
important book on architectural interpretation" of the previous decade.[3] In an attempt to understand patterns of critical
reception and canon formation, Bonta surveyed responses to
the Barcelona Pavilion from its inception to the early 1960s
and inferred a number of phases, which he assumed were ap-
plicable to other canonical buildings as well. Initial "blindness"
by critics was followed by "precanonic responses," then "official interpretations," and finally a generally agreed-upon set
of characteristics that defined a canonical position. In the case
of the pavilion these were: its new spatial quality (the "flowing
space" of its open floor plan), the preciousness of its materials,
its fine proportions and relationship to Cubism and De Stijl,
the reference to Germany's young democracy, and finally the
growing amount of praise it received.[4] This was, indeed, close
to the common textbook interpretation, which Rafael Moneo

would mock as "hackneyed" twenty-five years later: "invariably centered on spatial flow, on the presence of Neoplasticism, on the distinction between structural and merely formal elements, on the rareness and quality of the materials and so on. According to these interpretations, the Barcelona Pavilion is the paradigm of pure, abstract architecture, making the principles of modern architecture manifest with that very clarity with which Alberti's church of Sant'Andrea at Mantua once displayed the principles of Renaissance architecture."[5]

If one surveys in greater detail the period Bonta had analyzed and includes later responses, however, something more complex and unruly emerges: a continuous stream of different, often contradictory observations and opinions beyond the dominant view, some emerging at a certain point, others echoing earlier observations.

Contemporary Responses

While neither the official exhibition publications nor initial reports in Spanish and German newspapers after the opening were places for deep reflection and architectural analysis, they often provided important context.[6] Many listed the names of prominent attendees at the opening on May 27, 1929, and reprinted or paraphrased German commissioner Georg von Schnitzler's short remarks, where he had referred to the "hard times that we have gone through" and the resulting desire for simplicity, truthfulness and sincerity.[7] Since the unusual structure defied so many conventions, the confident words of an aristocratic, well-to-do businessman praising Mies's modern architecture on behalf of the German Reich carried considerable weight and guided those unsure of the pavilion's meaning. Most publications emphasized the building's simplicity and sincerity, the clarity of its lines, its asceticism, spirituality, and essentialism as a metaphor for Germany's reformed character, its young democracy with an honest desire to be a peaceful member of the family of nations after the catastrophe of the First World War. Von Schnitzler's humble words were recognized as a refreshing change of tone from the Kaiserreich's bellicose, aggressive assertions.

Architecture journals had seen explosive growth in Germany in recent years, and provided plenty of opportunities for more extended architectural criticism.[8] Just like their fellow journalists, few architecture critics could escape the lure of von Schnitzler's brilliant, if facile, link between the pavilion's qualities and the country's contemporary condition. The sheer number of reports and their often excited, even lyrical exuberance after the opening indicated that something truly extraordinary had happened in Barcelona. One senses the delight and relief over an ostensibly modern building, beautiful and self-assured, that boldly eschewed the mantras of standardization, rationalization, functionalism, and much of the established formal vocabulary of the modern movement, such as brick or white stucco walls and ribbon windows. Soon, the pavilion was hailed as the "most beautiful building at the entire exhibition,"[9] a victory for "a rebirth of the art of building,"[10] "a spatial work of art,"[11] "the manifestation of a higher spirit,"[12] even as "metaphysical architecture."[13] Numerous critics evoked musical metaphors, calling the pavilion "a pure sound from a new world,"[14] a "fugue,"[15] the "counterpoints" of modern polyphony,[16] or "music of eternal space."[17]

Critics carefully decoded the architect's work, describing spatial sequences, the structural system and surface qualities.[18] German reviewers, however, usually avoided commenting on the rich interplay of reflections in the pavilion and the illusionary effects of its semitransparent walls. German critics might have found a play with ephemeral reflections and optical illusions neither appropriate for an essential ethics of modern architecture nor a fitting association with the young German democracy. In great contrast, several foreign reviewers–unburdened by such concerns–delighted in describing the visual effects at play.[19] Catalan journalists Ángel Marsà and Luís Marsillach even called the pavilion a "palace of reflections" where "people of clear horizons" had "tamed light from above" and its freely crisscrossing rays of light were an apt metaphor for "the soul of the new Germany."[20]

The most exciting new tropes in architectural criticism in the early 1920s in Europe, however, were movement, dynamics, and spatial penetration. The ground had been prepared in the late nineteenth century by art historians such as Heinrich Wölfflin, who identified the key difference between the static Renaissance and the vibrant Italian Baroque architecture with the latter's "impression of continuous movement" and "spatial infinity."[21] Wölfflin's colleague August Schmarsow emphasized the central importance of the "kinesthetic sensations" of our spatial experience, in other words the need for the viewer to move in and around a building in order to comprehend it.[22] Wölfflin's student Paul Frankl noted in 1914 that a building can contain such "a great flood of movement that [it] urges us round and through."[23] He observed a "smooth flow of space"– the first time that this poetic metaphor was used–in English and German Baroque churches.[24] Shortly after, critics applied such dynamic terms to modern buildings as well–their planes, masses, and rooms described as if in motion–first in response to Frank Lloyd Wright's work[25] and by 1930, a "flow of space" was regularly diagnosed at the Barcelona Pavilion.[26]

What accounts for the easy transfer of such metaphors from the curved lines in church interiors by Borromini or Neumann to the straight lines of Wright or Mies? It might have helped that this vocabulary reached the mainstream just when modern architecture emerged and British astronomers found proof for Albert Einstein's theorem of gravity's impact on light's movement through space in 1919.[27] Einstein received the Nobel Prize in 1922. While the details of his work were hardly accessible to the public, it was generally understood that time and space were intricately connected, and time's "fourth dimension" complemented three-dimensional space.[28] Schmarsow's observation that spatial sequences reveal themselves through movement (which requires time), signaled to naive observers an indelible connection of space and time, and thus a demonstration of Einstein's theory.[29] It did not take long before the Barcelona Pavilion was, in all seriousness, presented as a demonstration of Einstein's theorem.[30]

Political positions apparently did not color critics' judgments in those years. A German writer like Guido Harbers, who had criticized Stuttgart's Weissenhof estate of 1927 as "anemic" and "un-German," and who eagerly join the National Socialist party in 1933, was just as enthusiastic about the pavilion as Justus Bier, a progressive Jewish critic whom the National Socialists relieved of his post as curator of modern art in Hannover in 1936.[31] Similarly, Spanish critic Francisco Marroquin, soon after a fervent supporter of General Francisco Franco, loved the pavilion as much as Nicolau Rubió Tudurí, a liberal critic and designer.[32]

Critical voices about the pavilion were rare at the time and far outnumbered by enthusiastic responses. A Stuttgart museum official found that the pavilion was merely an arrangement of "black or transparent glass panes," in fact, not "a building at all," and therefore "offensive" to the Spanish hosts.[33] Several critics feared that the pavilion might only appeal to an intellectual elite and be "absolutely incomprehensible" to the less well-briefed,[34] or similarly that a "shallow visitor" might wonder if he stood in front "of an unfinished building."[35] Such intellectual aloofness, a socialist critic noted, represented the "snobbish arrogance of the German on the intellectual world stage."[36] Others were disappointed with the building's luxurious execution, "superbly cool, precious, well-proportioned," but ultimately "dead pomp."[37] A Berlin daily paper found the pavilion "an oddity [...] original, entertaining, perhaps even practical in the southern climate, but basically not German."[38] Others similarly missed "the German spirit."[39] While some critics had praised the boldness of a modern building "without a purpose," merely "dedicated to representation, to empty space, and thus to space itself,"[40] conservative magazines happily pounced at this contradiction with the movement's much touted rationalism and functionalism: here, there was no "functional program (what are we building for?), nor can it be used for anything–as the embodiment of an abstract architectural idea (how does the New Objectivity deal with that?!)"[41] Another publication blamed progressive politics: "Whenever architecture or applied art is exhibited today it is always about radical, biased groups" and the "sick deformities in the German body politic." One should make sure that such "radical minorities" were not taken as "representative of the German people as a whole."[42] Not all members of such "radical minorities" were happy with the pavilion, either. Czech Marxist Karel Teige called it "nothing but a somewhat Wrightian architectural and sculptural flight of fancy, with its space arbitrarily subdivided by a few partition walls."[43] Mies's subsequent residential work, where he put formal elements of the Barcelona Pavilion to the test, received similar praise, but also more pronounced criticism. The Depression had hit hard in the meantime, and critics were sensitive to the urgent need for affordable housing. Mies's House for a Childless Couple at the Berlin Building Exhibition of 1931 was ridiculed by a critic as a "show-off apartment of the future."[44] Justus Bier, who had effusively praised the Barcelona Pavilion, was appalled by the "ostentation" of Mies's Tugendhat House in Brno and declared it "unlivable."[45]

Postwar Debates

Despite such occasional misgivings, the pavilion's appeal and formal language spread rapidly in the following years. The Museum of Modern Art's *Modern Architecture* show of 1932 made it well known in the US, and its imagery deeply influenced the work of Philip Johnson, Richard Neutra, Frank Lloyd Wright, Paul Rudolph, and others. In debates about the future of American architecture, critics weighed the impact of European immigrants against the homegrown modernity of Louis Sullivan, Henry Hobson Richardson, and Wright. Editor Elizabeth Gordon, for example, who considered Mies a "threat to the next America,"[46] found historian Vincent Scully's suggestion that Mies's Barcelona Pavilion had influenced some houses by the great Frank Lloyd Wright patently absurd.[47] Scully eventually gave in by stating that the concept of "flowing space" for which the pavilion was so well known had emerged much earlier in American country houses of the 1880s.[48] Historian Henry-Russell Hitchcock pulled the pavilion away from the perceived gravity fields of Neo-Plasticism and Frank Lloyd Wright to anchor it in classical antiquity. He read the "raised travertine base" as a "Greek stylobate" and saw "classical serenity" in the "exquisitely ordered" screens.[49] Perhaps inspired by Hitchcock's analysis, Mies took his first trip to Greece the following year (1959), and photographs show him contemplating the Acropolis and the ruins of Epidaurus.[50] Other critics adopted Hitchcock's approach and declared the Barcelona Pavilion "the specter of a classical temple"[51] or "a metaphor for a classical belvedere," including a reference to the "varying flute-widths of classical columns" in Mies's nickel-covered supports,[52] even recognizing it as *the* "temple" of the International Style.[53] While this reading of the pavilion continues to occasionally surface today, it had only transpired thirty years after the pavilion's inception[54] as part of a broader attempt to paint the modern movement not as a resolute break with the past, as both proponents and critics had charged, but rather as part of a long humanist and classical tradition.[55] Of course, in the case of Mies it helped that his recent American work had embraced symmetry, his columns gained gravitas, and allusions to antiquity seemed less far-fetched. Contemporary traits were projected back onto his earlier work.

The 1960s and 1970s

In any event, by 1960 there was general agreement that the Barcelona Pavilion was the "masterpiece of Mies's European career"[56] and "one of the few buildings by which the twentieth century might wish to be measured against the great ages of the past."[57] Its "absolute architecture"[58] provided "classic serenity,"[59] "harmony,"[60] and "intrinsic beauty."[61] "Mies could have died that summer," James Marston Fitch claimed, "at the age of forty-three, and his position as a world historic figure in architecture would have been secure."[62]

Modern architecture, however, faced increasing criticism at exactly that moment, and the pavilion's conventional interpretation began to be challenged. Arthur Drexler, director of the Department of Architecture and Design at MoMA, questioned the building's structural integrity, or rather the clarity of its message: the columns "announced a problem," he stated, since they were "superfluous."[63] The walls, he (wrongly) claimed, could have absorbed the load of the roof. Drexler probably knew Frank Lloyd Wright's letter to Philip Johnson of 1932 in the MoMA archive, where the American master had made exactly that argument.[64] But Drexler came to Mies's defense, explaining that there was a deliberate, didactic purpose for the columns, namely to "introduce an objective order," where "the eye could measure a space entirely subjective in its organization."[65] Drexler's argument found many followers in the following decades: the columns signified, we were told, "an interpolation, a caesura in a general space," invisible "corners of an en-suite sequence of square bays" and thus "their absent presences." The columns served as "a measured mediator of the infinite," or as "evidence of technology spiritualized, dematerialized, and annulled."[66] Of course, reading columns as didactic rather than functional happened after Mies had attached slender I-beams to the facades of the Lake Shore Drive Apartments and the Seagram Building as symbolic representations of a structural element that was invisible in its actual location. Once again, Mies's American work colored retrospective views toward his earlier approach.

Those who did not explain these structural contradictions away as a deliberate piece of Miesian pedagogy had to square such hybridity with their belief in Mies's structural purity. Sandra Honey harshly called the pavilion a "patched-up structure."[67] Robin Evans found columns next to a wall "deceitful and nonsensical." The general assumption of Mies's "sublime rationality" was a rumor, Evans concluded; Mies merely provided a "logic of appearance."[68]

Construction photographs of 1929 make clear that the columns did carry the roof structure, with the occasional minimal load at the end of a cantilever taken on by window frames or wall structure. A regular ceiling grid with columnar support was simpler and more practical than a load distribution on the irregular marble walls, and was probably introduced late when Mies and his engineer Ernst Walther faced enormous time pressure and uncertain delivery times. According to his assistant Sergius Ruegenberg, Mies was aware of the ensuing lack of clarity and at pains to make the columns as invisible as possible.[69]

Also in 1960, British architectural theorist Reyner Banham opened up an entirely new angle of interpretation, as he pointed to deliberate disharmonies in the pavilion: the stark contrast between modern (nickel and steel) and antique (marble and travertine) materials, or between Kolbe's romantic statue and its abstract environment, was akin to the provocative montages of "artistic and anti-artistic materials that runs back through Dadaism and Futurism."[70] Just like others at the time, Banham abandoned the well-rehearsed equation of the pavilion's "simplicity and clarity" with the noble goals of Weimar's young democracy. Instead, he linked it to irreverent countercultures of the 1920s. The moment was no coincidence: a renewed interest in the Dada movement had influenced the works of Robert Rauschenberg and Jasper Johns, whose style was termed "neo dada" in 1957.[71]

Banham had found a way to make Mies (or at least his most celebrated building) relevant and contemporary at a moment of waning enthusiasm both for his architecture and for the work of his epigones. Six years later, Robert Venturi published his famous plea for more *Complexity and Contradiction in Architecture*, a resounding rejection of much of classical modernism. Venturi seems to grudgingly acknowledge Mies's achievement, when he declared "flowing space" to be "the boldest contribution of orthodox modern architecture [...] used to achieve the continuity of inside and outside," particularly at the Barcelona Pavilion, where "flowing space produced an architecture of related horizontal and vertical planes" and ultimately a "continuity of space." Venturi then made a case for the opposite, stating categorically: "The essential purpose of the interiors of buildings is to enclose rather than direct space, and to separate the inside from the outside."[72]

By 1970 Charles Jencks and George Baird had examined *Meaning in Architecture* with the help of semiotics.[73] Jencks's PhD student, Juan Pablo Bonta, followed up with his abovementioned analysis of the Barcelona Pavilion's critical reception over time, and another contributor, Geoffrey Broadbent, provided a taxonomy of spatial divisions in the pavilion.[74]

Just like Venturi, Jencks had to acknowledge the Barcelona Pavilion as "the key building" of the modern movement and crucial for the transfer of modern architecture to the US. Based on "aesthetic rather than functional considerations," and a "romantic attitude toward style," as well as a rejection of functionalism and standardization, it became "characteristic of the way the modern movement was to be looked at in America for the next thirty years."[75] Jencks was a student of Banham's, and his PhD dissertation, published under the title *Modern Movements in Architecture* three years later, devoted an entire chapter to "The Problem of Mies." The Barcelona Pavilion was a rare exception, he averred, where Mies's "Platonic statements of pure form and transcendental technology are plausible and even appropriate, because the purpose and surrounding landscape provide the context for an 'ideal' solution." Everywhere else, however, Jencks saw that same "Platonic world view" had led "to an inarticulate architecture" marred by "damaging [...] technical and functional mistakes"[76] and a lack of connection to site, climate, and place. Jencks's magnum opus, *The Language of Post-Modern Architecture* (1977), consequently omitted the Barcelona Pavilion entirely, all the better to take Mies to task for his simplistic, "univalent" architecture in Chicago and New York, which he damned as "impoverished," "fetishized," and "confusing."[77]

Other new critical readings of the building, however, did emerge, in particular from politically engaged debates at Italian universities among critics such as Leonardo Benevolo, Giovanni Klaus Koenig, Renato Nicolini, and Manfredo Tafuri. The pavilion's structure, space, or materiality was of less concern here than its political and social context and the ideological aims it served. "The absolute vacuity of Miesian space would be a more fitting symbol of the artistic emptiness of Nazi Germany than of the artistically substantial Weimar Republic,"[78] Koenig stated; and Nicolini noted Mies's "impotence in the face of Nazism."[79] Manfredo Tafuri considered the pavilion an "empty stage set" where visitors wandered aimlessly and confused as in an urban labyrinth with meaningless signs—final proof that "utopia no longer resides in the city"[80] and that capitalism ultimately usurped all "meaningful cultural action."[81] Others noted Mies's "supreme indifference to dwelling"[82] and his retreat from "progressive commitment" into "the cold and timeless presence of precious materials."[83]

With his colleague Francesco Dal Co, Manfredo Tafuri had also picked up on Reyner Banham's twenty-year-old notion of the pavilion's "montage" of contrasting parts and materials of different linguistic qualities.[84] Tafuri's imprimatur gave Banham's observation new currency, and many critics gave Mies credit for the resulting complexity. For Catalan historian Josep Quetglas, this began with Mies's choice of the site behind an eight-column colonnade (since removed) as a provocative "collage,"[85] while American critic K. Michael Hays claimed that Mies's "montage of contradictory, perceptual facts" was intended to undermine our confidence in the "transcendent order of space and time"—columns were dissolved into light, polished planes of marble seemed transparent, and glass reflected like a mirror, in short the "fragmentation and distortion of the space is total."[86]

Mies's former collaborator Peter Carter had noted with regret a shift toward more complex readings in 1974 already, where a new appreciation of the "richness of the materials used in the pavilion" as well as its "transparency and reflectivity" merely produced "a fantasy of complex ambiguity," blinding critics to the pavilion's truly significant architectural values— namely its "clear distinction between structural and nonstructural elements; a free-flowing, open plan; a completely new kind of space."[87]

Twenty years later, American art historian Rosalind Krauss similarly declared herself bemused by the way Tafuri, Hays, and Evans had introduced her—via the Barcelona Pavilion—to a Mies she had not known before: "the antiformalist, anticlassical Mies," even the "politically correct," "poststructuralist," and "postmodernist Mies." Her argument was similar to Carter's: rather than the "classical logic of plan and elevation" she was now shown "a structure committed to illusionism, with every material assuming, chameleon-like, the attributes of something not itself—columns dissolving into bars of light, or glass walls becoming opaque, and marble ones appearing transparent due to their reflectivity"—in short, "a labyrinth."[88]

Postmodern Critiques

It was clearly no coincidence that critics became receptive to a more complex reading of the pavilion at the precise moment when many architects were maintaining that Mies's works were "distinguished by spatial monotony and formal poverty"[89] and turned "their backs on Miesian design in favor of postmodernism."[90] Ironically, in promoting a rival set of "contradictory" values, the same critics protected the Barcelona Pavilion from modern architecture's detractors. Likewise, when architect Robert A. M. Stern suggested in 1977 that Mies had "ornamented" the pavilion through the "richly veined, book-matched marbles, woods, polished chrome fittings, and tinted glass,"[91] he suggested that the building had exactly the visual richness missing in much of modern architecture. Not everyone was as generous in their judgment. Writing in 1982, postmodern architect Michael Graves cited the pavilion as the exact opposite of his own "figurative architecture." Modern architecture's emphasis on utility, abstraction, and machine imagery had—Graves claimed—led it to undervalue poetic form, with its rich allusions to previous architecture, to human scale, and cultural rituals. Thus, the Barcelona Pavilion "dissolved any reference to or understanding of figural void or space," producing a "feeling of alienation."[92] At the very moment when Graves was writing his critique, plans were under way to rebuild the Barcelona Pavilion, meaning his observations would soon be put to the test. Ironically, the very same critics who had, consciously or not, "postmodernized"

the pavilion by reading it as complex and contradictory, ornamented and multifaceted, had helped to prepare the
ground for this unusual undertaking. In the eyes of many, the
reincarnated Barcelona Pavilion became a truly postmodern
object.

Debating the Ethics of Reconstruction

The pavilion's reconstruction in 1986 inspired a body of writing focused on the new building's legitimacy and authenticity.
Probing these texts—undoubtedly among the most fascinating
within the literature on the pavilion's reception—one cannot
help but marvel at the richness of terms that the English language provided for this reproduction—*replica*, *clone*, *double*,
facsimile, *parable*, *maquette*, *simulacrum*, *pastiche*, *parody*,
etc.—all of them subtly revealing the allegiances of their authors.

Concerns about authenticity came in different shades: for one
group it mattered that the materials were different—stones
came from another quarry, stainless steel replaced nickel, the
colors of the new glass were less saturated, concrete stood in
for plaster-covered wood—thus, the pavilion was "a life-size
maquette."[93] Knowing about the scarcity of original plans and
drawings, one critic pointed out that "authenticity" was hardly
the issue, since "the real subject of the reconstruction is not a
building but the photograph of an artwork. The photograph
was built, rather than the building rebuilt, to affirm the belief
that architecture is an object of artistic contemplation."[94] The
three architects responsible for the reconstruction, Ignasi de
Solà-Morales, Cristian Cirici, and Fernando Ramos, who found
the rebuilding "a traumatic undertaking," were mindful of the

distance "between the original and its replica," and categorically declared their work merely an "interpretation."[95] This moved critic George Dodds to assign authorship of the new pavilion to Solà-Morales rather than Mies, but noted that, in any event, the replica did "more to obfuscate than to clarify the status of this cultural icon."[96]

Assuming that the new materials were close in character to the old ones, could the Barcelona Pavilion be considered "modern architecture's Ship of Theseus"? Lance Hosey pointed to Plutarch's famous thought experiment: if the mythical Greek king's ship was maintained and repaired so extensively over time that every board and nail had been replaced, was it still the same ship?[97] Famously, Plato and Aristotle disagreed on the answer. Plato assumed that form alone contained the essence, Aristotle insisted on the unity of form and matter. Of course, today's Barcelona Pavilion was neither the result of replacing parts over time, nor was it based on existing blueprints, but merely on a set of thirteen carefully composed photographs. Similarly inconclusive were attempts to apply philosopher Nelson Goodman's terms of *allographic* and *autographic* to the pavilion's reincarnation. In his *Languages of Art* (1968), Goodman had distinguished between singular works of art, such as a painting, sculpture, or a manuscript whose duplication would be forgery (*autographic*), and others, such as a cast, a piece of music, a play, or a dance, which were meant to be executed numerous times following a mold, score, plan, or text (*allographic*). Philosophers Maurice Lagueux and Remei Capdevila Werning both concluded that the application of Goodman's terms to the rebuilt pavilion had its limits. While at first sight the old and the new pavilions were "undoubtedly much more alike than are some interpretations of the same symphony," and thus allographic, the different materials, conditions of production and necessary additional input, ultimately suggested an autographic reading.[98]

Other critics looked to German philosopher and historian Walter Benjamin for help. Referring to Benjamin's most famous essay, "The Work of Art in the Age of Its Reproducibility" (1936), architect Dennis Dollens confirmed that "this is still an age of mechanical reproduction" and that the pavilion was an "eminently [...] reproducible work."[99] German critic Max Bächer, also responding to Benjamin, declared that the reconstruction of the new pavilion was authentic as a genuine copy–the distinction between original and copy would only be meaningful if it were a "sellable collector's piece."[100] Also echoing Benjamin, Dutch architect Rem Koolhaas regretted that "the resurrection of the pavilion destroyed its aura."[101] Benjamin had, indeed, written that in every "reproduction, *one* thing is lacking: the here and now of the work of art–its unique existence in a particular place." Without "the mark of the history to which the work has been subject"[102] it would lose its authenticity and authority. Variations on this theme abound among critics: "Without the original zeitgeist of the age that inspired it,"[103] the new pavilion was "merely a tourist attraction,"[104] devoid of its "revolutionary intent."[105] Reduced to the "aesthetic pleasure in the petrified beauty of Mies's rich, reflective materials," it became "a ruin emptied of utopian social meaning, a testament to the death of the avant-garde."[106] Catalan historian Josep Quetglas took the most extreme view: without "all the elements of the 1929 building in place," including traffic noise, the tread of gravel underfoot, the freshness of the air in Barcelona that summer, the perspectives of the visitors, their gestures and clothes, but also their astonishment at the sight of a chromium column, without all of that, "the building is not the same," he declared.[107] The author did not address the obvious counterargument that this distance from the moment of creation would also be the case if the building had simply survived—in fact it would disqualify us from passing judgment on any historic structure. And, in any event, more often than not, critics overlooked the fact that Benjamin had welcomed the loss of "authenticity" and "aura" as part of the "cathartic process" of the "liquidation of the traditional value of cultural heritage" and of "outmoded concepts, such as creativity and genius, eternal value and mystery"[108] that had helped the rise of fascism. For Benjamin, reproductions (in his case, photographs) freed the work of art from its ritualistic, exclusive context and made it available to everyone. In all likelihood, Benjamin would have welcomed the pavilion's reconstruction. While not reproduced mechanically, it certainly lacked the "aura" and "authenticity" of the original, and, thus liberated from its status as a cult object, it was available to everyone (who cared to come to Barcelona, that is) to explore, without the limits and prescriptive gaze of Sasha Stone's photographs.[109]

Countless architects and critics made their pilgrimage to re-examine, admire, sketch, and describe the building, unleashing plenty of additional interpretations and observations. Some were simply happy that they could experience the pavilion's spaces in person, in color, at different times of day and seasons. Unbothered by slight differences in the stone, glass, or metal used and only wanting to "applaud those responsible,"[110] French historian Jean-Louis Cohen found that "the opportunity of passing through the recreated space of the pavilion makes two-dimensional reproductions pale by comparison."[111] Former MoMA chief curator Barry Bergdoll similarly confessed that despite his opposition to "the idea of rebuilding something that had ceased to exist" he was emotionally touched by the experience.[112] Many others agreed that the reconstruction allowed them to convincingly experience Mies's design or to discover differences from what they had expected.[113] British architect Alison Smithson, for example, found the pavilion "one-third larger" than she thought, and the vast travertine expanse impressed her as "some sort of desert," suggesting Saint Jerome's hermitage in Syria, complemented by the pavilion's covered part, "his study." While she had been critical of the reconstruction as such, this reading helped her to accept "the Barcelona Pavilion as myth, an inheritance, by osmosis, of this western idyll."[114] German historian Wolf Tegethoff, who had provided the most matter-of-fact account of the pavilion's genesis in 1981, was inspired by his visit to ponder the question if Mies hadn't "intended the whole arrangement as a kind of allegory" of the Holy Grail.[115] Paul Rudolph, who had long preferred Wright over Mies, had a veritable epiphany: contrary to his expectations, the building was "one of the great works of art of all time," even "religious in nature," and overwhelmingly complex. He praised the "essential fluidity" of its spaces, the "reflections and refractions in the marble and glass," which for him augmented and embellished the "spatial organization," explaining "the mystery of the whole."[116] Similarly, British critic Robin Evans considered the reflections in the pavilion a central key for its understanding. While Tafuri, Quetglas, and Hays had read them as Mies's attempt to "fragment" and "distort" the "continuous surface of reality,"[117] for Evans they "created coherence" as they smuggled symmetries back into Mies's work (which he had officially abandoned when joining the avant-garde)—as if through a "veritable Trojan horse."[118]

Some of the selected texts by architects in this volume—be they Peter Eisenman, Toyo Ito, or Rem Koolhaas—make more sense when seen through the lens of their current preoccupation and building projects. Thus, a column might convincingly represent to them a sign rather than a symbol,[119] the pavilion's flowing space look as heavy as "molten liquid"[120] or the pavilion seem misused as a souvenir shop.[121] Frank Gehry misread (also somewhat self-servingly) the intersection between column and ceiling at the pavilion as merely a formal, not a structural solution. "It's so beautiful, this thin column hitting a roof that's just six or eight inches thick. But then you look at the drawings and you realize that it's not even a structural connection, it's just two things touching! And you start to understand all the structural gymnastics Mies had to go through to make that building look honest."[122] Gehry's own architecture, long devoid of any semblance of structural rationalism, was thus given additional pedigree.

Reception Histories

Perhaps the most common thread among critics' diverse responses, and one of architectural history's perpetual weaknesses, is the writers' neglect of the complexities of architectural production. This has led to frequent overestimating of an architect's agency and facilitated hagiographic impulses. Critics routinely assign to an architect the same artistic freedom and control over the final result as one might expect from a painter or writer. Unfamiliar with the realities in a planning office and typical structural, financial, and political constraints, writers generally have a hard time imagining and allowing for compromises, responses to limitations, and also human errors, indecision, and changes of mind—even if much evidence (and all our experience of how life usually unfolds) suggests otherwise.[123] Instead, a building's hidden "meaning" is freshly deciphered, read from its overall layout to its minutest details as the result of such agency and vision, and interpreted anew by each scholar, like readings of the Gospel. This strangely self-indulgent habit usually comes hand in hand with a lack of curiosity regarding the historical record in the archives. One cannot help thinking of Werner Hegemann, the German critic and Mies's contemporary, who noted sarcastically in 1925 (vis-à-vis his colleagues fawning over Wright and others): "the inability to differentiate between religion and architecture is quite common among architecture professors."[124]

Given the prevalence of reception histories and theory in other disciplines, it is surprising that they remain so rare in architecture.[125] Architectural historians (like literary critics, as Paul de Man noted) have typically preferred an "essentialist" approach, namely "studies of the production or of the structure [...] at the expense of the individual or collective patterns of understanding that issue from their reading and evolve in time."[126] As Naomi Stead and Cristina Garduño stated, "architectural history has tended to concentrate more on the production of buildings than their reception, and scholarship has frequently focused on the author and the work, rather than the reader and the 'text.' Buildings have been approached in terms of their patrons, clients, architectural authors, and design concepts before and during construction; once completed, the issue of their relation to society, or to the people who use them, receives less recognition. Given the power of the architectural canon, there is considerable attention to lineage and genealogical influence—that is, the way in which one architect's work and ideas carry through into the work of others. But this is rarely framed in relation to reception in the full sense."[127]

Sarah Williams Goldhagen noted in 2005 that critics of the rebuilt Barcelona Pavilion had all seen and described the same forms, but differed greatly "in their interpretation of the cultural, political, and social project that Mies meant to convey in the forms he chose and the way he composed them. [...] The battleground, then," she concluded, "is not over what these authors see at the Barcelona Pavilion, but over what they read into the forms that they see."[128] Similarly, the architect Rafael Moneo called the pavilion "a necessary emptiness, an inevitable reflection," a mirror or kaleidoscope "in which the viewer, the interpreter, the critic, is the new protagonist."[129]

Such results reflect the typical experience of reception histories in other fields. Historian Elliott Gorn, for example, found himself "deeply humbled" after he had completed a survey of scholarly writings on the American Civil War: "After much impressive marshaling of evidence and even occasionally fine prose by generations of talented scholars, your head spins with contradictions. [...] Historiography teaches us that all interpretation is limited by the cultural biases of our times, the skills of the individual historian, the limits of primary sources, the perspectives and blindnesses created by a scholar's social position."[130] Or, as Henry James observed, history "is never, in any rich sense, the immediate crudity of what 'happens,' but the finer complexity of what we read into it and think of in connection with it."[131] This, it seems, is one of the oldest observations about judgment in the arts and humanities. *"Pro captu lectoris habent sua fata libelli"* (books' destinies depend on the minds of their readers) was how the Roman author Terentian Maurus put it in ca. 200 AD. Even older is the wonderful parable that first appears in the Sanskrit *Rigveda* text (1500 BC.), and tells the story of a group of blind men who come across an elephant for the first time and try to figure out its shape by touching it. Since everyone touches a different part and deducts its overall appearance from this limited experience, their descriptions vary wildly.

But still, even if we agree that works of art or architecture (or historical events) might elicit a wide range of different interpretations over time and reflect the position and predilections of the critic, is there no way to distinguish good from bad interpretations, more plausible from less plausible ones? That is exactly the question that the abovementioned American philosopher Nelson Goodman tried to answer with his essay "How Buildings Mean" (1985),[132] published, probably not coincidentally, at a time when structuralism, postmodernism, and deconstruction had given critics unprecedented interpretative license. It was also the year when the reconstruction of the Barcelona Pavilion was nearing completion, inviting new rounds of critical scrutiny. In this context, Goodman asked: "Does a work mean just whatever anyone says it means, or is there a difference between right and wrong statements?" He conceded, "a work of art typically means in varied and contrasting and shifting ways and is open to many equally good and enlightening interpretations." Those interpretations, he explained, usually occupy a middle ground between extremes. One view holds that there is only one correct interpretation, which coincides with the artist's intentions (which often are not known to the critic—as in the case of the notoriously taciturn Mies). "At the opposite extreme from such absolutism is a radical relativism that takes any interpretation to be as right or wrong as any other." Between these two extremes, Goodman positioned his "constructive relativism," recognizing that some interpretations of a work are better than others. Of course, both the detailed historical record and an understanding of how buildings come about can help to distinguish between more and less plausible arguments. And even seemingly far-fetched interpretations provide important insights into critical approaches at particular moments in time. They reveal, with seismographic precision, contemporary upheavals in the critical landscape—while the conventional textbook narrative, which Juan Pablo Bonta had identified in 1975, has of course, continued. Nine decades of critical writings present an exhilarating variety of different viewpoints over time and record the continuing fluidity and uncertainties in our knowledge and understanding of the modern movement.

1929

GEORG VON SCHNITZLER
Remarks at the Opening of the German Pavilion

Your Majesties, Your Royal Highnesses, Ladies and Gentlemen: Allow me, first of all, to express my deepest gratitude for your presence at this festive ceremony in order to hand over the representational German pavilion to the Directorate of the International Exposition in Barcelona. Allow me to also warmly thank the city of Barcelona and the Exposition management for their generous gesture of friendship as they offered us the space needed for the German pavilion and to present the products of German industry in the exhibition palaces. It was our purpose and desire to present here a sample of German industrial diligence, in accordance with the grandeur of the local context and represent the export goods Germany can offer in exchange for the products of Spain. Our strength has not yet reached its full potential. This undertaking also had to struggle with the difficult economic circumstances that currently affect Germany. There are several industries which, following their desires and sympathies, had wanted to be part of this event, but, due to circumstances, had to abandon the idea; also the entire installation and decoration of the German sections had to be confined to more modest means than what a richer country than Germany could have offered. It is our mission to show in this simple framework examples of essential products exported from Germany, and to display them in such a way as to produce an overall impression and give a detailed idea of the structure of our economy in its thinking and activity. You can find the most visible expression of this mission in this pavilion, designed by the architect Mies van der Rohe, one of the most outstanding and original architects of the new generation in Germany. In a country less favored by the sun than this beautiful land of Spain, where the winter is long and dark, and the sky is almost always full of clouds, a new spirit of light and clarity has emerged, and can be reflected as much as natural conditions permit. We reject anything that is labyrinthine, obscure, over-wrought, and numbing, we want to think and act clearly, and we want to surround ourselves with things that are clear and straight. The utmost simplicity has to be accompanied by the deepest profundity. The hard times that we have gone through have led us to consider simplicity as essential, and to reject anything that is not precise as superfluous. To be able to show such simple forms under the blue sky of your Medi-terranean country, amid its natural beauty, has emboldened us. Perhaps everything we show here produces an impression of exaggerated simplicity and involuntary asceticism, but we would not have been honest if we tried to present ourselves here differently from how we see things at home. Our pro-gram seems to be lacking a theme, but please consider it the expression of our desire to be absolutely truthful, giving ex-pression to the spirit of the new era, whose theme is this: sin-cerity.

Georg von Schnitzler, typescript without title (1929), private archive. This text corresponds to a Spanish translation that appeared in "Inauguracíon del Pabellón y Sección de Alemania," *Diario Oficial de la Exposición Internacional Barcelona 1929*, no. 12 (June 2, 1929): 4.

GEORG VON SCHNITZLER
Opening Remarks, German Week

For the second time during this exhibition the doors of the German pavilion open for a ceremony. When it was publicly inaugurated on May 27, in the presence of the king, there had been weeks of intense work day and night by everyone involved, in order to present—on time—a visible result of our efforts. The king, who had been watching the progress of our work, magnanimously showed his satisfaction at all that our activity had produced in a very short time here and in the many German sections.

Today we look at the finished work and we can now consider its meaning—after we had earlier merely been able to show the idea of what we wanted to realize. Given the existing premises, and following the example of other great nations, Germany also had to distribute all the products we wanted to show among many different palaces. Assembling them all in one building would have exceeded the funds even of financially stronger nations than Germany. In our representative pavilion, then, we wanted to provide a synthesis of the overall approach to production which each industry will present in their respective sections.

Consider, then, this pavilion as a spiritual demonstration of our serious efforts to contribute to the world economy and as a bridge to new forms in the decorative art of space. You can begin your visit at this pavilion. It might be better, however, to consider seeing it after you have visited the different German sections. You will then find again, in an abstract fashion, what is demonstrated in examples in each of the exhibits.

Today is the beginning of our German Week, a celebration of the German community here, just as we had acknowledged German work on the day of the opening. Our meetings are inspired by the desire for reforms and new ideas, both inside and out. Our thanks go, first of all, to our friends in Spain, whose hospitality has provided us with the space to show our work, and whose efficacious sympathy has inspired us to celebrate a German Week on Spanish soil.

"Barcelona i l'Exposición 1929: La Setmana Alemanya: Inauguració Oficial de la Setmana al Pavelló Alemany." *La Publicitat,* October 20, 1929.

Georg August Eduard von Schnitzler (1884–1962), a high-ranking manager in the chemical industry, was the General Commissioner of the German representation at the Barcelona International Exposition. Together with his wife, Lilly, he was instrumental in hiring Mies van der Rohe and Lilly Reich to oversee the design and construction of all German sections and in particular the German pavilion. Von Schnitzler was also instrumental in framing the narrative about the pavilion's purpose and meaning at his short speech at the opening. Von Schnitzler gave his second speech at the pavilion at the opening of German week on October 19, 1929 in front of a larger crowd of visitors, several dignitaries and the military band of the battle ship Königsberg which had travelled to Barcelona for the occasion.

The pavilion had been completed in the meantime (at its official opening on May 27, the small office on its southern end had not been finished, the luminous wall did not yet function, the red curtain had not been delivered and the word Alemania had not yet been applied on the outside), and a number of positive critiques had appeared in the meantime. Von Schnitzler now declared the pavilion the centerpiece, even the summary of Germany's presentations.

1929

KING ALFONSO XIII
Remarks at the Opening of the German Pavilion

I greatly appreciate the kind words we just heard from the Commissioner General of Germany in this exhibition. And now I must express how very pleasantly impressed I am to see this pavilion completely finished, because if I was not convinced of the industriousness of the German people, I would have thought that only a miracle would have been able to accomplish what we are seeing here. When, during my visits to the exhibition over the last weeks and days, I passed by the site and looked at the work on your pavilion and saw the laborers at work, I could not fathom how it could be done in time for the planned inauguration. But as you know, the miracle has happened. For this, I congratulate you.

"Inauguración del pabellón y sección de Alemania," *Diario Oficial de la Exposición Internacional Barcelona 1929*, no. 12 (June 2, 1929): 4.

Alfonso XIII (1886-1941) was king of Spain until the proclamation of the Second Republic in 1931, when he went into exile to Italy. Though not known to be interested in cultural issues, he was apparently a spontaneous and witty conversationalist. According to Lilly von Schnitzler, at the opening he deviated from the official text and joked that the Germans he delayed finishing the pavilion on purpose in order to show the world how much they could accomplish in one week.[1]

1 Lilly von Schnitzler, «Weltausstellung Barcelona», in: *Der Querschnitt*, Jg. 9, Nr. 8, August 1929, S. 582–584, quote: S. 584. (See text p. 64–65)

PAUL JOSEPH CREMERS
Germany at the Barcelona Word's Fair

Barcelona was literally attacked by a barrage of French culture, which the Spaniards found a bit intrusive and unelegant, perhaps with the exception of the pretty models. The strangest fact comes last: Mr. Citroën[1] himself paid an enormous multimillion-dollar amount which made this week possible. It is certainly not irrelevant to mention this, since in Germany we have had debates in the Reichstag about the question if the amount of a little more than one million Reichsmark for the participation in Barcelona wasn't too much. Of course, the discerning mind of our parliamentarians managed to reduce the amount to 500,000 Reichsmark, while dozens of German cities pay annual subventions to their theatres of 1.5 million Reichsmark without thinking twice about it. The German participation in Barcelona cannot be mastered for less than 1.25 million Reichsmark. In the end, industries and some other source (which will not be hard to guess) will find the money. But we have to emphasize how inconceivable it is that the government and industries have, either through their criticism or lack of interest, delayed the work of the German representation by several weeks, and have also limited the German achievement to just about the barely possible.

Mies van der Rohe, known as one of the leaders of the new architecture, was commissioned to build the pavilion and to design the interiors. The German pavilion, a low building clad in travertine and Greek marble, is in its form and volume a balanced and noble composition, whose style is dominated by the sequence of covered space, interior court, and garden. Simplicity and dignity of the German approach to the exhibition were displayed here most fortuitously. In the German sections of the individual exhibition palaces, Mies van der Rohe's work sometimes appeared almost revolutionary. Wherever possible, he calmly knocked off occasional ornamental consoles and capitals from concrete columns[2] and strived for the sleek and striking planes that we prefer for exhibition architecture in Germany.

[...] At the moment, where the German sections are about to be finished, Spain still shows almost uninhabited exhibition palaces and other nations present mostly empty halls. Perhaps Spain will be able to show what it has planned in one or two months. Only two Spanish sections are complete which one can call the sensations of the world's fair: the National Palace and the Spanish Village.

Dr. Paul Joseph Cremers, "Deutschland auf der Weltaustellung Barcelona," *Rheinisch-Westfälische Zeitung*, May 28, 1929.

Paul Joseph Cremers (1897-1941) was a German journalist and writer. From 1922 to 1937 he regularly wrote for the culture section of the *Rheinisch-Westfälische Zeitung* in Essen, Germany. In 1928 he had published a major biography of the architect Peter Behrens. Several books on lesser-known local architects followed. He also wrote a number of historical plays during the Third Reich, and was engaged in National Socialist politics. The *Rheinisch-Westfälische Zeitung* was the premier daily paper in the industrialized Ruhr area, the home of many of the exhibiting industries— among them Mies's clients the silk producers Josef Esters and Hermann Lange in Krefeld, who had both come to Barcelona just before the opening.[3]

1 The French car manufacturer André Gustave Citroën (1878–1935) was Commissioner General of the French section at the exhibition.

2 There is no indication that Mies and his collaborators made any permanent alterations to the structure of the exhibition halls.

3 "Internationale Arbeiten der Seidenindustrie: Tagung auf der Weltausstellung in Barcelona," *Industrie- und Handelszeitung* (May 26, 1929).

1929

ANONYMOUS (*LEIPZIGER NEUESTE NACHRICHTEN*)
The German Pavilion in Barcelona: Inauguration of the German Section

(From our correspondent in Madrid.)

"Stop! That's eight pesetas, please." A jolt and the car comes to a stop. "Eight pesetas? Again? For what?" It is the admission fee to the exhibition grounds for cars. Five, six uniformed civil guards surround the vehicle. Only after the yellow receipt has been issued can the car continue its journey. But, we were invited to an official event, the inauguration of the German section at the exhibition! Never mind. First you pay, then you inaugurate.

If only everything else at the exhibition were just as well organized as this toll booth! Unwittingly, one considers this as the car approaches the German pavilion. And then one remembers that all entrance fees at the exhibition, in their entirety, have been taken over by a society, which paid a lump sum to the Spanish government or the city of Barcelona, and whose president is a supposedly well-known Catalan who used to be very much against Primo, but has now been given a golden handshake for his silence. So, the dictator isn't such a bad politician after all, and he knows his people. The family of another influential man, who also hadn't been a friend of

Primo's, apparently received the exclusive rights for photography at the exhibition. And thus, suddenly we have an explanation why photography is strictly prohibited and the illustrated journals of the world have such meager access to images. But people talk so much ... and we have just reached our destination.

Surrounded by trees and bushes, the flat building of the German pavilion at the Barcelona International Exposition radiates a festive glow in the morning sun. Only a few of those who have been invited to the opening celebration have appeared, and so we can assess once more the serious, dignified language of its yellow and gray marble, the large glass walls, the black marble tables and the snow-white leather upholstery. Everything is grand, simple, and straightforward; nothing distracts the gaze or thought. The hand of a master has created it, made it the fitting expression of our time and its spirit. Thus, this pavilion can be dedicated to representation in the word's truest sense, while unfortunately many of the German stands inside the international exhibition pavilions are far from ready. Oh you Reichstag committee! You suddenly did not want to approve any more funds for the Barcelona exhibition, and now the delay comes back to haunt you. Even the marble pavilion had to be finished with the help of a loan—but it looks splendid now, as if nothing had ever happened.

How the halls have filled up in the meantime! Two hundred, three hundred guests, Spaniards and Germans mixed together. In front of the great glass wall at the entrance there is Primo de Rivera, of course surrounded by plenty of beautiful ladies, and he has the production process of the glass walls explained to him. Directly behind him, Don José Vanguas, the president of the Spanish National Assembly, deep in thought, considers the expanse of marble; the Duke of Alba lovingly caresses the nickel frames of the walls with his fingers. Or does that only look like nickel? Now the crowd falls silent, as the royal family appears at the entrance stairs. King Alfonso smiles as he greets the crowd, Queen Victoria Eugenia waves her hand lightly here and there, and Don Jaime, the king's second son, and his two charming sisters clearly feel at home right away among so many familiar faces. The royal couple signs the leather guest book of the exhibition and then, standing, with Primo de Rivera to the right of the king, and the German ambassador, Count von Welczeck, on the left of the queen, listens to the opening remarks of the German commissioner Dr. von Schnitzler, who speaks first in Spanish and then in German of the German willingness to contribute to the exhibition, of the dire German economy, which even limits our resources for foreign exhibitions, and finally of the overall meaning of the marble pavilion and the German parts of the exhibition: they want to present simplicity, sobriety, and clarity as essential German characteristics.

King Alfonso expresses his thanks, not just with a gaze or a handshake, nor through the words of the dictator, but, unexpectedly, the emperor shares his own impressions by giving ample credit to the German rise after bitter misery and to the forceful dedication of the German industry. The king speaks calmly and steadily; he does not offer empty formulas but rather personal words of empathy.

The German pavilion as a work of art is the subject of unmitigated admiration of the royal family. The great interest in Germany's representation in Barcelona seems to grow even further, as the royal family listens attentively in the chemical section to the explanation of how artificial diamonds are produced, as King Alfonso has motors, machines, and models

taken apart and demonstrated to him in the machinery exhibit, and as he studies the models of airplanes, in particular the
flying restaurant car, in the transportation section. Among the
models of a suspended tram system and a hydroelectric dam
he recognizes copies of structures in Spain that he himself
once inaugurated. He takes a seat in a giant omnibus in order
to examine the level of comfort for travelers, and, finally, in
the special pavilion of the German electricity producers he
discusses the drawings and details of a giant management
operation. The opening visit lasts more than two hours and it
was certainly not just politeness when the king expressed his
deep satisfaction with the German achievements when he
said farewell to the German commissioner and the German
ambassador.

Primo de Rivera also expressed a lively interest in Germany's
striving to regain its previous level of achievements. At the
festive dinner on the evening of the opening day, he announced, after the German ambassador had read President
von Hindenburg's telegram expressing gratitude to King Alfonso, how happy he was to join in the ensuing applause, as
he also admired the president of the German Reich. The dictator, too, spoke spontaneously and warmly, inspired by the
mood of the moment, and praised in particular the work of
the German ambassador in Spain. The openness and cordial-
ity of all these Spanish words, including those of the exposition director, the Marqués de Foronda, about his extraordinarily pleasant collaboration with the German Commissioner
von Schnitzler, and the German women whose blue eyes reflected the Spanish sky, let the German delegation forget its
many misgivings of the last days. They even gave rise to the
hope that the beautiful events of the opening celebration
would after all lead to something like political results for Ger-

many in the important weeks to come. Let's hope so anyway; meanwhile we are nervous about the fact that Barcelona's newspapers haven't done anything beyond merely reporting about the German festivities.

"Der deutsche Pavillon in Barcelona: Einweihung der deutschen Abteilung," *Leipziger Neueste Nachrichten, June 1, 1929,* 5.

The *Leipziger Neueste Nachrichten und Handels-Zeitung* was founded in 1892 and continuously appeared until 1945, when its publishing house was destroyed during the Second World War. The conservative paper had the most modern printing machines in Europe and appeared daily in a print run of over 150,000, which made it the biggest German daily paper outside of Berlin.[1]

1   A shortened version of this article appeared three days later in the *Münchner Neuesten Nachrichten.* This version contained neither the reference to Primo's purchasing of political goodwill among Barcelona businessmen, nor the Marqués de Foronda's praise of the women in the German delegation, "whose blue eyes reflected the Spanish sky"—a thinly veiled reference to the blue-eyed Lilly von Schnitzler, who had developed an intense friendship with the Marqués. "Der deutsche Pavillon in Barcelona: Die feierliche Eröffnung," *Münchner Neueste Nachrichten,* June 4, 1929.

1929

LUDWIG MIES VAN DER ROHE
Excerpt from an interview

Life has changed in the last few years. Today we live different-ly, and what satisfied us yesterday leaves us indifferent today. We have other needs and it is logical for architecture to change as the way we live also changes.

Life today demands simplicity and brevity. The complications of the past no longer have reasons to exist. It is therefore nat-ural that our buildings, our furniture, the interior of our homes respond to this new way of life, which becomes apparent more and more every day.

The danger of this new kind of architecture is the possible elimination of artistic taste. Modern architecture, so thor-oughly accepted in Germany, tends to combine art and sim-plicity. There can and should be art in the new architecture. Using true and simple lines and smooth planes, one can solve the problem of architecture without compromising its aes-thetic. For that we have to employ rich materials. Marble in different colors, bronze and glass are obligatory elements of the modern style.

When I constructed the German pavilion at the international exhibition in Barcelona, I was given complete freedom. Only then can an architect carry out his work.

The furniture complements, in my opinion, the architecture. I have designed a new type of furniture made from materials not previously used. The results are very comfortable and resonate with the building.

"El arquitecto Van der Roch creador del Pabellón de Alemania," *Diario Oficial de la Exposición Internacional Barcelona 1929*, no. 12 (June 2, 1929), 25.

In this interview at the opening, Mies was unusually candid about the formal and material appeal of modern architecture, a decisive change from his earlier claims about form being merely the result, not the goal, of his work. The article notes that Mies spoke with confidence and was probably unaware that he was talking to a reporter.

1929

HEINRICH SIMON
World's Fair 1929: German Section I

It is by no means chauvinism that has placed this section at the beginning of our report. While the French departments inside the exhibition palaces had opened earlier, the unfinished state of their exhibits had to be hidden carefully behind screens. In contrast, the Germans were truly finished. Our cabled report had already mentioned that, next to the German commissioner Dr. von Schnitzler and his office, it is mainly the architect Mies van der Rohe who deserves credit for this. Anyone who had seen the degree of incompleteness of both the German pavilion and the German sections in the individual exhibition palaces on the day of the general opening will understand the widespread astonishment that they were entirely finished, minus a few minor details, just eight days later. Besides those already mentioned we have to heap praise on several others, in particular on Mrs. Lilly Reich, who had the artistic supervision of all the German sections—we will talk more about her work when we cover the textile palace—and the other collaborators of Mies van der Rohe, engineer [Ernst] Walther and architect [Sergius] Ruegenberg, and in particular the German and Spanish craftsmen. It was an example of true and immediate international collaboration, accomplishing something together in record time: twenty-four-hour workdays were accepted as entirely normal. There was one goal for all: to be ready on the announced day! [...] The German pavilion only serves representative purposes—as do similar buildings for other nations. They are, in a way, the calling card which each nation presents to the Spanish people.

[...]

The unified lettering is entirely convincing: large black Antiqua letters on a white wall, or, if a company's exhibition stand is at the center of a space, the lettering runs between two wires, thus hovering in midair. In all German sections one finds the same Miesian chairs: instead of wood, curved steel tubes, corresponding with the tubes surrounding the individual stands, and black caning for seats and backrests. In the pavilion they are very elegant, with white leather. One sits well on them, just well enough for short moments of rest during an exhibition. Anything more comfortable would be dangerous!

Now let us talk about the German pavilion itself. It is a true statement: At the press gathering, its builder spoke about a "spiritual demonstration." But it is far from the usual representative architecture that is commonly offered at these occasions in most European countries. Next to the heavily ornamented design of these areas, it could have seemed ascetic and sober, if its material wasn't so precious (beautiful yellow, white travertine, and moss-green marble), and if the building weren't surrounded by lavish plantings (which tone down its severity). It consists of two space formations: an uncovered room, open to the front, enclosed on two sides by a wall, in which you sit on marble benches at the edge of a large water basin, offering coolness. Above the wall you see green leaves and colorful flowers. The fourth, perpendicular side provides the transition to a second space formation, whose walls are built partially from marble and partially from colorful or matte (luminous) glass. It is covered by a flat roof, and inside divided by two additional walls, relieving the space of its limitations, creating paths from spaces almost as if in an orchard. There is another small pool, at the axis parallel to the great basin, surrounded by a high wall, open to the sky. In it, a magnificent stone figure by Georg Kolbe, a *Venus Anadyomene* of 1927, emerges upward, as it were, from the ocean's depth.

Mies van der Rohe is not unknown in Germany. He is rightly considered one of the most talented among the younger generation of architects. He has taste, a fine sense of proportions and color. Of course, he has a theory—you have to have one nowadays—but it isn't gray: in this case it is enchantingly realized from green, yellow, glass, water, flowers, and the Spanish sky.

How will such radicalism impress the inhabitants of this country? We will have to wait and see. The first responses were almost enthusiastic. In any event, the contrast to everything else seemed sensational. The limitations of the means available certainly suggested striving for results through originality and progressiveness. Since such progress was not established through radicalism at all cost, but presented in such tasteful and expensive garb, the ultimate success will surely follow, at least among those souls among the Spaniards and other visitors open to contemporary tendencies.

And, besides, if this pavilion, based as it is entirely on the horizontal line, will succeed in distracting the architects of this country a bit from the verticalism of the skyscraper, which, under the influence of South American taste—or rather lack thereof—threatens to destroy the regularity even of multistory cityscapes in Spain (and in Madrid it has already destroyed it), then a positive effect, even if unintended, would have been achieved.

Heinrich Simon, "Weltausstellung 1929: Deutsche Abteilung I," *Frankfurter Zeitung,* June 5, 1929, 1.

Heinrich Simon (1880–1941) was for many years the editor-in-chief of the *Frankfurter Zeitung*, one of the most distinguished daily papers of the Weimar Republic. It had a print run of about 80,000 and counted Walter Benjamin, Siegfried Kracauer, Theodor Adorno, and Ernst Bloch among its contributors. Simon was a close friend of Lilly and Georg von Schnitzler and, according to Lilly, a frequent guest at their Frankfurt home. Simon's five-part report on the German participation at the Barcelona International Exposition in the *Frankfurter Zeitung* in June 1929 was republished shortly afterward as a separate booklet. It was the most extensive report about the fair in any German publication—and clearly supportive, while elegantly skirting several sensitive issues surrounding the German representation, such as its lack of completion and the pavilion's emptiness. A few months after the appearance of Simon's long testament of praise, Georg von Schnitzler's employer, IG Farben, secretly began funding the *Frankfurter Zeitung*, which had gotten into financial difficulties during the Great Depression. Simon, who was Jewish, left Germany in 1934, emigrated to Palestine, and later to the US. He was murdered in an attempted robbery in Washington, DC, in 1941.

1929

EDUARD FOERTSCH
Germany in Barcelona

The German exhibitors are the only ones who present themselves in truly modern garb. The Reich's finances were used to cover the overall establishment of the German exhibits, which are spread over eight exhibition halls and cover 16,000 square meters. As different as the exhibited objects are, the same approach has been maintained everywhere: simplicity, clarity, good taste, omission of anything that is not essential or necessary. The lowering of the light, executed generally via a canvas ceiling, was a very good idea.

The official representation of the German Reich (general commissioner: Dr. von Schnitzler, artistic director: Lilly Reich) deserves credit for the fact that the German sections, notwithstanding their particular purpose, represent both a cultural and spiritual accomplishment. In the German pavilion this becomes particularly apparent; it is a purely representative building, which, being hardly useful for any practical purposes, is intended merely as a spiritual demonstration. This marble and glass building (architect: Mies van der Rohe) is completely incomprehensible to an innocuous visitor, but a true experience for someone sensitive to modern artistic manifestations. The material emptiness of the space is filled with the harmony of its colors and forms. The view through the green glass wall onto the water basin, where Kolbe's *Bath-er* stands, is of sublime calm and uplifting silence. It is, indeed, a refuge for anyone who feels burdened by the crazy commotion and loud noise of the buildings, towers, and fountains that crowd in on one another near the entrance of the exhibition.

Eduard Foertsch, "Die Weltausstellung in Barcelona," *Vossische Zeitung*, June 11, 1929, 4.

Eduard Foertsch (1890–1973) was a journalist and writer who translated the works of the bestselling German author Erich Maria Remarque into Spanish (most famously *All Quiet on the Western Front*, which had first appeared in serialized form in the *Vossische Zeitung*). His numerous contacts in Spain make it likely that Foertsch saw the exhibition with his own eyes. The present selection represents the central section of Foertsch's text, which continues with an enthusiastic description of the Poble Espanyol (Spanish Village). The *Vossische Zeitung* was a Berlin-based liberal bourgeois paper of national importance. Before it was closed down by the National Socialists in 1934, it had continuously appeared since the mid-eighteenth century.

1929

JOSEP MARIA DE SAGARRA
Marble and Crystal

On the margins of the nocturnal pyrotechnics of the exhibition, I have seen the silent rectangles of the German pavilion. This pavilion has to be experienced in low light, which is why the night is perhaps the most recommendable hour for the visitor who wants to extract the most delicate juice from things.

The particular moment I observed this geometric invention, tables and chairs were piled up in a corner, and guards defended the entrance. In spite of this I could see the new installation perfectly. I saw it in a way much more precisely than if I had walked comfortably, or if I had crossed my legs in the seat of a chair, with my eyes distracted by the dangling of a few earrings nearby, and with the tickling of this little white and fugitive moustache that a well-administered gulp of beer leaves on the lips.

The entire pavilion is of gray marble and lightly opaque glass. There is neither a molding, nor an ornament, nor a curve. Right angles are everywhere, polished surfaces, splendid geometry. The glass has a transparency of a bitter, watered-down drink, the things inside are seen as if through disinfectant. There are two large pools of moribund liquid, a water that looks like a softened glass full of invisible larvae; and a single large statue as the only decoration; the folds of the stone figure's nude flesh are a succession of indolent, asexual, and miserable grimaces. The arms and legs of the chairs, all of them simply made from nickel, make one think—even if one does not want to—about medical laboratories.

Now imagine all the anarchy of color, all the physiology of a fan and a romantic umbrella, and all the paper cut and painted with the scenes that we have contemplated with our heart since the hour we were born. The past moves us away from this clinic of pure rectangles, but a kind of new sense exists within us that we wouldn't know how to define, as it pulls our eyes to the glass and marble in its diabolic proportions and leads us to think that this German pavilion is perhaps the sharpest, most sensual, most enthralling example of everything we have contemplated this night in June.

Josep Maria de Sagarra, "Mabre i cristall," *Mirador* 1, no. 20 (June 13, 1929): 2.

Josep Maria de Sagarra i de Castellarnau (1894-1961) was a prominent Catalan novelist, poet, critic, and translator. As a journalist he had been a correspondent in Germany and contributed numerous essays to the new cultural weekly magazine *Mirador* (1929-37). Sagarra counted the painter Salvador Dalí among his friends, and as his text on the Barcelona Pavilion makes patently clear, his writing had Surrealist tendencies.

1929

LENORE KÜHN
German Work at the International Exhibition in Barcelona

Germany did not, as the other states, assemble a number of representative spaces for the main display of a country's products and character (apart from the presentation in the different sections), but has placed emphasis on these thematic sections and focused the purely representative function at the German pavilion, a strange, strictly modern and factual creation by the architect Mies van der Rohe. It is a not exactly large, but made from very beautiful dark green marble and light brown travertine, adorned with some kind of garden court and pools, while the building's straight lines display a rich array of steel and clear and tinted glass. A beautiful statue of a young woman by [Georg] Kolbe is the only figurative ornament; in the interior, which—designed to achieve its effect merely through material and its planes—a few pieces of steel furniture with snow-white leather upholstery, a black carpet, and black cloth offer the only lively element; an office for the general commissioner has found a place in a far corner of the court. This creation might speak to the "spirit of sobriety, honesty, and clarity" of the new Germany and the abundance of light and air might reflect the modern German sense of life. But one might regret, in the interest of psychological empathy and a true, characteristic representation of the country's spirit (as it is easily detectable for the visitor at other national representations at the exhibition), that the German presence at this world's fair is so strictly divided into separate parts—pure representation on the one hand, real achievements on the other. Thus, the plurality of the disparate German sections, as strong and important as they are, never come together to form a coherent statement. Those who don't know Germany will only be able to speculate about the country and the people behind these achievements of hard, somber, and determined work. Given the fact that unsympathetic interpretations of the German spirit abroad have often led to one-sided impressions, perhaps it would have been appropriate to aim for a bit more empathy and understanding for such a rich and lively people and a country full of beautiful landscapes, in order to complement the impression of simply sober and impressive accomplishments. Without a doubt, the other national pavilions, with their display of characteristic and beautiful interior furnishings, crafts, works of art, typical dress, and traditions of all kinds, lead to a subtly sympathetic impression and an increased understanding of their countries.

But there might have been spatial and financial reasons for this, and given Germany's impressive appearance almost throughout, also in the field of assured elegant taste, we will be content with the understanding that the German tends to step back behind the cause and on the inside we are still more than we might appear from outside.

Lenore Kühn, "Deutsche Arbeit auf der Internationalen Ausstellung in Barcelona," *Der Auslandsdeutsche* (June 1929): 400–402.

Lenore Kühn (1878–1955), a conservative German philosopher and writer, was a member of the DNVP (the German National People's Party), where she was in charge of furthering women's rights, and was later close to National Socialist ideas and organizations. Her book on female sexuality, *Diotíma: Schule der Liebe* (1930) became a bestseller. She published numerous travel accounts and art historical essays. Her report from Barcelona is one of the few voices critical of the pavilion's role as representative of German culture. The biweekly magazine *Der Auslandsdeutsche* was the newsletter of the DAI (Deutsche Ausland-Institut) which, since 1917, had reached out to Germans living abroad.

L. S. M. (LILLY VON SCHNITZLER)
Barcelona World's Fair

The arrangement of the exhibition, accomplished by the German architect Mies van der Rohe and his collaborator Lilly Reich, distinguishes itself from that of other countries by the complete coherence of its furnishings, the division of space, the lettering, and the material of the vitrines. All is kept in black and white: nickel tubes, nickel frames, the Mies-Reich-Bauhaus furniture, using bent chromium-covered steel pipes with black wicker fabric (which was particularly applauded by the Spaniards). Both this strict limitation of the exhibition design and the German exhibition's emphasis on quality and functionality of the object might perhaps seem too cold, too cerebral to the Latins. Perhaps those unfamiliar with our culture will see in it mostly a calculating will to power and a steely discipline.

At least the German Pavilion, a representational building in the best sense of the word, has received full recognition in Spain. Here the German architect Mies van der Rohe has complemented the cool sobriety of the industrial displays with the beauty and refinement of the noblest materials. The building is made from green marble, yellow onyx, from white-, black- and olive-colored plate glass walls, travertine floors and water basins (in one of them, a female figure by Georg

Kolbe is the only ornament). As if from a fairy tale, not of the *Arabian Nights*, but from an almost supernaturally inspired music of eternal space, Mies's work stands, not to be considered a house, but a drawing of lines in space by a hand that defines the human reach toward infinity. We Germans owe gratitude to Mies van der Rohe, for he has succeeded in casting our spiritual existence into form under the southern sun, on the distant Iberian peninsula.

L. S. M. (Lilly von Schnitzler), "Weltausstellung Barcelona," *Europäische Revue* 5, no. 4 (July 1929): 286–88.

L. S. M. (LILLY VON SCHNITZLER)
The World's Fair Barcelona 1929

Eight days later the inauguration of the German Pavilion and the German sections. The German architect Mies van der Rohe and his collaborator Lilly Reich have formed these into a masterpiece of German art and German character. Simple and matter-of-fact in color and form, they present the German will to the world, the chemical industry, machines, cars, telephones, textiles, book arts, toys […] modest, serious, strict. The German commissioner Dr. von Schnitzler says: "We wanted to show what we can do, who we are, how we feel and see today. We don't want anything but clarity, simplicity, honesty." This explanation of sentiments can be applied to the entire German exhibition; it provides the basis for German architect Mies van der Rohe's approach—representational architecture of the highest order. It is here, between these walls from green marble and onyx, between black, olive, and white plate glass, large slabs of travertine, pools of the most elegant expansion, in which a female figure by Kolbe is reflected as the only piece of ornament, it is here that we also sense and experience exquisite beauty in the quality of space and in the selection of materials.

The king responds in his own welcoming speech: in one week he had seen this building rise, he had driven by daily and wondered if it would ever be finished. Today he believes that in a certain sense the German leadership intended this brilliant and perfectly detailed work to be improvised.

L.S.M. (Lilly von Schnitzler), "Marginalien: Die Weltausstellung Barcelona 1929," Der Querschnitt 9, no. 8 (August 1929): 582-84.

Lilly Bertha Dorothea von Schnitzler, née Mallinckrodt (1889–1981), was a prominent member of Frankfurt's society in the 1920s. In 1910 she had married Georg August Eduard von Schnitzler (1984-1962), a high-ranking manager in the chemical industry. From 1922 on she supported the painter Max Beckmann and collected his work. In 1924 she founded the pan-European cultural magazine Europäische Revue together with the conservative Austrian publicist Karl Anton Prinz Rohan (1898–1975). She was very much involved in her husband's efforts as Germany's General Commissioner at the Barcelona International Exposition, including his choice of Mies van der Rohe and Lilly Reich as the appointed architects. She published two essays in July and August 1929 (one in the Europäische Revue, the other in Querschnitt) under her pseudonym L.S.M. In the former she conjured up some of the most lyrical formulations celebrating Mies's achievement. The art magazine Der Querschnitt (The Cross-Section) had a print run of 20,000 and reached an affluent intellectually sophisticated, centrist audience in Germany from 1921 until 1936, when it was banned by the National Socialists. Lilly von Schnitzler detailed her impressions of the opening and mentioned the upcoming conference in Barcelona of the European Cultural Association (Europäischer Kulturbund), under the topic "Culture as a Social Problem," just before German Week at the fair. "The exhibition will be completed in all its parts, and the organization entirely accomplished," she promised.

1929

JUSTUS BIER
Mies van der Rohe's Pavilion of the Reich in Barcelona

The task was truly unusual for today: a building without a purpose, or at least without a visible, tangible, obvious purpose. A building, dedicated to representation, to empty space, and thus to space itself. Architecture as a free art, as an expression of a spiritual commitment. It must be welcomed that this task ended up in the hands of Mies van der Rohe, and that Germany was represented by an example of the new architecture.

The selection of the architect was particularly felicitous, as it concerns one of the men who has developed the elements of the new architecture from the ground up, and has fought for decades for its realization. He is a pioneer and also an artist with an elevated, humanistic approach to life, with the inner capacity to "say something important with dignity."

The building that Mies van der Rohe has erected in Barcelona points thus to new directions, which might become immensely important for the future development of architecture. It demonstrates that representation is possible without false pathos, that nobility and a lively fullness of appearance does not require decorative additions, and that the rigorous tools of the new architecture can cause an immense richness of spatial experiences, an extraordinary change of sentiments as one wanders through its spaces.

To begin: the building lacks axial symmetry. Just as the inner sequence of spaces allows for idle wandering, the outer appearance also contributes to a free equilibrium of masses, in which the cool, sober lines of the roof plate set the tone together with the austere planes of the surrounding walls. The stairs leading up to the terrace are placed toward the side. The interior beckons with a strangely enticing darkness, from which glass and chrome tubes sparkle in front of a noble marble background.

Mies van der Rohe comes from a family of stonemasons and has acquired his knowledge of different marbles and minerals since childhood. This, as much as his passion for precious stones and noble materials in general, led to sensible calibrations of color and structure at the Barcelona Pavilion, and to an application that is appropriate for their use. The terrace and the entire plinth, including the staircase and all light-colored walls, are made from travertine, harmonizing with the appearance of the white solid ceiling, which rests on eight slender, sparkling chrome supports. They correspond with the chrome frames of the glass walls, separating the main room from the exterior and the water in the court. In these glass walls color already makes an appearance. While the glass wall at the front consists of large colorless panes of plate glass, the wall in the back is made from gray plate glass, and the wall in the water court of olive-green plate glass. These walls define the space without closing it, and are of a strangely indeterminate materiality. The larger and brighter one of the two pools contains plants, shimmers in a light green, and is freely positioned on the terrace, while the smaller one, lined with black glass—uncanny as a nightmare—is surrounded by walls of

green Tinos marble. From this basin a female body sculpted by Georg Kolbe emerges, not in the center, but moved to the side on axis with the hallway beyond the gray glass wall, facing the interior. The figure, in light-colored stone, emerges from the darkness of its setting: the gesture of her right hand turning upward—seemingly shielding her against the flood of light entering the open court—is of a mysterious beauty.

This green enclosure around the courtyard is the most unassuming of the marble walls. A similar one, more noble in its dappled patterns of verde antique, stretches beyond the front row of steel supports. The most precious wall has been moved deep into the interior: it consists of honey-yellow onyx dorée with a wonderfully lively surface. It was the only block of this kind of marble available anywhere in Europe. The height of the space was determined by this wall, from a block that was sliced four times. In front of it a black carpet stretches across the floor, offering both a strong contrast to the delicate and luminous colors of the travertine and onyx, and a prelude for the water court opening up behind it in black and green. The settees inside—new, very simple, and noble from chromium-covered steel band—are covered in white *glacé* leather pillows, while the tables carry black opal glass plates.

Our description can only hint at the distinguished impression of the building, the care and confidence of the selection of materials, deliberately enhanced toward the interior, the strange interplay of spaces, which impress through the serious sobriety of their forms, just like a noble vessel, without ostentation. It is essential that the preciousness of the applied materials does not affect the clarity of the architecture; on the contrary, every single member of the building's organism has its unique function. The walls do not have the usual dual purpose: they are merely dividers of space: wall as itself, without being used as a load-bearing element. Unburdened, as if simply slid into place, they stand in the space, often directly behind the steel supports, which have to carry the weight of the ceiling. Ceiling and wall are without a close relationship: the roof plate hovering above its slender supports covers the large central section of the terrace, unconcerned about spatial overlaps. As one walks through the rooms, spatial coherence has been entirely maintained, every impression is tied to its sequence; at every moment the whole addresses our spirit as a fantastically assembled spatial work of art.

While Mies van der Rohe's building presents itself boldly and future-bound, the nobility of its appearance has overcome any opposition and has won many friends for a new Germany. A pure sound in the midst of hapless exhibition architecture, inspired by romantic reminiscences, a beginning, which, for those with an unbiased eye, establishes a new, appropriate tradition.

Justus Bier, "Mies van der Rohe's Reichspavilion in Barcelona," *Die Form: Zeitschrift für gestaltende Arbeit* 16, no. 4 (August 15, 1929): 423-30.

Justus Bier (1899-1990) was a German-American art historian. After completing a PhD thesis (1924) on the medieval Franconian sculptor Tilman Riemenschneider, he began writing essays on modern architecture, notably for the Werkbund journal *Die Form*. From 1930 to 1936 Bier was a curator at the Kestner Society and Museum in Hannover, where he mounted contemporary art exhibitions with its director Alexander Dorner. The National Socialists closed the Kestner Society in 1936 and Bier, who was Jewish, had to leave Germany. He emigrated to the US in 1937 and taught art history at the University of Louisville between 1937 and 1960, when he was appointed director of the State Art Museum in Raleigh, North Carolina (until his retirement in 1970). Bier's extensive review of the Barcelona Pavilion in *Die Form* was much noted and paraphrased in abbreviated form in other newspapers.[1] As a student of Heinrich Wölfflin's, Bier was particularly sensitive to the importance of movement for an experience of space.

1 Justus Bier, "Der deutsche Pavillon auf der Ausstellung in Barcelona." *Rheinisch-Westfälische Zeitung,* August 18, 1929.

1929

WALTHER GENZMER
The International Exhibition in Barcelona

Most architects failed when faced with the task of creating an architectural setting for several exhibits and to lend those volumes a characteristic expression of their country or state. Only the house of the Swedish state represents a convincing solution to this task: a modest, horizontal cube of a building with excellent proportions, which carries as the only symbol of today's Sweden a large, colored state coat of arms above the door of its main entrance and whose continuous, wood-clad white exterior walls obtrusively suggest the cultural-architectural history of the country. The architects of the other state pavilions either succumbed to the temptation to give in to an arbitrary artistic folly without any general validity, or they have copied more or less skillfully one or several building ideas from the art history of their country.

Contrary to the other states, Germany did not exhibit anything in its pavilion, but left it to the architect to advertise Germany merely through the architectural design. Since in our time types of a general validity have not yet been found for such buildings which are essentially without function, this simplification of the basic program requirement did not make the task easier, but considerably more difficult.

Mies van der Rohe, who had been commissioned to design and oversee the building of the pavilion by the German exhibition commission, began his work with the search for an appropriate site. The site offered by the Spanish exhibition leadership—of course with the best of intentions—in the interior corner of the protruding wing of the Palacio Alfonso XIII, at the foot of the stairs to the national palace, was rejected, because Mies van der Rohe saw that here, in the middle of the world's fair commotion, with its overly colorful and uncritical agglomeration of architectural and other ornamental motifes, a lasting effect could not be achieved. He thus selected a spot a bit off to the side, but still conveniently located close to the general traffic, in front of the lower longitudinal wall of the Palace Victoria Eugenie, between this and a broad boulevard, which turns off the main axis to the right and leads in a slender curve to the stadium behind the national palace. The calm, high wall of the palace provides an effective background for the pavilion, which was kept low and horizontal in careful contrast to this mighty vertical. Its footprint is roughly 60 by 20 meters, and its longitudinal direction runs perpendicular to the palace walls. The floor sits about 1.5 meters above the surrounding ground along the longitudinal side which faces the main boulevard; the other longitudinal side opens on the same level to a garden section, which was created on a low slope by applying additional soil.

A part of the floor area lies underneath a reinforced concrete ceiling plate, which is carried by eight chromium-clad iron supports with a cruciform footprint. With the exception of the walls surrounding the office addition, which hardly registers overall, the walls have no load-bearing function, but only enclose or suggest space. The marble walls consist of metal scaffoldings, on both sides of which thin marble slabs have been fixed.

Since no doors were necessary, the architect could let the outer and inner spaces interact freely—a game which is reinforced for the eye by the intelligent use of the reflectivity and transparency of the employed materials. In the relationship between the reflective and transparent areas an enhancement can be noted. In an open area that is not covered, only the large horizontal water area is reflective; the rest of the floor and the surrounding walls clad with unpolished Roman travertine are dull. In the covered part, adjacent to the right, all vertical building parts (walls and supports) are reflective or transparent or both, while the horizontal parts—namely the stuccoed ceiling and the floor, which is partially covered by a black carpet—are dull in the small partial space; open to the sky at the far right, which the visitor normally enters at the very end, both the horizontal and vertical parts are reflective: a black expanse of water and the surrounding walls of bottle-green glass and green Tinos marble.

Seen from the outside, the artistic impression is determined by the appearance of the two planes located 3.1 meters from each other; the floor plate and the reinforced concrete ceiling plate of half the size, which relates to the floor plate in such a way that all the interior and exterior walls reach up to that height. The vertical plates present surprisingly new connections between the two horizontal planes. Nevertheless, there is nothing arbitrary, but one senses a regulatory framework. It seems obvious to draw comparisons with contemporary music, whose most essential characteristic is, in contrast to the music before the war, the avoidance of ornate but empty masses of musical accords, but instead guides each voice in counterpoint and thus reaches a new spirituality of "forms moved by sound." The clarity in the arrangement of voices is mostly the result of an honest, realistic striving; the parallel phenomenon in the area of building lies in the spiritualization of the building elements from the technical, static side, as it already happened during the gothic period under different conditions. The special meaning of the German Pavilion in Barcelona in fact probably lies alongside—or if you like, despite—a strict technical logic, which appears mostly in the reduced, just barely permissible dimensioning of the load-bearing and non-load-bearing parts; effects of a purely artistic kind have been achieved.

Walther Genzmer, "Die Internationale Ausstellung in Barcelona," *Zentralblatt der Bauverwaltung* 49, no. 34 (August 21, 1929): 541–46.

WALTHER GENZMER
The Pavilion of the German Reich at the International Exhibition in Barcelona

Only the pavilion of the German Reich is exciting somehow. It requires a spiritual engagement, it establishes challenges and it responds to them—as far as we can yet ascertain—with a generally valid solution. The task: the pavilion was not supposed to contain exhibits (all the German products are accommodated throughout the Spanish exhibition palaces); it should merely invite the passing visitors to shorter or longer contemplative stays and to serve occasionally as a gathering place for festive events. Especially the fact that there were no spatial requirements, the rational response to which would have forced the building mass in the architect's hand, provided weight and responsibility.

Mies van der Rohe was allowed to select the site. It lies between the lower longitudinal wall of the previously mentioned Palace Victoria Eugenie and the main road that turns right from the entrance promenade. This selection of the building site was, perhaps, the architect's most important creative act: the clarity of this location helped to essentially determine the overall form of the building. It seems almost obvious that the main direction of the pavilion is perpendicular to the palace's wall behind it, that in contrast to the significant height of that wall the pavilion is kept very low, and in contrast to its uninterrupted calm it is kept open and airy. The fact that the architect could forego enclosing doors allowed him to let exterior and interior spaces transition almost imperceptibly into each other. With this possibility, the architect played a very spirited game, which found its characteristic essence in the use and distribution of opaque, reflective, and transparent areas.

The floor plan shows the main spatial areas, and the most important materials used. The reinforced concrete slab above the central part is carried by eight iron supports, cruciform in section and clad in chromium. The walls are 3.1 meters tall throughout and are not load-bearing (with the barely noticeable exception of the perimeter walls of the building). The marble slabs are attached to iron supports.

The minimal—statically just about permissible—dimensions of all load-bearing and non-load-bearing parts is a general distinction of the new architecture. On a technological foundation, effects of a purely spiritual and irrational nature were achieved here in superior fashion, and in particular without any reference to the building ideas of the classicist past. This allocates to the pavilion of the German Reich in Barcelona a position in the front row of those buildings of our time, which let us hope for a rebirth of the art of building in the not-too-distant future.

Walther Genzmer, "Der Deutsche Reichspavillon auf der Internationalen Ausstellung in Barcelona," *Die Baugilde* 11, no. 20 (October 1929): 1654–55.

Walther Genzmer (1890–1983) was a German architect, administrator, and preservationist. He was a somewhat atypical reviewer for the pavilion, as his main architectural interests lay with the medieval and Baroque. He became a civil servant at the architecture department of the Finance Ministry in Berlin in 1928 (in charge of gardens and palaces) and edited its *Zentralblatt der Bauverwaltung*, a weekly journal focusing on government-funded projects. Genzmer wrote two complementary essays about the pavilion in August and October 1929 (after his visit to the German Week in Barcelona). His essays stand out for their careful spatial and material analyses.

1929

NICOLAU MARIA RUBIÓ I TUDURÍ
Germany's Pavilion at the Barcelona Exposition by Mies van der Rohe

It contains only space. It has no practical purpose or material function. People say it is useless, but it is representative architecture, just like an obelisk or a triumphal arch. In order to represent Germany with a commemorative structure, some architects might have evoked the form of a large Zeppelin. In a subtler approach, Mies van der Rohe has given his representative monument the quiet shape of a home.

Certainly, we no longer agree on what constitutes the form of a house. When you build a real house, it remains a house, whichever way you look at it. But if you make something that is not a house, but wants to look like one, you have to design your building close to the well-known forms of the architecture of the house. There you have it—a traditional element, a conservative principle, which we should not ignore, and which we find again very conspicuously in Mies van der Rohe's pavilion. Tourists and the local avant-gardists might complain: "This pavilion is not at all in the latest fashion!" They like to blame the architect: he should not offer anything that is not exactly new at an international exhibition. But I leave those opinions and return to my subject.

The pavilion contains only space, and yet it has a geometric dimension, which is neither real nor physical. It has no doors and, even better, each room is only imperfectly closed, on three sides by three walls, for example. These walls are mostly great pieces of continuous glass, which limit the space only partially. Some of the glass, of a dark hue or neutral, reflects the objects and the visitors in such a way that what you see behind the glass gets mixed up with what you see reflected. Some rooms have no ceilings: they are really half patios, where the space is limited only by three walls and the horizontal surface of the water in the pool, but anchored by its geometry.

When you approach the pavilion, and then again when you enter, you are shocked by the impression of purposelessness that emanates from these open and empty rooms, these beautiful marble walls, nude and abandoned, the uninhabitable patios, and I daresay you immediately feel the shock of a metaphysical architecture.

But I should stop here for a moment to make my case clearer. The normal interpretation of the words "metaphysical architecture" would be something like an architecture of intelligence or of intellectual abstraction. Everyone would understand it if one spoke of proportions, numerical relationships, of clarity and an almost cruel precision of architectural reasoning, etc., etc. However, in the German Pavilion in Barcelona, architecture, as it overcomes the physical, moves toward the evocative and symbolic. In representative architecture that is inevitable. The German commissioner addressed this in his remarks. "Here is the spirit of the New Germany: simplicity and clarity of means and intentions—everything is open to the wind, just a real openness, where nothing limits the access to our hearts. A work honestly done, without arrogance. Here is the quiet home of a peaceful Germany."

This evocation has a clear sentimental tendency: all the materials and even their geometry are subjugated under this tendency. It may seem surprising to find the sentimental in a work of architecture that is very modern and very technical, but we have to recognize that architecture can hardly escape the social influences which gave rise to it.

Nicolau M. Rubió i Tudurí, "Le Pavillon de l'Allemagne à l'Exposition de Barcelone par Mies van der Rohe," *Cahiers d'Art*, nos. 8/9 (August/September 1929): 408–11.

Nicolau Maria Rubió i Tudurí (1891–1981) was a Catalan architect, landscape designer, and author, since 1917 director of parks and gardens in Barcelona. He had designed the gardens at the Royal Palace of Pedralbes and Turó Park before working with his former teacher Jean-Claude Nicolas Forestier (1861–1930) on the Montjuïc Gardens for the international exposition. In 1929 he had built one of the first modernist buildings in Catalonia, the Barcelona Radio Station (Estación Unión Radio Barcelona) at the Tibidabo hill above the city. His essay about the pavilion in the French art and literature journal *Cahiers d'Art* (founded in 1926 by Christian Zervos) showed a redrawn floor plan, which ignored the steel columns in the pavilion—probably in order to support his point that the pavilion "contains only space." In response to the great enthusiasm for Le Corbusier in Barcelona, in 1931 Rubió i Tudurí published a manifesto called *Actar* against "pseudo-machinist functionalists" which he sent to Mies in recognition of his work.[1]

1 Nicolau M. Rubió i Tudurí, *Actar: Discrimination des Formes de Quiétude, Formes de Mouvement dans la Construction* (Paris: Imp. Union, 1931). Mies kept a copy of this book in his personal library.

ALFREDO BAESCHLIN
Barcelona and Its World's Fair

Germany presented itself formidably, especially in its special exhibitions in the different palaces, which pleasantly stand out through their restrained, modern decoration. The design of those spaces comes from the architects Mïes van der Rohe and Lilly Reich.

Regarding the pavilion, which officially represents Germany, so to speak, and was also created by the architect Mïes van der Rohe, opinions vary, however. I personally find this flat, utilitarian architecture, in which only noble or interesting building materials are displayed, not at all unpleasant.

The pavilion contains no exhibits whatsoever, as it is merely meant as a kind of gathering space for the German colony in Barcelona and German visitors to the exhibition. With new and original materials interesting effects were achieved, but, unfortunately, an idea was not presented. The visitor stands perplexed in front of this pavilion and is doubtful if he is looking at a building that is still being assembled.

The pavilion is much impacted by the neighborhood of one of the palaces by Puig i Cadafalch,[1] which completely overpowers it. I would have preferred a different location, for example in the area where the other countries have erected their pavilions.

The structure of the pavilion is made out of aluminum and the walls are out of darkly colored plate glass, which does not allow a gaze from the outside to penetrate inside. From the interior, the visitor sees, as if through a tender veil, the gardens and palaces surrounding the pavilion. A pool, entirely straight, without any ornamentation, seems harsh. A second pool receives an extraordinarily beautiful effect thanks to a naked figure rendered in brown clay, especially through its multiple reflections.

All in all, this is an interesting exercise in the application of forms entirely independent from conventional styles; but as an exhibition pavilion representing a nation such as Germany, it is not entirely convincing.

Alfredo Baeschlin, "Barcelona und seine Weltausstellung," *Deutsche Bauzeitung* 63, no. 57 (1929): 497–504; and no. 77 (1929): 657–62.

Alfredo Baeschlin (1883–1964) was a Swiss architect, painter, and poet. He studied architecture in Zürich, worked as an architect in Bern, and wrote for a number of Swiss and German architectural magazines, in particular *Die Schweizerische Baukunst*, which he also edited. He wrote several books about vernacular architecture in Switzerland and Spain, where he settled in 1928, first in Valencia and then in Barcelona.

1 Josep Puig i Cadafalch (1867–1956) was a Catalan architect and politician. Initially working in the style of *modernisme*, not unlike Antonio Gaudi, he had moved on to the historicist *noucentisme* style when he was given the commission to design the Montjuïc fairgrounds. Due to his engagement in Catalan political and cultural independence, he was relieved of his commission, but the palaces adjacent and across from Mies's pavilion had already been built.

HELEN APPLETON READ
Barcelona

As to the contribution made by the exhibiting nations, it would seem as if Germany alone had given the art of display serious considerations or exerted censorship on the material chosen to represent her. By means of her distinguished little pavilion, designed by Mies van der Rohe (the national pavilions are in no case used as exhibition halls, but merely serve as symbols of national cultures), she is also the only exhibiting nation to demonstrate that a new chapter is being written in the history of architecture. The pavilion is built of black-and-white marble with silver metal trimming. An inside garden makes effective use of a life-size bronze by Georg Kolbe. Clarity, simplicity, and emphasis on the thing exhibited, rather than elaborate trimming, characterize the German method of display. It is understandable that Germany should make a special effort, in this her first appearance in a world's fair since the war, to make a convincing and arresting demonstration of her postwar cultural and economic status. The exhibition technique and discipline are however, of the same order which she has exhibited in her local postwar exhibitions.

Helen Appleton Read, "Barcelona," *Vogue* (September 28, 1929): 74–75, 106, 108.

HELEN APPLETON READ
Germany at the Barcelona World's Fair

Of all the nations represented, Germany alone symbolized her industrial and cultural status in a modern gesture. England and America are not officially represented; France gave the matter scant consideration and is represented by inferior material badly arranged; Russia, due to diplomatic reasons, was not there. The Scandinavian exhibits were well done, national in feeling, unimportant. Italy showed a bombastic Roman modern pavilion.

Germany naturally made a special effort in her first entry into an international affair since the war. Her contribution is more than putting her best foot forward. Her austerely elegant pavilion designed by Mies van der Rohe, pioneer in the modern movement in architecture, is a symbol of Germany's postwar *Kultur*, a convincing exposition of the aesthetic of modern architecture. The technical and industrial displays, also arranged by Mies, have that clarity and objectivity characteristic of Germany's present point of view. They symbolize the German *Kommissar*, Dr. von Schnitzler's explanation of the intention of Germany's representation: "We have wanted to show here what we can do, what we are, and how we feel and see today. We do not want anything more than clarity, simplicity, and integrity."

To plan a building which shall represent purely the idea of *Sachlichkeit* and shall serve no utilitarian purpose is an unusual, difficult assignment because it necessitates working without a disciplinary control entailed by a specific practical problem. That German officialdom had the good judgment to choose Mies is significant of her postwar culture.

Radical rationalist that he is, his designs are governed by a passion for beautiful architecture. He is one of the very few modern architects who has carried its theories beyond a barren functional formula into the plastically beautiful. Material and space disposition are the ingredients with which he gets his effect of elegant serenity. Evincing in his work a love for beautiful materials and textures, he emphasizes this predilection.

The outer walls of the pavilion are olive-green and black marble; honey-colored onyx is used for the inner walls and floor; great panes of plate glass, some clear, some black and smoke-gray, set in silver-metal frames, are used both for windows and partitions. A female figure in bronze, by Kolbe, is placed effectively at one end of an inner garden pool. The vitality it imparts to the austerity of the scheme, the enhanced plasticity and grace which the setting in turn imparts to the figure, is a brief for the use of sculpture in modern arrangements. The interior is equally simple and effective—metal chairs upholstered in cream leather, a black carpet, honey-colored floors, and tables with black glass tops.

Helen Appleton Read, "Germany at the Barcelona World's Fair," *Arts* (October 1929): 112-13.

Helen Appleton Read (1897–1974) was an art critic for the *Brooklyn Daily Eagle*, one of the most popular American daily papers during the 1920s, associate art editor for *Vogue*, and director of the Art Alliance of America. Read was a friend of Philip Johnson and shared his enthusiasm for modern European architecture. Johnson's might have alerted her to Mies's pavilion, although he never managed to see it for himself. Her articles for *Vogue* and *Arts* were among the first to report about the architecture at the Barcelona International Exposition in the American mainstream press. Read also has the dubious distinction of having introduced Johnson, when both were in Berlin in the summer of 1932, to the visual splendors of a National Socialist rally. Hitler spoke to a crowd in Potsdam; Johnson was mesmerized.[1]

1   Franz Schulze, *Philip Johnson: Life and Work* (Chicago: University of Chicago Press, 1996), 90.

EDMUNDO T. CALCAÑO
Germany at the Great International Exposition of Barcelona

Our visit begins with an architectural delight—the official German pavilion, built right next to the palace of Queen Victoria Eugenia. It was designed by the architect Mies van der Rohe, who has a well-deserved reputation in his country as an ingenious innovator. It was made here in Barcelona, a creation admirably representative of the modern German spirit and the new outlook on life in that thriving country. The hard years of the war and after, bristling with difficulties and disastrous economic consequences, have inspired German architects to create a new style—simple, severe, with straight lines, avoiding all ornamentation and seeking beauty only in the harmony of proportions and the preciousness of the materials used. This ideal has been fully achieved in the German pavilion with its beautiful travertine, marble, and glass. It consists of three parts: the primary building opens on one side toward a small enclosed courtyard with a pool in which a statue by modern German sculptor [Georg] Kolbe stands; and on the other side, to a large courtyard, which is open and also contains a large pool. Despite its severe simplicity, this pavilion offers a variety of impressions thanks to the diverse tints of its glass walls reflecting the daylight always differently, and by the hues of the marble. Color effects play a major role in the decorative scheme: a red curtain contrasts with the immaculate brightness of the sky; the green marble harmonizes with the black carpet. But there are no violent contrasts. All these effects are quiet, expansive, and strong.

From the entire pavilion a feeling of tranquility, sincerity, and nobility emanates, which according to Mr. von Schnitzler, "depicts well the current spirit of a country that, after having suffered much, tries to limit its art to the absolutely essential."

Edmundo T. Calcaño, "Alemania en la Gran Exposición International de Barcelona," *La Razón*, October 5, 1929.

This text is part of a longer article by the Argentinian journalist and publisher **Edmundo T. Calcaño** (1885–ca. 1960), who acted as Argentina's consul general in Barcelona since 1926 and reported as a foreign correspondent for *La Razón,* the second-largest newspaper of Buenos Aires.

BONAVENTURA BASSEGODA I AMIGÓ
At the Exhibition: More Foreign Pavilions

At one end of the great Plaza of the Magic Fountain, the official pavilion of Germany shows its wealth and noble composition and its, in many ways, interesting concepts. Above an
extensive high podium, clad entirely in polished travertine,
independent, smooth wall panels have been arranged,
formed by slabs of marble and beautiful grayish glass. They
hide from the passerby the view of the reception room, whose
studied severity seduces and simultaneously perplexes us;
the flat roof, supported by a metal framework of nickel-plated
posts, does not cover the entire area of the pavilion but ex-
poses the smooth rectangular mirror of the large pool, occupying much of the terrace, and the shallow waters in which
Georg Kolbe's clay-colored nude is reflected; in the southern
corner, another piece of flat roof protects the small office. If
this great creation of the eminent architect Mies van der Rohe
has stunned the occasional shallow visitor, who might have
wondered if he is in front of an unfinished building, every cultivated and lively spirit will bow with admiration and respect
and understand the significance of a hard and tenacious
struggle for liberation from the tutelage of artistic conventions and the pressure of established forms. Its purpose was

to manifest, as stated so eloquently by Baron von Schnitzler, the Reich's commissioner, to whom the exhibition owes much gratitude: "the burning desire of modern Germany—characterized by its clarity, simplicity, and sincerity."

Bonaventura Bassegoda, "En la Exposición: Más pabellones extranjeros," *La Vanguardia*, October 31, 1929, 5.

Bonaventura Bassegoda i Amigó (1862–1940) was a prominent Catalan writer and architect. He taught at the architecture schools of Barcelona and Madrid and built a number of significant structures in the *modernismo* style in Barcelona, such as the Casas Rocamora and Berenguer and Salle Comtal College. He regularly contributed to journals and newspapers such as *La Renaixença, La Ilustració Catalana, L'Avenç, Diario de Barcelona*, and *La Vanguardia*. His grandson Joan Bonaventura Bassegoda Nonell (1930–2012), a historian and expert on the work of Gaudí, tried in the 1960s to further the rebuilding of the pavilion.

LIESEL ELSAESSER
Letter from Barcelona

The German exhibition structures look excellent. They are really the only ones that provide a clear framework. The others are … entirely confusing and tiresome. The German pavilion by Mies van der Rohe (all exhibition buildings are by him) is a superbly cool, precious, well-proportioned thing. An important-looking frame that lacks content. Empty—what for, one asks. One doesn't know. Mrs. von Schnitzler and the people surrounding her are enthusiastic. Large panes of plate glass, illumination behind an opal glass plate, 4 by 2.5-meter walls of travertine. Black velour, red silk curtains, white kid-skin pillows on nickel … everything excellent and undeniably beautiful and precious; but I cannot fall on my knees in front of such dead pomp. And locals haven't the slightest bit of understanding for it, they turn the other way, horrified—just like the cultured French are stoning their own Le Corbusier. Martin [her husband, the architect] is often asked for his opinion about the unappreciated pavilion. He does so very effectively, standing firmly with M.v.d.R. and yet still responding tenderly to the hurt feelings of those who asked.

I am grateful to Professor Thomas Elsaesser (1943-2019) for sharing this and the following document from his family's archive with me.

Elisabeth (more typically, Liesel) Elsaesser (1890–1980) was the wife of Frankfurt architect Martin Elsaesser, who had designed the city's central market hall and, in 1928, renovated the house of Lilly and Georg von Schnitzler. Liesel maintained a close friendship and correspondence with socialist landscape architect and writer Leberecht Migge, to whom this letter is addressed. Elisabeth and Martin Elsaesser were in Barcelona in October 1929 for the conference of the *Europäischer Kulturbund* and for *German Week*, during which Martin Elsaesser gave a lecture on modern architecture. This private letter, not meant for publication, provides the unfiltered observations of a highly educated German visitor close to the circles of both architect and client.

LEBERECHT MIGGE
Why the (Cultured) World Doesn't Fall for the German Pavilion

Essen (20.11.1929)
hitting the sack late
doing repetitions

Why the (cultured) world doesn't fall for the German pavilion. The reason is the same as it was when it didn't want to swallow the prewar Werkbund arts and crafts of those days. It only accepts intellectually processed, settled forms as valuable for life. Whatever is constantly in motion and dealt with, it ignores.

The pavilion is good. Modern architecture is "good." But the question is: For what? It is the oblique (and if—albeit rarely—asked with intelligence, dishonest) questioning that makes the New Building culturally dead and irrelevant. If even the cultured Frenchman is building his Corbusier, and—he at least knows to present his rationalities as rarities—what will the intellectual man of the world make of our well-behaved Gropiuses and M. v. d. Rohes!

But even if that pavilion over there and the utilitarian architecture over here were really good, the world would still not swallow them—unless it was forced to. While intellect exists anytime and anywhere, it will only be noticed under pressure (and with some luck). World cultures are power cultures (of the French, English, American kind). Which does not necessarily mean that world powers have always produced culture. The German pavilion is a demonstration—more than one of the art of building—of the unabashed mentality and snobbish arrogance of the German on the intellectual world stage. He invents new clothes, which in reality are only bathing trunks—while the world does not expect either one but instead wants a profound epigram.

Leberecht Migge, "Warum die (Kultur) Welt den Deutschen Pavillon nicht frisst," letter to Liesel Elsaesser, 20 November, 1929 (Thomas Elsaesser Archive).

Leberecht Migge (1881-1935) was a German landscape designer, regional planner, and critic. Working with architects such as Ernst May and Bruno Taut, he introduced socialist gardening ideas into the housing movement of the Weimar Republic. A close friendship with Elisabeth Elsaesser, the wife of prominent Frankfurt architect Martin Elsaesser, produced a voluminous correspondence. This letter responds to her account from Barcelona in October. His political background shines through when he critiques the "snobbish arrogance" it represents.

HANS BERNOULLI
The Pavilion of the German Reich at the International Exhibition Barcelona

Among the opulent exhibition palaces of Barcelona—with their towers, portals, exedras—one finds a curious object: low, flat, very quiet. It is the pavilion of the German Reich, designed by Mies van der Rohe.

A kind of Japanese house: walls placed in relation to each other in open constellations, at times standing separately in space, in selected materials. Partially covered, partially under the open sky; firm ground and then again water.

There was no program to complete; there were no needs, no functions for which the building had to provide. On the contrary, the building was supposed to show a certain lack of purpose: it was only there to represent, to represent the German Reich. These are the most difficult tasks for the art of architecture, which essentially strives to faithfully fulfill a program whose main focus is usually the choice of the most useful construction, the most appropriate material.

The pavilion of the German Reich, however, shows—and this seems important to us—that our time is capable of rising above the most basic utilitarianism without having to deny its identity. The open spaces it provides contain possibilities where playful imagination, rich invention, absolute abstraction, can establish their place. Those don't necessarily have to follow the lines that Mies van der Rohe has established here. This first hint suggests so many possibilities, greatly diverse but still essentially related, that with them an entire new world emerges.

And another thing: the figure appearing in the background seems to suggest to us a path, opens a clearing toward a potential form of decoration that is possible today—a decoration which is meant as a counterpart to the tectonic, space-forming elements. Here, sculpture adopts—open and courageous—a role which has hitherto been played by leafy plants: the plant was a replacement borrowed from nature. The manmade sculpture has to hold its own in the surrounding structure, it has to enrich and enliven it—and it has to be understood as essential.

Hans Bernoulli, "Der Pavillon des Deutschen Reiches an der internationalen Ausstellung Barcelona 1929," *Das Werk* 16, no. 11 (1929): 350-51.

Hans Benno Bernoulli (1876-1959), an important Swiss architect, critic, and theoretician, worked as chief architect in the city of Basel and was a professor at the Eidgenössische Technische Hochschule (ETH) in Zürich. He was a major protagonist of the Neues Bauen in Switzerland, and was the first critic to evoke a Japanese house for comparison with the Barcelona Pavilion—followed fifty years later by Ludwig Glaeser and Werner Blaser[1]—and to assign a central role to Kolbe's sculpture, an observation that the architect Paul Rudolph would pick up again much later. (See texts pp. 197, 273.)

1   See for example Werner Blaser, *West Meets East: Mies van der Rohe* (Basel: Birkhäuser, 2001). Japanese architect and critic Hajime Yatsuka convincingly demonstrated the decisive differences between the structural ambiguities in Mies's pavilion and the ancient rules of Japanese architecture. See Hajime Yatsuka, "Mies and Japan," *Cornell Journal of Architecture* 7 (2003): 52-62. (See text p. 316)

1929

ARNE LAURIN
Images of the World's Fair in Barcelona

It was much discussed in the papers of the German Reich: the erection of the German Exposition in Barcelona cost 4 million Reichsmark in state subsidies alone, thus a little more than 32 million crowns. The statistics are silent about how much the individual firms invested in their installations and how high other contributions were. But what was installed here is worth a debate. It would be blindness if one wouldn't emphasize that there is hardly a building here that does not contain a German section, with the same inscriptions, the same tubular steel everywhere furniture—one gets so used to it that one automatically looks out for these tubular steel furniture and inscriptions.

This is focused propaganda which is not easily matched any-where. The visitor receives an impressive demonstration of how one penetrates the world, in which ways and through which framework. The frame is an important element of this penetration, not just the quality of the work. Already the in-scription "Alemania" on every second wall captures your at-tention with its severe, characteristic fonts; the appearance of the exhibition—the exhibition itself, all of the German sec-tions, represents a unique arrangement, thanks to the quasi scientific presentation of the exhibits.

There was much, at times malicious, discussion about the height of the costs. No exhibition of such dimension and quality can be assembled for free. But this type of propaganda is the only thing in the world that yields an almost criminally high return.

This being said by a foreigner to the address of the protesting parties.

Arne Laurin, "Bilder von der Weltausstellung in Barcelona," supplement, *Prager Presse*, November 10, 1929, 3.

Arne Laurin (born Arnošt Lustig, 1889–1945) was a Czech journalist and editor-in-chief of the *Prager Presse*, a liberal German-language newspaper in the young Czechoslovak Republic. Founded in 1921, the paper was closed down by the National Socialists after Germany invaded Bohemia in 1939. The sum of four million Reichsmark, which Laurin mentions in the article, caused some concern among the pavilion's organizational team. Georg von Schnitzler was asked to respond that the actual costs were much lower, namely 1.35 million. It is likely that the Tugendhats read this article in Czechoslovakia's largest German-language paper with great interest, as the construction of their villa, designed by Mies in a similar formal language, had just begun.

1929

RICHARD VON KÜHLMANN
View from Barcelona to Germany

Whoever saw the exhibition in Barcelona took home the impression that Germany has played an honorable role here, and that the nation's gratitude is owed to those who succeeded, under enormous difficulties, in creating a lively image of the Germany of today—at the German sections of the exhibition in general, and at the German pavilion in particular. The Reich's commissioner, one of the best minds among the leading figures of our major industries, has produced a formidable result, and the architect Mies van der Rohe has shaped its outer forms most fortuitously. How, then, does the new Germany appear to other nations?

The form is confident, restrained, sober almost—while being modest. The abstinence from ornamentation has been pursued to the point of being ascetic. What speaks to us, however, are the clarity of space, its clear lines, and the sensual pleasure from the mysterious magic of true materials, which, despite this austerity, renders the overall impression friendly and inviting.

The goal which the prophets of a new age, such as van de Velde, aspired to in the prewar period—namely that beauty should emanate from clearest functionality—seems to have been brought close to its realization in the German exhibition.

Recent events, whose destructive storms swept away much that was historically grown, inherited, and beloved but also limiting, have made it easier to approach formal problems with fewer preconceptions. What appeared so convincing in Barcelona was that these forms did not seem elaborately attached from the outside, but rather had evolved—with serene self-confidence—from within. The German hall of honor with its miraculous effects of a pool's reflections and colorful marble, be it a large German airplane above the city, or the Zeppelin on its short but impressive visit, the slim, beautifully proportioned battleship *Königsberg*—they all seem an almost unconscious expression of a free, confident, and natural culture.

How different are the impressions when one returns from abroad and observes the people and their day-to-day life in a big city in Germany. How much uncertainty, how many complaints, how much true hopelessness, and how little understanding there is of the enormous achievement of Germany's position today, of how much it has endured but also accomplished in the ten years since the war.

Richard von Kühlmann, "Blick von Barcelona auf Deutschland", *Berliner Tageblatt*, December 1, 1929, 5.

Richard von Kühlmann (1873-1948) had been a high-ranking politician during the last years of the empire, foreign minister, and ambassador in Turkey. During the Weimar Republic he wrote political commentary and authored several books, while serving as a board member and trustee for major German steel companies. Kühlmann was a close friend of Lilly von Schnitzler's and served as head of the *Deutscher Kulturbund* (German Cultural Association). At the 1929 Barcelona Conference of the *Europäischer Kulturbund*, he delivered an impassioned defense of individualism versus "American, Bolshevik, and Fascist Attempts at Forming Man." His essay in the fall of 1929 has to be seen in the context of the ongoing discussions about the unsolved financial problems of the exhibition. The *Berliner Tageblatt* was, together with the *Vossische Zeitung*, the most important newspaper of the German capital, with a daily readership of about 100,000.

1930

GUSTAV EDMUND PAZAUREK
Is the Werkbund Moving in the Right Direction?

The official German representation at Europe's most artistical-ly conservative nation, the Spaniards, at the Barcelona International Exposition of 1929, was particularly strange. The arrangement of the different exhibition objects in the individual palaces, in particular in the hall of machines, was simple, noble, and faultlessly tasteful. In contrast, the so-called representational house that Mies van der Rohe, the second vice president of the Werkbund, built far away from the section with the other national pavilions was incomprehensible. If it was the Reich's intention to offend the Spaniards, then it could not have accomplished this in a better fashion; the Spaniards did not know if they should consider us crazy, or if we were making fun of them. This was not a building at all, but an open arrangement of black or transparent glass panes, surrounding some shallow water basins, into which one would fall in all likelihood if one were without guidance, since there was no railing. Some tubular steel furniture, where one could perhaps recover from the shock, was the only contents of this strange architecture, which, thank God, was placed in such a hidden location that most visitors never found it. Before the war, people had repeatedly criticized the German embassy in

St. Petersburg by Peter Behrens for being an alien object in the city fabric, particularly in its exposed location. When the relevant authorities in Barcelona allowed this project to go forward, they turned out to be even worse psychologists.

Gustav Edmund Pazaurek "Ist der Werkbund auf dem richtigen Wege?," *Münchner Neueste Nachrichten* 83, no. 308 (November 12, 1930): 1.

Gustav Edmund Pazaurek (1865-1935) was a German art historian and critic and a member of the German Werkbund. As director of the arts and crafts department at the Landesgewerbemuseum (Museum for Applied Arts) in Stuttgart he introduced a "kitsch" department for educational purposes. While Pazaurek had, in the same article, expressly approved of the Weissenhof housing estate in Stuttgart as "one of the most important and interesting experiments of recent years," his rejection of the Barcelona Pavilion was approvingly quoted as a condemnation of modern architecture in the conservative magazine *Baukultur* (jointly edited by, among others, Werner Hegemann, Paul Schmitthenner, and Paul Schultze-Naumburg). The editors of *Die Baukultur* added: "That's right! Whenever architecture or applied art are being exhibited today it is always about radical, biased groups. While we do indeed know that there are extreme, perhaps even sick deformities at the German body politic, foreign countries will rightly assume that they represent the entirety of the German people. And this would be the task of a responsible foreign office: to prevent Germany's being misjudged because of radical minorities."[1]

1 "Deutsche Kunstausstellungen im Ausland und Deutscher Werkbund," *Die Baukultur* 3, no. 2 (January 17, 1931): 1.

1930

FRANCISCO MARROQUIN
Towards a New Architecture:
The German Pavilion at the Barcelona Exhibition

In the Plaza de Bellas Artes at the Barcelona exhibition stands the German pavilion with its harmonious proportions, serene, luminous—water, glass, marble—partly closed, partly open. Blocks of dark veined marble and huge glass panes in nickel frames form dividing elements—vertical rectangles—and above them a horizontal rectangle, like a huge board, flat roof, and soft whiteness. White leather chairs—large seat, large backrest—mounted on thin nickel-plated steel, a table— moon metal—black carpet, and in the corner of an open court- yard, a nude female statue provides the only embellishment. Outside, two long walls of polished white stone form a corner with another emerging wall in order to create space. Along the lateral wall there is a long bank of stone. At its feet there is the still water of a pool. Some exotic plants, shying away from the exhibition, emerge from its far end. Pure lines, geo- metric lines. Greatness and austerity. All is beauty and para- dox in this pavilion that looks bare and superbly rational, while it also seems sober and displays a wealth of materials. The poor couldn't have built it nor a fool imagined it; it is the manifestation of a higher spirit not flaunting its gifts.

The creator of this wonderful artistic work is a young architect, already famous in Stuttgart and Berlin: Mies van der Rohe. The German government was very successful when it put the design of its pavilion in the hands of such a modern creator, officially marking the artistic trend of a country that has advanced like no other toward new architectural directions. This unique approach, whose spirit—simplicity, elimination of the superfluous—is visible in all German installations, has imposed a sober and aesthetic uniformity on their displays, keeping in check any potential fantasies of individual exhibitors. German discipline in the service of art has won here a noble and necessary battle.

Of all the arts, architecture is most resistant to progress—static, outdated, apparently trapped under ancient stones without access to the present. The mechanized home of modern man cannot be the same as that of our ancestors, the warrior, the mystic, the romantic. To seek retrospective inspirations one would have to go further, to the primitive man, who built rationally, out of necessity, without cerebral or emotional complications. The superfluous is absurd today; life is too precise; the house should be, according to Le Corbusier, "a machine for living in." Plenty of room, a minimum of decoration, and an intelligent organization which gives everything its right place. No more "furniture warehouses": instead, shelves built into walls for clothes, dishes, books, pictures [...] it is more convenient, cleaner, nicer than the unsightly ancestral closets. The chairs at the German exhibition stands, which every visitor has admired [...] and tested (also a work by the architect Mies van der Rohe), are a perfect example of the synthesis that modern art is looking for.

Such simplification is applied to the walls, intended to provide light and not to perpetuate styles. Turning an inhabitable house into a museum distorts the rational order. Balconies, medallions, friezes, and other architectural meringues must give way to crystal clarity and hygiene.

We must return to the archaic, revolutionize the methods, and build in response to our time, without anachronisms. Why look at centuries-old architectural models? Our style is here already, clearly rendered in airplanes, ocean liners, cars—those results of mechanics, fruits of our time, free and ignorant of any terrible traditions.

However, the human eye is addicted to a stale mold unfit for new concepts. As a result, modern architecture has suffered two crucial failures that will continue to haunt those responsible: first, the project to build the palace of the League of Nations, where modern architects lost a fierce battle with the academics; and second, the reconstruction of northern France, where innovators' plans were also cast aside.

For this reason Germany's gesture at the International Exposition of Barcelona is particularly laudable. Officially sponsoring and providing such a great example of modern architectural art no longer seems an experience, but a consecration.

Francisco Marroquin, "Hacia una nueva arquitectura: El Pabellón de Alemania en la Exposicion de Barcelona," *ABC*, January 26, 1930, 13-14.

Don Francisco Marroquín y Pérez-Aloe (1887-1957) was a cultural critic for the monarchist daily paper *ABC* and the magazine *Blanco y negro*. For many years he lived in Paris and was an honorary attaché at the Spanish embassy. In France he was heavily engaged in the political right, in particular with the group and publication *Action Française*, under the leadership of his friends Charles Maurras and Léon Daudet, which supported Mussolini and Franco. The title of his essay in *ABC* "Hacia una nueva arquitectura," seems to gesture towards Le Corbusier's publication, *Vers une architecture* (1923), whose English edition had appeared with the title *Towards a New Architecture* (1927).

ÁNGEL MARSÀ AND LUÍS MARSILLACH
The Illuminated Mountain: Spiritual Guidebook to the Barcelona Exposition 1929-1930

All styles, all nations.

With its characteristic fusion of architectural styles and patterns, Montjuïc represents an index of peoples and racial temperaments. That is why it is so interesting to visit the exhibition, which has turned into an international assembly of disparate architectures, and to collect physiognomies of pavilions, just as people collect beautiful exotic trading cards.

Next to exuberant Eastern fantasies—small Indian palaces, Chinese pagodas—one can find a cold and piercing scheme out of reinforced concrete, the latest reflection of Le Corbusier's influence. Beside a rustic wooden house—glimpses of Finland or Romania—stands a Renaissance palace. Opposite the oval of the sports stadium, we find the pure Flemish art of the Belgian pavilion. Between a synthetic building—smooth walls, strong colors—and an iron tower stands a small and delicate Japanese house. In front of the pompous and grand lady of the National Palace, there are those crystals and smooth and succinct marbles of the German pavilion. All styles, all nations. As a powerful adjunct to the study of political and spiritual geography of nations gathered in the hanging gardens of Montjuïc, a synthesis of the exhibition could result in this axiom: Show me your architecture, and I will tell you who you are. The German pavilion–the palace of reflections–is the most authentic expression of Cubism, the chief manifestation of that dead, quartered aesthetic which Picasso invented one gloomy day. The black marble walls drink up the sunlight insatiably, eagerly; and this very sunlight, in its turn, has deigned to kiss the burnished floor and the glass roofs, only to splinter into a thousand flecks of scattered reflections. Sunlight, in the German pavilion, is one of the foremost decorative motifs. Indeed, it may be the most important, in this labyrinth of large planes, straight lines, and bare, plain walls.

To have tamed light from above is a great achievement. If a people should adopt this architecture, they will be a people of clear horizons. Such is the German pavilion: the architecture of reflections. Walls, paving stones, and roofs form a prodigious blending of rays of light which crisscross freely. And this, precisely, is the soul of the new Germany.

Ángel Marsà and Luís Marsillach, *La montaña iluminada: Itinerario espiritual de la Exposición de Barcelona 1929-1930* (Barcelona: Ed. Horizonte, 1930), 11, 14.

Ángel Marsà (1900-1988) was a Catalan journalist, writer, and critic. He worked for the newspapers *Las Noticias*, *La Vanguardia*, and *El Correo Catalán*, and during the 1920s wrote about the bohemian "Barrio Chino" of Barcelona. **Luís Marsillach** (1901-1970), a Catalan journalist and theater critic, worked for *La Vanguardia* and *Diario de Barcelona*. Many of the essays collected in the book *La montaña iluminada* previously appeared in the *Diario Oficial de la Exposición Internacional de Barcelona 1929*. As they tried to decipher how the pavilion represented its country's qualities, the two authors settled on the complexity of its multiple reflections.

ELISEO SANZ BALZA
Notes from a Visitor: The International Exposition in Barcelona 1929

Official German Pavilion

The architect van der Rohe has achieved something very modern—characterized only by straight horizontal and vertical lines, with rich materials like marble from Spain and Italy and double walls of mysterious crystal. The result is very distinguished: an unusual arrangement with two pools, a formal living room, and wide corridors. It has been said that the glass is mysterious because a person standing in front of one of these transparent walls sees himself reflected as in a mirror, but if he moves behind it, he will see the outside perfectly. Not all the visitors notice this curious particularity, whose cause remains unknown.

German Electric Utilities Pavilion

Through the portico one enters the Plaza de la Luz where Germany has erected a rare cubic pavilion, with straight lines, and the excessive sobriety of the modern Teutonic style. It demonstrates convincingly the power of its hydroelectric industries and the distribution of industrial energy, of domestic uses and lighting. Murals, reliefs, and charts are all persuasive and convincing, but, due to German idiosyncrasies, they are also relentless and heavy-handed.

Eliseo Sanz Balza, *Notas de un visitante: Exposición de Barcelona 1929* (Barcelona: Tip. Olympia, P. Yuste, 1930), 140.

Eliseo Sanz Balza (1870–1946) served as an officer in the Spanish army. After he retired, he wrote several books on military strategy, history, and geography, and his account of his visits at the Barcelona International Exposition stands out as an exception. Like other foreign critics, Balza made a particular point of mentioning the reflective quality of the expansive glass in the pavilion, but he was the only one who explicitly compared the Barcelona Pavilion with Mies's pavilion for the electric utilities (to the latter's detriment).

ANONYMOUS *(THE SPECTATOR)*
A Visit to the Barcelona Exhibition

The German national pavilion, designed by Miles [*sic*] van der Rohe, must surely impress students of the art of display as the outstanding feature of the exhibition. This strange building, covering no considerable space, merges insensibly into its immediate surroundings and is yet in sharp contrast with all the other exhibition pavilions. It is impossible to describe it in terms that would bring it before the mind's eye of an Englishman who had not seen it. For it is a gesture rather than a building, deriving its effects from a sense of severe, spacious, and efficient simplicity which we rarely find except in an up-to-date hospital or a modern power house. Its design is throughout rectangular. Its floors and its roof are of white stone. Some of its walls are also of white stone; others are of green marble. Along one side of it runs a wall that is also a window—a sheet of black glass, through which in daytime one may look out without being looked upon from outside. It contains a small stone pool in which is set a single statue. It leads out to a larger bathing pool [sic], at the extreme edge of which a cluster of water plants has been permitted. Here and there upon the floors a few steel chairs surround a steel table. Otherwise its only decorations are the black-lettered word "Alemania" upon its front, and the four German flags at the borders of its domain. A visitor remarked that a colored hand-kerchief, dropped on its white floor, would be hastily swept up as an insult to its austerity. Essentially this pavilion is the expression of a lonely, powerful and forward-looking spirit. It is a gesture, incomplete in itself, the significance of which finds its fulfillment in the displays of German industry else-where in the exhibition.

For you may follow the same theme through fourteen other displays which, in nine different pavilions of the Exhibition, enforce a sense of the industrial power of modern Germany. In some of these the task of the exhibitor has been made dif-ficult by the diversity and even by the triviality of the material for whose display he must provide. Certain features, however, are common to them all. The lowered roof of white canvas, the white walls, the single word "Alemania" in red, the black lettered titles of the exhibitors, the red lettered numbers of the exhibits, the steel or aluminum rails which protect or sup-port the exhibits, the steel tables and chairs, the spaciousness and the absence of irrelevant detail—all these repeated fea-tures are common to the fourteen other German displays. At one end of the exhibition is the Graphic Arts pavilion. Here in showcases of glass and aluminum, laid flat or set upright as screens, are arrayed examples of the finest German printing in the shape of books or of designs. In the German section in the pavilion of Communications and Transport giant ma-chines are set against a background of huge photographs, each the size of the wall of a room. You look upon a city as seen from an aeroplane, upon a huge factory, upon the gi-gantic machinery and cable network of a mine. Those black-and-white presentations of reality add incalculably to the force of the exhibits behind which they have been set. The same method is employed in the display of the German National Ministry of Electricity in its special pavilion. Elsewhere you pass through arrays of steel shelves and fittings for libraries, of safes, of office furniture, of typewriters and adding machines and addressographs and cash registers, and you end amid German machinery, black and dustless, spaciously displayed in a horizontal and rectangular order which conveys at once the sense of a powerful present and the inescapable suggestion of a yet more powerful future. So speaks at Barcelona the industrial ambition of Germany.

"A Visit to the Barcelona Exhibition," *The Spectator* (January 18, 1930): 84–85.

The Spectator is a weekly British cultural and political magazine continuously published since 1828, which, though conservative, was outspoken against the rise of National Socialist politics in Germany. Editor and owner from 1925 to 1932 was John Evelyn Leslie Wrench, a writer and avid traveler, founder of the Over-Seas Club in London (and possibly the author of this article). While playing to time-worn stereotypes about Germany when emphasizing the pavilion's "severe, spacious, and efficient simplicity" and meticulously maintained "austerity," the author stressed its outstanding importance. He had come late enough to the exhibition to notice the word "Alemania" in the front, which had been applied in October and was missing from all official photographs.

1930

GUSTAV ADOLF PLATZ
Architecture of Our Time

There can be no doubt that abstract space represents the most noble, the most cultivated form for our time. Its only embellishment might be, for example, the lively appearance of well-designed furnishings. This "empty"—flowing as it were—space, created from precious, partially transparent surfaces, is the result of the new art of building, to which Mies van der Rohe has made essential contributions. His pavilion of the German section at the world's fair of 1929 in Barcelona is a result of this approach to architecture, which envisions clarity and purity paired with richness and sensuality. The Pavilion is 60 meters long and consists of a travertine plinth on which chromium-covered steel posts with a cruciform footprint stand and carry, together with individual pieces of wall, the deep cantilevers of the reinforced concrete plates. Into this floating construction, walls of precious materials (marble, onyx, plate glass of different colors in metal frames) have been placed freely, so that they form a sequence of open spaces of vastly different lighting conditions, which one enjoys as one passes through them. A complete lack of axiality and conventional space enclosures, the transparency of the walls, the increasing twilight inside contrasting with a surprising flood of sunlight in certain areas, the size of the uninter-

rupted planes, and the stark beauty of the colors (for example honey-colored onyx, a black velour carpet, and nickel-covered metal furniture with white *glacé* leather cushions) are combined to form a strangely festive impression. "Ceiling and wall are without a close relationship; the roof plate hovering above its slender supports covers the large central section of the terrace, unconcerned with spatial overlaps. As one walks through the rooms, spatial coherence has been entirely maintained, and every impression is tied to its sequence; in every part the whole addresses our spirit as a fantastically assembled spatial work of art.

While Mies van der Rohe's building presents itself boldly and future-bound, the nobility of its appearance has overcome any opposition and has won many friends for a new Germany. A pure sound in the midst of hapless exhibition architectures inspired by romantic reminiscences, a beginning, which, for those with an unbiased eye, establishes a new, appropriate tradition." (Justus Bier, 1929)

Gustav Adolf Platz, *Die Baukunst der Neuesten Zeit*, 2nd ed. (Berlin: Propyläen Verlag, 1930), 80–81.

Gustav Adolf Platz (1881–1947), a German architect and critic, had worked with Fritz Schumacher in Hamburg before becoming Mannheim's municipal building director (1923–32). His 1927 book *Die Baukunst der neuesten Zeit* (Architecture of our time) was the first major attempt at a history of modern architecture, from its predecessors in the utilitarian buildings and engineering structures of the nineteenth century to the latest examples of the *Neues Bauen* (New Building) in Germany. The volume quickly sold out, and Platz prepared a new edition, which he finished in March 1930. It included examples beyond Germany (a detailed discussion of Le Corbusier, for example) and the most recent German buildings, such as the Stuttgart Weissenhof exhibition and Mies's Barcelona Pavilion. The volume has had a major influence on the historiography of modern architecture. The quote at the end comes from Justus Bier's text in Die Form of August 1929 (see pp. 66–71).

MARCELLO PIACENTINI
Architecture of Today

Mies van der Rohe, who is by nature both quiet and shy, is one of the young German architects with a great future ahead of him; his pavilion at the exhibition in Barcelona last year displayed an impressive uniqueness. It does not contain specific and precise spaces: some walls, less than four meters tall, are made out of glass; others, marble. They alternate with completely free spaces, sometimes connected by a solid ceiling, sometimes left uncovered, almost a series of unmovable screens.

No objects are exhibited; there is no symbolism. Instead: rhythms. Symphony of lines and color and nothing else. Rather than building a pompous pavilion with a hall of honor, galleries, and arcades, as all the other nations have done, Germany has announced its presence with this simple calling card, with this modest romance without words. Expression (oh, how ostentatious!) of a modesty of life, even of misery? Of a spiritual anti-imperialist direction?

Marcello Piacentini, *Architettura d'Oggi* (Rome: Paolo Cremonese, 1930), 39.

Marcello Piacentini (1881–1960), an Italian architect and urban theorist, became the official architect and planner of the Fascist regime under Benito Mussolini. While his own style evolved from neo-Renaissance historicism to the stripped-down classicism of buildings such as the administrative center for the university La Sapienza in Rome, he was also supportive of the International Style used by the Italian rationalists of the Gruppo 7. He developed the master plans for Rome's EUR district and for the Via della Conciliazione from the Castello Sant' Angelo to St. Peter's.

WALTER RIEZLER
The New Sense of Space in Art and Music

Enclosed spaces with clear, quiet proportions recede more and more in favor of parallel and penetrating spaces, which open up toward each other and toward the surrounding, unformed space. How the art of such spaces can be formally satisfying and filled with inner music is proven particularly well by the designs and executed spaces of the architect Ludwig Mies van der Rohe. For a long time, nothing as formally stringent as these very memorable creations has been built or designed. The most consistent among the executed examples was the German pavilion at the world's fair in Barcelona. How its different spaces flow into each other and how the entire building opens up toward the environs has no equal in the entire history of architecture. Only buildings by the French Le Corbusier can be considered its equal. It is of particular significance that frequently very large areas of semitransparent glass are used to limit the spaces, which underlines the impression of a new spatial reality. This reality not only is different from the spatiality of the Renaissance, but also that of the gothic age: while a gothic spatial arrangement can only be perceived by the visitor in motion, and thus in time, the basis of its plan and elevation is still a "static" idea, so to speak. All dynamics are eventually based on a calm essence, which is revealed in the symmetry of the whole and basically dominates every spatial section, so that even a person moving through space will be aware of it. [...] The spaces by Mies van der Rohe and Le Corbusier [...] can be comprehended by the visitor only in moving through them, and their entire essence is based—independently from the impression on the viewer—in their mutual penetration, the flowing into each other, and thus in a temporal event. To a much higher degree than with other architecture, the harmony of these buildings is based on music.

The only figural ornament in the German pavilion in Barcelona was a bronze figure by Georg Kolbe. Anyone who had gotten attuned to the essence of the space would consider this otherwise very beautiful figure as not truly fitting: it still stemmed from the world of the old space. Even though a sculpture is primarily about a body and not about space, the kind of spatial configuration into which this body is inserted is crucial. And in the case of a figure by Kolbe or another sculptor from that circle, the clarity and determination of its spatial configuration still differs little from that of the Renaissance or the Baroque. Clearly, sculpture, whose subject always remains the same, is more bound by tradition than painting. Thus it is even more important that the new sense of space will also eventually enter sculpture. This applies not just to the sculpture of Archipenko and his circle, with its affinity to Cubistic forms, but also to sculpture much closer to naturalism. Since [Wilhelm] Lehmbruck and [Ernst] Barlach a new sculptural attitude is gaining ground which contemplates nature from the position of a new spatial idea: it is based on a less concise constellation of order and a complicated system of axes. And the old rules of statics don't apply to it anymore—parallel to the new sense of statics in architecture; these figures don't stand solidly on the ground anymore, even where their motif has nothing to do with weightlessness, they seem to be levitating. And here too, one can find that the old Renaissance demand for visual comprehension—which Adolf Hildebrand had emphasized for sculpture in particular—does really not exist anymore, that, in any case, no form is chosen in order to fulfill this demand, but instead that these figures lead their lives, so to speak, unbothered by the viewer, in a single-minded allegiance to nature that lends their faces an entirely new and strange expression. [...]

With the definition of four-dimensional space, moving in time, the sciences [...] have created a concept, which directly connects to both atonality in music, and the new sense of space in the fine arts.

Walter Riezler, "Das neue Raumgefühl in bildender Kunst und Musik," in *Vierter Kongress für Ästhetik und allgemeine Kunstwissenschaft*, Hamburg, October 7-9, 1930, *Zeitschrift für Ästhetik und allgemeine Kunstwissenschaft*, no. 1 (1931): 179-216, quote 202-204.

The occasion of **Walter Riezler's** (1878-1965) lecture was the Fourth Congress for Aesthetics and General Art History in Hamburg, dedicated to "Design of Space and Time in Art" in October 1930. It had been organized by Germany's most prominent art historians: Aby Warburg, Erwin Panofsky, Ernst Cassirer, and Fritz Saxl. Riezler, an art and music historian, had been a cofounder of the German Werkbund and was editor of its journal *Die Form*. He was among the first to comment on the "flowing space" inside the pavilion, as an example of the "new spatial reality" (in which, however, he found Kolbe's sculpture misplaced). Riezler also emphasized the visitor's movement as the basis of modern spatial experience, an idea which had been applied by art historians like Heinrich Wölfflin and August Schmarsow since the 1890s initially to the architecture of the Baroque period.

1931

CARLO ENRICO RAVA
The Need for Selection

Mies van der Rohe—among the best known of the uncompromising German architects—demonstrates what high results the interpretation and courage of an independent intelligence can give us. In fact, this rationalist among rationalists, who is regarded as one of the great figures of Germany's architectural revolution, was in charge of building Germany's (official, it should be noted) pavilion, at the exposition at Barcelona. He dared to imagine a building in which the only material used, in addition to large sheets of glass and small amounts of metal in the slender pillars, doors and windows, is marble for all walls and floors; this marble, "the most outdated" thing, which all the hard-liners believed had been relegated to the attic, together with the old traditional styles. Now, with this flat pavilion, Mies van der Rohe has managed to create one of the most perfect and modern pieces of architecture that we've seen in recent years, with a conception of simple grandeur (albeit in a small space), which suggests an Aegean inspiration: Knossos and Hagia Triada; with a clarity of line and profile, with a crystal-clear, mysterious transparency, with a sober wealth of precious reflections, which have made it a unique example of its kind, precise as a machine, clear as a diamond.

Carlo Enrico Rava, "Necessitá di Selezione," Parte Prima, *Domus* (1931): 36-40, 84.

Carlo Enrico Rava (1903–1985) was an Italian critic, furniture designer, and architect. He graduated from the Politecnico di Milano in 1926 and then founded Gruppo 7 together with Giuseppe Terragni, Luigi Figini, Gino Pollini, and others. In 1931, however, he left the organization in order to join RAMI (Raggruppamento Architetti Moderni Italiani), which had been founded by the Fascist architects' syndicate. He visited the Italian colonies and tried to develop a "modern colonial architecture," and a "Mediterranean rationalism." In the late 1930s he also worked as a set designer for Cinecittà in Rome. Rava is one of the earliest critics who saw classic Mediterranean connotations in the pavilion.

1932

RAYMOND MCGRATH
Looking into Glass

The German pavilion at the Barcelona exhibition. Walls of black glass reflecting a garden and water, shining stanchions, a polished ceiling, and a terrace of travertine combine to make Mies van der Rohe's "metaphysical pavilion" one of the most beautiful, poetical, and stimulating pieces of building ever associated with the ordinary vulgarities of an exhibition. [...] To Mies van der Rohe belongs the credit of imbuing modern architectural forms with the genuine spiritual qualities of great design. His magnificent simplicity, his sensitiveness to form, and his understanding of special relationships combine to make his rare works outstanding. He is known particularly by his interiors at the Plate Glass exhibition at Stuttgart, by his German pavilion at the Barcelona exhibition, and most recently by his Haus Tugendhat in Brünn. At Stuttgart he discovered the value of black glass in creating depth and space. At Barcelona the black glass wall of his terrace reflected in dark tones the foliage of the whole garden. This pavilion was clean and empty, in strange contrast to other exhibition stands. Its rooms and patios were uninhabited. Sudden encounter with metaphysical architecture brought home its beauty. The house at Brünn is an arrangement of connected and related spaces. The living room, with its screens of waxed wood and honey-colored onyx, is divided only by plate glass walls from the garden and along one side of it, as in a glass avenue, runs the winter garden.

Raymond McGrath, "Looking into Glass," *The Architectural Review* (January 1932): 29-30.

1934
RAYMOND MCGRATH
Twentieth-Century Houses

Miës van der Rohe is an architect who says little about himself and has put up only a small number of houses. But such is the surprising quality of what he has done that his name is second to nobody's in present-day building. [...]

In his design for a brick country-house (1922) he first made use of the free plan, in the later development of which he went far in front of anything so far attempted by Wright in America. In his Garden House at the Barcelona Exposition he put the idea into full effect. The limiting and seeming expansion of space in building are facts to be taken into account not only physically but in theory. The architects of the old days took great pleasure in the designing of buildings on an important scale with solid columns and rooms as high as houses. [...] But this sort of building has given way to the straightforward use of space and the free balancing of the parts—design not with outside walls but with inside space. To Mies van der Rohe, to-day's Brunelleschi, goes the credit of giving new building-forms the true qualities of great design. His houses are examples of a simple, delicate and certain feeling for form and material, of a clear knowledge of space relations.

At Stuttgart in the Plate Glass exposition he gave an example of the value of black glass in making space and giving a feeling of greater space. At Barcelona the black glass wall of the terrace darkly gives back the moving leaves of the garden. This Garden House was clean and open—unlike the other buildings of the Exposition. Its rooms and walled square had nobody living in them. To see it was like coming face-to-face with someone strange and beautiful. This building, with its glass and water, its bright columns and its quiet girl in stone, was a place for the mind's play more than for the business of living.

Raymond McGrath, *Twentieth-Century Houses* (London: Faber & Faber, 1934), 168.

Raymond McGrath (1903–1977) was an Australian-born interior architect and writer who worked in London before becoming principal architect for the Office of Public Works in Ireland in 1940. As he had not visited the pavilion, he mistook the black marble for glass when he described it in *The Architectural Review*. In his book *Twentieth-Century Houses*) he extended his text with a new interpretation of the pavilion as a "garden house" and juxtaposed it with a modern garden house with a flat roof in Stuttgart by Otto Valentin (1930). His friend and collaborator Christopher Tunnard, a garden designer, adopted this view in his famous book *Gardens in the Modern Landscape* (1938).[1]

1   Tunnard showed the Barcelona Pavilion, identifying it merely as "a garden house by Mies van der Rohe." He lauded its "bright metal columns" and observed that the "black glass walls reflect with curious depth the pattern of the surrounding water garden." Christopher Tunnard, *Gardens in the Modern Landscape* (London: The Architectural Press, 1938), 103,104.

GUIDO HARBERS
The German Reich's Pavilion at the International Exhibition in Barcelona 1929; Architect Mies van der Rohe, Berlin

This collection of contemporary single-family homes would show a distinctive gap if it would not also report on the conclusions that German architects have come to at the currently final step in the genealogy of a country house's floor plan. Its characteristics are: dissolution of the enclosed room, spatial interlacing, deep connection of the protected living room with the adjacent garden or open nature. Mies van der Rohe was the one who gave to this, not exactly new, demand of English country house architecture, which the American architect Frank Lloyd Wright also repeatedly tried to realize, its appropriate constructive execution and formal appearance; most purely so far in his programmatic pavilion of the German Reich at the Barcelona exhibition of 1929, and again at his Tugendhat House and the single-family home at the Berlin Building Exhibition of 1931. The exhibition pavilion, however, is still unmatched. It provided a framework for cultivated entertainment in a southern country. The structural elements are essentially two plates—floor and ceiling—and supports, which hold the ceiling plate at a certain height above the floor plate, plus non-load-bearing screens, which could be out of any material, from Japanese cane weave to glass and marble. Essentially, they could be moveable and be placed anywhere. The required piece of land can be astonishingly small. The common denominator is the placement of such walls, be they defining outer walls or divisional screens inside, directly in front of or behind the metal supports, whose static system provides the ground plan with regularly placed sections. From this rational grid and its irrational and rhythmically free placement of walls stems the basic counterpoint of confinement and freedom, which might inspire the art of architecture, in particular in the field of residential design.

Guido Harbers, *Das freistehende Einfamilienhaus von 10,000–30,000 Mark und über 30,000 Mark* (Munich: Callwey, 1932): 94.

Guido Harbers (1897–1977) was a German architect, critic, and publicist. He was trained at the Technical University in Munich and initially worked in the office of Munich modernist Robert Vorhoelzer, before becoming a high-ranking administrator in the municipal building department. As the editor-in-chief of the architecture journal *Der Baumeister* (from 1927 on) and author of several monographs, he had significant influence on the German architectural debate. Stuttgart's Weissenhof exhibition had been extensively critiqued as formalistic in his magazine,[1] but he was enthusiastic about the Barcelona Pavilion. "Mies's newest creation is destined to represent Germany's culture in the now peaceful competition of nations. It is well positioned to inspire and initiate German architectural culture. We embrace this work wholeheartedly."[2] A more detailed analysis followed in his book about single family homes in 1932. When the National Socialists came to power in 1933, Harbers joined the NSDAP and embraced a more traditional formal language. In this style he designed in 1934 the experimental Ramersdorf estate in Munich, for the Deutsche Siedlungsausstellung, a Nazi response to the Stuttgart Weissenhof estate. The positive account of this conservative (and soon National Socialist) critic show the ambivalent political position that Mies's pavilion could command at that moment.

1   Rudolf Pfister, "Stuttgarter Werkbundausstellung 'Die Wohnung'". *Der Baumeister* 26.2 (February 1928): 33–72.
2   Guido Harbers, "Deutscher Reichspavillon in Barcelona auf der Internationalen Ausstellung 1929," *Der Baumeister* 27, no. 11 (November 1929): 421–27.

FRANK LLOYD WRIGHT
Letter to Philip C. Johnson

Someday let's persuade Mies to get rid of those damned little steel posts that look so dangerous and interfering in his lovely designs. He really doesn't need them as much as he thinks he does.

I am sending some plans of the Home on the Mesa which should be enlarged if possible so others can understand the organic simplicity of a design wherein style arises from the nature of construction. A design intended to show how machine-age luxury might compare with that of the Greeks or Goths.

Carbon copy of letter from Frank Lloyd Wright to Philip Johnson, February 26, 1932, fiche #M029B03, Frank Lloyd Wright Archive, Avery Library, Columbia University, New York.

This letter is part of an extended correspondence between Wright and Johnson during the somewhat chaotic buildup to the *Modern Architecture* exhibition at the Museum of Modern Art in 1932. Wright had been a reluctant and difficult participant, and his project arrived only at the last minute. In this letter he criticized Mies's pavilion and presented his own project as a counterproposal, but many critics would later charge that Wright's House on the Mesa owed several design ideas to Mies's projects for the Concrete and Brick Country Houses of 1923 and 1924.

1932

PHILIP C. JOHNSON
Ludwig Mïes van der Rohe

In his peculiar treatment of space and in his keen sense for decoration and materials Mïes is unique. For him a building is a series of partially enclosed spaces opening into one another and opening to the exterior without the intervention of a solid screen as a defining facade. The planes which define these spaces he makes independent and apparently intersecting by the use of a different material for each plane: plate glass, marble, or screens of wood. These varying planes of rich materials form the basis also of Mïes' scheme of decoration. [...]

It was not until 1929, however, in the Barcelona Pavilion that Mïes really added to the aesthetic innovations of his Country House of 1922. The new element is the rigidly regular system of steel posts and the simple rectangular roof slab, which replace the arbitrary brick walls and irregular roof slab of the earlier project. Space flows around this rigid system. Partial screen walls, so placed as to create the feeling of space beyond, form separate rooms. The posts stand away from the walls in order to allow freedom of planning and to emphasize aesthetically the rhythm of the structure. So strong is the feeling for one space, rather than separate rooms, that Mies often continues the wall screens beyond their intersections except at the four corners of the entire plan.

Philip C. Johnson, "Mies van der Rohe," in *Modern Architecture: International Exhibition*, exh. cat. Museum of Modern Art, New York (New York: Museum of Modern Art, 1932), 111–20, here 115.

Philip Cortelyou Johnson (1906 – 2005) was an influential American architect, curator and critic. He was a prolific designer, best known are his Glass House in New Canaan, Connecticut, and the AT&T tower at 550 Madison Avenue in New York. He won both the Pritzker Prize and the AIA Gold Medal. Together with Henry-Russell Hitchcock he organized the 1932 „Modern Architecture" Exhibition at the Museum of Modern Art, in which Mies was one of the major protagonists and a solo show for Mies at MoMA in 1947. Johnson would later collaborate with Mies on the Seagram Building in New York City. The chapter on Mies in the catalogue of MoMA's "Modern Architecture" exhibition in 1932 was the only one written by Johnson. The other eight chapters (on Wright, Gropius, Le Corbusier, Oud, Hood, Howe & Lescaze, Neutra, Bowman Brothers) were written by Henry-Russell Hitchcock. In great contrast to Wright, Johnson welcomed the grid of the steel columns as an aesthetic improvement. Johnson had initially hoped that Mies would "plan the installation of the exhibition," such as "designing bases for the models, tables for the literature, chairs, photograph racks, and partition screens of glass and metal" in order to "show to some extent in actual objects what has been achieved in modern architecture."[1] While this particular collaboration failed to bear fruit, Mies's work was very much a centerpiece of the exhibition.[2] The Barcelona Pavilion was shown in several of Stone's photographs but not as a model since, according to Johnson, "one would see nothing but the roof."[3]

1 Philip Johnson, "Built to Live in" (New York: Museum of Modern Art, 1931), n.p., accessed August 28, 2017, https://www.moma.org/documents/moma_catalogue_2044_300153621.pdf.
2 For the prehistory of the exhibition, see Terence Riley, *The International Style: Exhibition 15 and the Museum of Modern Art* (New York: Rizzoli, Columbia Books of Architecture, 1992), 74–78.
3 Philip Johnson to Alfred Barr, 7 August 1931, MoMA, 1932 Modern Architecture exhibition correspondence.

1936

GEORGE HOWE
Abstract Design in Modern Architecture

We are all familiar with the well-conceived and delicately designed groups of workmen's houses, community buildings, hospitals, and churches erected by such men as [J. J. P.] Oud and [Alvar] Aalto. They do not flaunt their abstract quality but show it rather in the reduction of an architectural-social complex to its simplest terms. It is not, however, in such useful buildings that we find the space-time idea most clearly expressed. It was to be seen rather in Mies van der Rohe's German pavilion at the Barcelona exposition, where all utilitarian considerations were absent. The past tense is used advisedly, for the pavilion has long since been demolished. Its disappearance is perhaps prophetic of a period when we shall have reduced the time element of our lives to a complete abstraction and nothing will remain of architecture but pure conceptual space. At the present moment we are still dealing in realities, though realities reduced to their most abstract form. In the pavilion of Mies van der Rohe, floors, coverings, supports, and vertical subdivisions have ceased to be space enclosures and become mere planes and axes of reference by which space and time relations may be registered. In architecture, as has been said, movement, the movement of human beings through space, corresponds roughly to time in

mathematics, and physical space delimited by one or more axes or planes to theoretical space. In this building the contemporary space-time idea as flowing, continuous, and relative is carried to the furthest limits of architectural expression. A system of tenuous steel posts, constituting no more than a diagram of lines, supports a roof slab of no great extent approximating an ideal plane without thickness. Through this structure movement takes place in principle freely in all directions, inside and out. There are no enclosing walls. This is the frame of reference within which a line of movement must be determined by specific magnitudes. These magnitudes are established by subdividing the space under and immediately outside the roof slab by a system of straight vertical screen walls, as thin as possible, which form a very single meandering pattern quite independent of the supporting posts. They give the impression of being movable to new positions almost at will, while at the same time they are disposed with consummate skill so as to carry the observer along the most agreeable curves of movement. They overlap, are unequal in length, and differ in material, some being of glass and some of solid substances. At no point is the space under the roof completely enclosed, so that in wandering through and around the screens one is at times in the full light and air, at times behind glass, at others in partial obscurity. At one end, where three walls determine a half-turning movement, they project beyond the roof slab so that the eye is carried for a moment up to the sky. At the other end a large open enclosure, walled on two sides only and containing a broad reflecting pool, determines a transition between the limited space under the roof slab and the unlimited space around. There are no doors, nor is there any definite point of access to the enclosure, yet there is never anywhere nor at any time a sense

of vagueness or formlessness. The absence of integral decoration, such as sculptured ornament or mural painting, is an
inevitable consequence of the space-time idea. Such elements would destroy the effectiveness of the planes of reference, first by giving them an appearance of fixity improper to
their function and second by introducing distinct space relations of their own, confusing the essential line of movement.
The surfaces of the various planes consist necessarily of uninterrupted polished materials, glass, marble, and stone, so that
the observer's eye is never too long distracted by local interest from its proper task of registering space-time movements.
As in Greek and Gothic architecture the visible elements are
an obligatory development of the space idea, not a mere
whim of personal taste. There is only one pure ornament in
the Pavilion, a single statue standing in a small pool at one
end of the turning-point, already referred to, at the further
extremity of the composition. It stands freely in space without
architectural frame or rigid axial position, and serves only to
retard momentarily the flow of the general movement where
it changes direction and form. This building, as has been said,
represents probably the furthest point to which the abstract
space-time idea has been carried, liberated of all the purely
material restrictions which usually govern architecture.

George Howe, "Abstract Design in Modern Architecture," *Parnassus* 8, no. 5 (October 1936): 29-31.

George Howe (1886-1955) was an American architect and teacher. Thanks
to his collaboration with William Lescaze on Philadelphia's PSFS building
(1929-32), the first International Style skyscraper, he is considered one of
the first modernists in American architecture, despite his many buildings in
an Arts and Crafts–inflected vernacular.
Howe's text was delivered as a lecture on April 9, 1936, at the annual meeting of the College Art Association in a session held at the Museum of Modern Art. It coincided with the museum's exhibition *Cubism and Abstract Art*
(March 2-April 19, 1936), in which both Mies's country house design and his
Barcelona Pavilion were included.

1940

ELIZABETH MOCK AND
J. M. RICHARDS
An Introduction to Modern Architecture

Another of the great original figures who emerged in post-1918 Europe is the German Mies van der Rohe, an architect who handles materials with absolute logic, absolute precision, and develops his ends from his means with startling consistency. His structural purity is unique in modern architecture. Perfection, of course, can be a great bore and it is only Mies's consummate artistry and subtle feeling for spatial relationships that preserve him from this pitfall. Most characteristically he defines the flow of space by a free arrangement of screen-like walls, kept completely independent of the parallel rows of columns that do the work of supporting the roof, and achieves a fine rhythmic relationship between the broad flat planes of the walls and the regularly repeated verticals of the supports. Often he has made his wall-planes of rich, smoothly polished materials—exotic woods or veined marble, a very satisfactory modern substitute for applied ornament. The beautiful pavilion at Barcelona [...] is an excellent illustration of the serene elegance of his developed style, and its ground plan [...] deserves particularly careful study. Expression of materials and construction generally took a very secondary place in this period, and not occasionally the structure and even the function of a building were verily tortured to achieve the fashionable effect of paper-thin, plane-like walls and overall geometric purity. Often it was the self-styled functionalists who were most ruthlessly doctrinaire in their design—an irony worth mention in connection with the argument [...] that modern architecture never has been literally functionalist.

Elizabeth Mock and J. M. Richards, *An Introduction to Modern Architecture* (London: Pelican Books, 1940), 70-71, 110-11.

Elizabeth (Bauer) Mock (later Kassler, 1911–1998) was an architect, historian, and publicist. Trained at Vassar College in Poughkeepsie (NY) in English and at Frank Lloyd Wright's Taliesin in architecture, she worked for the Museum of Modern Art in New York and served as director of the department of architecture and design from 1942 to 1946. Among her exhibitions are *What is Modern Architecture?* (1938) and *Built in the USA: 1932-1944* (1944). **James Maude Richards** (1907–1992) was trained at the Architectural Association School of Architecture in London and worked for the engineer Owen Williams before embarking on his career as a writer on architecture. He served as the editor of *The Architectural Review* from 1937 to 1971.

1947

PHILIP C. JOHNSON
Mies van der Rohe

The culminating achievement of Mies's European career was
the German pavilion for the International Exposition at Barcelona in 1929. The Barcelona Pavilion has been acclaimed by
critics and architects alike as one of the milestones of modern
architecture. It is truly one of the few manifestations of the
contemporary spirit that justifies comparison with the great
architecture of the past, and it is lamentable that it existed for
only one season. Here for the first time Mies was able to build
a structure unhampered by functional requirements or insufficient funds. In doing so he incorporated many characteristics
of his previous work, such as insistence on expert craftsmanship and rich materials, respect for the regular steel skeleton,
and preoccupation with extending walls into space. Critics
have seen in the hovering roof and open plan a reflection of
Frank Lloyd Wright's prairie houses; in the disposition of the
walls, the influence of De Stijl; or in the elevation of the structure on a podium, a touch of Schinkel. But the important fact
is that all of these elements were fused in the crucible of
Mies's imagination to produce an original work of art.
The design is simultaneously simple and complex: its ingredients are merely steel columns and independent rectangular
planes of various materials placed vertically as walls or hori-

zontally as roofs; but they are disposed in such a way that space is channeled rather than confined—it is never stopped, but is allowed to flow continuously. The only decorative elements besides the richness of materials are two rectangular pools and a statue by Georg Kolbe, and these are inseparable components of the composition.

The independent walls and flowing space are developments of motifs which Mies first evolved in the Brick Country House of 1923, and on which he has been composing variations ever since. Sometimes this effect is only part of a larger design, as in the well-known Tugendhat House in Brno, Czechoslovakia, of 1930, where space can be said to flow only on the main living floor. Here the overall plan, devised to meet the needs of a growing family, is closed rather than open.

Philip C. Johnson, *Mies van der Rohe*, exh. cat. Museum of Modern Art, New York (New York: Museum of Modern Art, 1947), 58, 60.

Besides a smaller show at the Chicago Art Institute in 1938 and an exhibition at the Renaissance Society at the University of Chicago earlier that same year (May 16–June 7, 1947), this exhibition was the first major monographic show on Mies van der Rohe's work, and its catalogue the first book-length study on his oeuvre. Mies collaborated closely with **Philip C. Johnson** (biography see p. 131) on all aspects of the exhibition and catalogue and designed the layout. With Mies's prewar drawings still in Germany, the exhibition was dominated by wall-high photographs of his earlier work, among them Sasha Stone's view toward Kolbe's statue along the back corridor of the pavilion.

1947

FRANK LLOYD WRIGHT AND LUDWIG MIES VAN DER ROHE
Two Letters

October 25, 1947

My dear Mies,

Somebody had told me you were hurt by remarks of mine when I came to see your New York show. And I made them to you directly I think. But did I tell you how fine I thought your handling of your material was?

I am conscious only of two "cracks." One: you know you have frequently said you believe in "doing next to nothing" all down the line. Well, when I saw the enormous blow-ups the phrase "Much ado about next to nothing" came spontaneously from me.

Then I said the Barcelona Pavilion was your best contribution to the original "negation" and you seemed to be still back there where I was then.

This is probably what hurt (coming from me) and I wish I had taken you aside to say it to you privately because it does seem to me that the whole thing called "Modern Architecture" has bogged down with the architects right there on that line. I didn't want to classify you with them—but the show struck me as sharply as reactionary in that sense. I am fighting hard against it myself.

But this note is to say that I wouldn't want to hurt your feelings—even with the truth. You are the best of them all as an artist and a man.

You came to see me but once (and that was before you spoke English) many years ago. You never came since, though often invited.

So I had no chance to see or say what I said then and say now. Why don't you come up sometime—unless the break is irreparable—and let's argue.

Affection,

Frank Lloyd Wright

November 25, 1947

My dear Frank,

Thank you so much for your letter.

It was an exaggeration if you heard that my feelings were hurt by your remarks at my New York show. If I had heard the crack "Much ado about—next to—nothing" I would have laughed with you. About "negation" I feel that you use this word for qualities that I find positive and essential.

It would be a pleasure to see you again sometime in Wisconsin and discuss this subject further.

As ever,

Mies

Frank Lloyd Wright to Mies van der Rohe, 25 October 1947 and Mies to Wright, 25 November 1947, Museum of Modern Art, Mies van der Rohe Papers.

This exchange between Wright and Mies unfolded weeks after both men had attended the opening of the Museum of Modern Art's exhibition on Mies van der Rohe on September 15, 1947. It documents Wright's ongoing attempts at defining his own architecture as distinctly separate from that of his European peers. The opening of the exhibition was the last time the architects saw each other.

1955

BRUNO ZEVI
History of Modern Architecture

Finally, in 1929, the Barcelona Pavilion, Mies's masterpiece. The method of composition of his spatial concept gets more precise: a regular series of steel posts supports the roof panel; under this premise, the immaculate walls are free to divide the space or serve as hinges. A figurative dictionary: isolated floor plates, crisp sheets of the most diverse materials and colors. Outside, the base plate and the background are Roman travertine; the wall around the statue, green marble. Inside, we find a crystal gray septum, a luminous double glass sheet, a diaphragm of green glass between the atrium and the space of the statue, a mirror of onyx, and finally the coating of the pool in black glass. We can see a clear definition of Mies. [...] The slab of onyx slides underneath the roof slab to fit between it and the sheet of the floor construction; this type of composition applies to floor plans and cross sections. It is appropriate to point out what is implied with this language. Since the prismatic stereometry has been torn up, and the geometry of rectangles has been abandoned in plan and facade, what are the expressive instruments of Mies's language? Evidently, his visions, as they don't arrange volumes and surfaces, but only terse isolated planes, point to space. [...] Only in Mies van der Rohe's work the architectural vacuum directs, space flows between walls, brings the ambience together, and extends outward. If one stops to observe the segmented weave of the plans, the relationship with the neo-plastic painters, in particular Piet Mondrian, will seem decisive, and, in fact, the historians of Mies systematically point this out. But if one instead thinks of architecture—except that the grid lines of Mondrian always end at the frame of the picture, while the directions of Mies go beyond—you will find that he is a poet of the rationalist period. [...] This is precisely the genius of the Barcelona pavilion.

Bruno Zevi, *Storia dell'architettura moderna* (Turin: Einaudi, 1955), 143.

Bruno Zevi (1918–2000) was an Italian architect and historian. He studied under Gropius at Harvard and, in 1945, became professor of architectural history at the University of Venice, before later teaching at the University of Rome. He wrote a daily column for the weekly magazine *L'Espresso* and, for forty-six years, edited the magazine *L'architettura: Cronache e Storia*. He wrote books about organic architecture, architecture as space, modern architecture, Michelangelo, and Erich Mendelsohn and was a major proponent of Frank Lloyd Wright's organic architecture. In his 1957 publication *Architecture as Space* (based on *Saper Vedere l'Architettura* of 1951), Zevi had merely spoken of "continuous space" and "an uninterrupted flow in the succession of visual angles" at the Barcelona Pavilion, while in this publication he embraced the term "flowing space" for the first time.[1]

1 Bruno Zevi, *Architecture as Space: How to Look at Architecture* (New York: Horizon Press, 1957), 144.

1956

LUDWIG HILBERSEIMER
Mies van der Rohe

Architecture is placed in space and at the same time encloses space. Therefore, a double problem arises—the handling of exterior space, as well as interior space. These two kinds of space can be unrelated to each other, or they can, by various means, be united. The outer space can merge with the inner, the inner space with the outer. Or both can flow into one space. With the Brick Country House, Mies van der Rohe made his first contribution to the solution of our space problem, to which he has contributed so greatly. In a way this house symbolizes his space concept, the flowing together of inner and outer space. The long, low walls extending into the open bring the outdoors in the house, which, with its large apertures is in turn open to the outside, while the rooms inside are open to each other. [...]

With infinite eloquence he expressed his space concept in the Barcelona Pavilion. It was a building without the usual practical limitations. Its sole purpose was to represent Germany at the International Exposition in Barcelona. It was based on a skeleton structure and consisted of three equal rectangular bays with cantilevered ends. Between the two horizontal planes of the floor and the ceiling, vertical planes were disposed in an unusual way. They differed in material, size, and proportion, dividing the enclosed space at the same time they united it optically. The result was a simplicity which was, as always, complexity itself. The building was embellished not only by the richness of the colorful marbles used but also through the succession of different space compartments. None was closed. All led from one to the other. The space seemed to be in motion, flowing from one part to another, merging with the enclosed water court and finally with the outside space. As the inside and the outside space united, so did the rational of the structure with the irrational of the space concept, resulting in a masterpiece of architecture, in a great work of art. It is a sad loss to architecture that the Barcelona Pavilion was demolished. It could have remained as great a source of inspiration as any building of our age.

Ludwig Hilberseimer, *Mies van der Rohe* (Chicago: Paul Theobald & Co., 1956), 41–42.

Ludwig Karl Hilberseimer (1885–1967) was a German-American architect and urban planner. He taught at the Bauhaus from 1929 to 1933 and then followed Mies van der Rohe to the US to teach urban planning at the Illinois Institute of Technology. For a number of years, he served as director of the city planning office of Chicago. Just like Philip Johnson, Hilberseimer identified the first realization of Mies's spatial concept in the Brick Country House, but he is noticeably more observant and careful in his description of the pavilion.

1957

ULRICH CONRADS
From Exhibited Buildings to Exhibition Buildings

Vis-à-vis nature, pure architectural form appears as something distinct; as representation of an attitude. For this we can point to the famous example of the pavilion which Mies van der Rohe built for the International Exhibition in Barcelona in 1929. Here, neither functional demands nor insufficient funds set limits to the creative freedom. Here, pure architecture was realized—in an exhibition building: rectangular planes—vertical as walls and horizontal as ceilings—and steel girders were arranged in such a way that the result was not contained space, but built space; a continuous, seemingly simple, but truly very complicated spatial assemblage, elevated toward the festive and unusual thanks to its precious materials: chromed steel, onyx, gray, and bottle-green transparent glass, black and etched glass, Roman travertine, and green marble. This pavilion, a piece of absolute architecture, a masterpiece, was permitted—we choose our words carefully: was permitted—to represent the German Reich in Barcelona in 1929. One had courage, and one believed, for the first and only time in twentieth-century Germany, that an architectural statement, given form in a building, would assume symbolic power and represent the attitude of a people. And this all by itself, without emblems and ornaments, and particularly without "displays," without a "presentation of accomplishments." While certainly the thought and autonomous achievement of 1929 cannot be repeated, we nevertheless want to recall that event, in the face of the *horror vacui* of our time. Today we would see—of that we are certain—ministers, lobbyists, managing directors travel to Barcelona by the trainload. After all, there is unused, empty space. Seemingly empty space. And we have so much to show. And when much has to be shown—following the rules of internal fairness—even more needs to be shown. Until the shop is really full.

The Barcelona Pavilion wasn't a shop, but still, the world has given it more and in particular longer-lasting attention than any other German exhibition building of the past three decades. It was not only, like Joseph Paxton's Crystal Palace for the London world's fair of 1851, a stepping stone for a new architecture, but also key for a new attitude, a new kind of representation.

Ulrich Conrads, "Von ausgestellten Bauten zu Ausstellungsbauten," *Bauwelt* 48, no. 31 (August 5, 1957): 777.

Ulrich Conrads (1923-2013) was a highly influential German publicist and architecture critic in the second half of the twentieth century. He edited the architecture magazines *Baukunst und Werkform* (1954-57), *Bauwelt* (1957-88) and *Daidalos* (1981-92) and published a series of 150 foundational texts about modern architecture (Bauwelt Fundamente). In 1961, on the occasion of Mies's seventy-fifth birthday, Conrads began a campaign to invite Mies to Berlin to design a gallery of the twentieth century, which resulted in the commission for the Neue Nationalgalerie (New National Gallery).[1]

1   Ulrich Conrads, "Mies van der Rohe 75 Jahre," *Bauwelt* 52, no. 13 (March 27, 1961): 363.

1957

NIKOLAUS PEVSNER
An Outline of European Architecture

If one were compelled to choose one work as the most perfect, it ought probably be the German pavilion at the Barcelona Exhibition of 1929 by Ludwig Mies van der Rohe (born
1886 at Aachen), low, with a completely unmolded travertine
base, walls of glass and dark green Tinian marble, and a flat
white roof. The interior was entirely open, with shiny steel
shafts of cross section and divided only by screen walls of
onyx, bottle-green glass, etc. In this pavilion, unfortunately
long since demolished, Mies van der Rohe proved what the
enemies of the new style had always denied, that monumen-
tality was accessible to it by means not of columnar shams
but of splendid materials and a noble spatial rhythm.

Nikolaus Pevsner, *An Outline of European Architecture* (London: Penguin Books, 6th Jubilee ed.,
1960), 415–16. (The expanded section that contains the text quoted here appeared first in the
German 1957 edition of *Europäische Architektur von den Anfängen bis zur Gegenwart.*)

Nikolaus Pevsner (1902–1983) was a German-born British architectural
historian and critic. While perhaps best known for his forty-six-volume *The
Buildings of England* (1951–74) he also played a major role in the historiography of modern architecture through countless essays in the British architectural press and major publications, *Pioneers of the Modern Movement:
From William Morris to Walter Gropius* (1936), *An Outline of European Architecture* (1943) and *A History of Building Types* (1974).

ORIOL BOHIGAS
Sensational News: Mies van der Rohe Offers to Rebuild the Famous Pavilion of 1929

In October, 1954, we wrote a few lines in these pages recalling the architectural marvel that was the Pavilion Mies van der Rohe built for Germany at the 1929 Barcelona Exhibition, the most important, culturally transcendent work built in Spain in recent centuries. We regretted its immediate disappearance after the Exhibition closed, while so many sadly mediocre palaces remained, and we pointed out the possibility of a reconstruction that could be the first archaeological project carried out for modern architecture and the first monument raised to the great pioneer of the new art. [...]

Given this growing interest, we wrote to Mies van der Rohe, now residing in Chicago and Director of the School of Architecture at the famous Illinois Institute of Technology. Mies's reply was rapid and specific. He put himself at our service with great enthusiasm and promised to carry out this reconstruction, freely donating his personal involvement in the project's planning and management. This letter, which we are preserving with special feeling, has a tremendous importance for Barcelona. At the present time, Mies van der Rohe is surely the world's most sought after architect, the man for whom you have to wait months and months in order to commission anything of importance. His generous cooperation in the reconstruction of the famous Pavilion would be the most important gift offered to the city of Barcelona in many years.

It seemed to those of us who were more or less committed to this enterprise that before making anything public it was advisable to specify the possibilities precisely. So, taking advantage of a recent trip, the architect Francesc Bassó, professor at our School, visited Mies at his school at the IIT to approach him definitely with this subject on behalf of all of us.

Bassó relates how Mies, the venerable and famous Mies, dispensed with the waiting periods that are generally required before being able to see him, and Bassó received an extraordinarily cordial reception when it was learned that he was going to speak about the early work in Barcelona.

Mies explained that, when the 1929 Exhibition closed, there was an attempt made to preserve the Pavilion and the German government was asked to give it to the city of Barcelona. The German government refused to do this and so it was dismantled. Most of the materials were shipped to Germany, with the probable exception of a part of the metal supporting structure that remained stored in our municipal warehouses. The materials that returned to Germany were kept for a time, but were later scattered and are presumed totally lost. Another interesting thing to establish was the existence of the original design. Mies explained that the blueprint for the Pavilion, whith all the details for construction was filed in a studio he had kept in Germany, and this was destroyed during the last war. So, the slightest trace of the plans were lost. This, Mies makes clear, is not going to be an obstacle to the completion of the reconstruction; because as he assures us, he recalls all of the details, all of the elements, all of the materials necessary to recreate the blueprints that will permit the work to be built again with absolute accuracy. He is therefore, willing to get down to work as soon as he receives the definite commission. Regarding the overseeing of the work, he states that it will not present any problems since the organization of his studio permits him to do it perfectly well from a distance. In any case, he wishes to make known his desire to return, for this purpose, to Barcelona—of which he has such fond memories—and wants to take advantage of the opportunity of this interview to convey his cordial greetings to our entire city and to all of those, from near or far, who care about his vanished work.

This is the concise news of the interview, according to what the architect Bassó has told us. The activities regarding Mies, seriously proposing the reconstruction, have gone this far. Now it is the city's turn to speak. The city must realize the importance of all of this. It must be above all convinced of the cultural transcendence of Mies's work, in which the Pavilion is one of the fundamental pillars of the new architecture that constitutes the most important cultural movement of our generation. If today there are streams of tourists to see the ruins of the Acropolis in Athens, for the French cathedrals, for the Ville Radieuse in Marseilles or the Hansa in Berlin, one day they will come in larger numbers to visit Mies van der Rohe's small Pavilion in Barcelona, the essence and summation of the new architecture. The name of our city is double famous among artists around the world thanks to Mies. It is impressive to confirm that in any volume on architecture Barcelona gloriously appears twice: when Mies's Pavilion, one of the three buildings that established the new style, is mentioned, and in references to the famous "Barcelona Chair," also designed by Mies for the 1929 exhibition and popularized around the world under that name, becoming today the high-est-quality furniture sold by the Knoll establishments.

The great master's generous offer of cooperation cannot fall on deaf ears. The opportunity must be seized, and quickly. Mies van der Rohe is gradually retiring from his professional activity, due to his advanced years. At present he is able to give his cooperation. We can put this matter off no longer because it would be tragic if, after we came to a decision, we were no longer able to count on his help. And without Mies, without his being responsible, we would no longer be able to think seriously about reconstructing the Pavilion.

Oriol Bohigas, "Una Noticia Sensacional: Mies van der Rohe se Ofrece a Reconstruir El Famoso Pabellon de 1929," *Destíno*, no. 1080 (April 19, 1958): 36-37. English translation adapted from: Rosa Maria Subirana i Torrent, *Mies van der Rohe's German Pavilion in Barcelona 1929-1986* (Barcelona: Mies van der Rohe Foundation, Ajuntament de Barcelona, 19877), 58-59.

Oriol Bohigas i Guardiola (*1925) is a Spanish architect and urban plan-ner. He was one of the founders of Grup R (1953-63) and a professor of the Architecture School of Barcelona since 1971. In his role as head of urban planning of the City of Barcelona (1980-84) he finally was able to put in motion the idea to recreate Mies van der Rohe's 1929 Pavilion, which he had formulated in the 1950s. *Destino* was a weekly illustrated journal that had been founded by the Fascist Falange in 1937, intended to bridge the cultural differences between the centralist regime in Madrid and the inde-pendently minded Catalans. Both a decisive lack of local political support, and high cost estimates from Mies's office for a recreation of the lost plans foiled Bohigas's efforts in the 1950s.

HENRY-RUSSELL HITCHCOCK
Nineteenth- and Twentieth-Century Architecture

In 1929 came Mies's masterpiece, one of the few buildings by which the twentieth century might wish to be measured against the great ages of the past. The German pavilion at the Barcelona exhibition, although built of permanent materials—steel, glass, marble, and travertine—was, like most exhibition buildings, only temporary. But few structures have come to be so widely known after their demolition, except perhaps Paxton's Crystal Palace. Set on a raised travertine base almost like a Greek stylobate, in which lies an oblong reflecting pool, the space within the pavilion was defined by no bounding walls at all but solely by the rectangle of its thin roof slab. This was supported, almost immaterially, on a few regularly spaced metal members of delicate cruciform section sheathed in chromium.

The covered area was subdivided, rather in the manner of the project of 1923 for a Brick Country House, by tall plate glass panels carried in light metal chassis, some transparent, some opaque, and also by screens of highly polished marble standing apart from the metal supports. The disposition of these screens is asymmetrical but exquisitely ordered; yet it has none of that neo-plasticist complexity evident in the placing

of the partitioning elements in the project of 1923. As a result, the articulated space of the pavilion has a classic serenity quite unlike the more dynamically flowing interiors of Wright's houses. At the Berlin Building Exhibition of 1931 Mies repeated the Barcelona Pavilion in less sumptuous materials, making only slight changes in the plan so that it might provide a model for a house.

Henry-Russell Hitchcock, *Nineteenth- and Twentieth-Century Architecture* (Harmondsworth: Penguin Books, 1958), 376.

Henry-Russell Hitchcock (1903–1987) was an American architectural historian who taught at Smith College and New York University. As one of the first historians of modern architecture (see his *Modern Architecture: Romanticism and Reintegration* of 1929), he became a cocurator with Philip Johnson and Alfred Barr of the Museum of Modern Art's *Modern Architecture: International Exhibition* show in 1932, and coauthor with Philip Johnson of *The International Style: Architecture Since 1922*. Books on Henry Hobson Richardson (1936) and Frank Lloyd Wright (1942) followed, emphasizing the American roots of modern architecture, whose further development he chronicled in another MoMA show with Arthur Drexler in 1952 titled *Built in USA: Post-war Architecture*. His scholarly interests were far-ranging, including the publications *Early Victorian Architecture in Britain* (1954), *German Renaissance Architecture* (1981) and *Rococo Architecture in Southern Germany* (1986).

ARTHUR DREXLER
Ludwig Mies van der Rohe

Mies suddenly equaled the brilliance of his early theoretical projects with an executed building. As a result of his efforts for the Deutscher Werkbund, he was commissioned to design the German pavilion for the International Exposition at Barcelona in 1929. Destroyed when the exhibition closed, the building can have been seen by only a few architects or historians concerned with the new style. Subsequent publication established his fame. At the age of forty-three Mies had produced the masterpiece of his European career.

The Barcelona Pavilion, as it has since been called, was without practical purpose. No functional program determined or even influenced its appearance. No part of its interior was taken up by exhibits: the building itself was the object on view. The "exhibition" was an architectural space such as had never been seen. The building consisted of walls and columns arranged on a low travertine podium. Like the 1923 project for a brick country house, it channeled space between separate vertical and horizontal planes. But this time the flow of space was held within clamp-like walls at each end of the podium. Between these walls the building "happened" like a slow dance on a stage.

Apart from the intrinsic beauty of its travertine, gray glass, and green marble, the pavilion's only adornments were furniture specially designed for it by Mies, two reflecting pools lined with black glass, and a sculpture by Georg Kolbe. One other detail was given decorative value: steel columns carrying the roof were sheathed in chrome.

Columns were notably absent from the project for a brick house. In 1922 Mies had seemed indifferent to a major aspect of the new architecture. Steel or concrete columns regularly spaced allowed a new freedom in the disposition of walls, if indeed "walls" were any longer necessary. Le Corbusier's famous diagram of 1914 illustrated what had become the irreducible framework: floor slabs and a flat roof carried by slender columns. Within such a framework walls could be arranged like furniture; on it they could be hung like curtains. But Mies had gone directly to this freedom of composition without the aid of a separate skeleton structure. Its appearance in the Barcelona Pavilion announced a problem.

The pavilion's walls were placed only a few feet from columns they might just as well have absorbed. The columns were superfluous, and were eliminated from the caretaker's shelter at one end of the podium. But as fixed, regularly space elements they introduced an objective order. Against them the eye could measure a space entirely subjective in its organization. The Barcelona Pavilion can fairly be described as one of the first modern buildings able to withstand comparison with the best work of the past. Such a comparison would be to Mies's advantage. Like Le Corbusier's Villa Savoye or Wright's Robie House, the Barcelona Pavilion is more than a unique masterpiece. It is the grammar of a complete style, an ordering principle capable of generating other works of art. But within its discipline is the beginning of that conflict between subjective space and a wholly rational order that has since come to mark Mies's work.

Arthur Drexler, *Ludwig Mies van der Rohe* (New York: George Braziller, Inc., 1960), 19-20.

Arthur Drexler (1926–1987) was curator and director of the Department of Architecture and Design at the Museum of Modern Art in New York from 1951 to 1985. During this time, he curated many exhibitions and edited their catalogues. He also arranged for the Mies van der Rohe Papers and Drawings to come to the museum after the architect's death and edited the first four volumes of *The Mies van der Rohe Archive*.[1]

1 Arthur Drexler, ed., *The Mies van der Rohe Archive: An Illustrated Catalogue of the Mies van der Rohe Drawings in the Museum of Modern Art* (New York: Garland Pub., 1986-92).

1960

PETER BLAKE
The Master Builders

The first thing that needs to be said about the Barcelona Pavilion is that it is considered by many—to this day—the most beautiful modern building to have been constructed anywhere. This is so for several reasons: first, Mies decided that the German exhibit was going to be the pavilion itself, not something displayed inside it. (After all, who could remember what had been exhibited inside Paxton's Crystal Palace, or inside Sullivan's Transportation building at the Chicago Fair in 1893?) As a result there were practically no functional requirements worth mentioning, so that the pavilion could, in fact, be a pure exercise in spatial composition.

Second, there was the fact that money seems to have been no object: somehow, Mies was able to specify Roman travertine, Tinian marble, gray transparent glass, onyx, chromium-plated steel columns—in short, the most precious materials available to any architect. And, finally, there was Mies's phenomenal display of genius. No doubt the Barcelona Pavilion showed the usual "influences"—some stronger than others. But it showed, above all, the hand of an artist of such elegance and perfection that no modern building put up since—except, perhaps, one or two of Mies's later works—has been able to escape invidious comparisons with the detailing of this lovely structure!

Here, at last, was the fulfillment of the promise of Mies's glass-tower projects. Here was the tangible evidence of the genius that had lain dormant during the years of the well-proportioned, well-built (but rather dry) brick villas and stucco apartments. Here, at last, was the emergence of a master equal in every way to Wright and to Le Corbusier—a master with so sure a hand that no one would ever again be able to question his prowess.

The Barcelona Pavilion was a small, one-story jewel of a building placed upon a wide pedestal of travertine, part of which held a pool lined in black glass. The building itself consisted of a sweeping, horizontal roof plane supported on eight chromium-plated steel columns, cross-shaped in section (rather than H-shaped like most standard steel columns). Below this roof, there was a rectangular composition of glass and marble walls that formed a series of beautiful spaces, all open to one another and open to various outdoor areas beyond the glass. The only objects shown inside these spaces were several elegant chairs and tables especially designed by Mies. The glass walls were divided by slim, vertical bands of chromium-plated steel; some of the glass was a transparent gray (a shade in increasing use in American buildings since 1945 to reduce sky glare); other walls were of etched glass, two sheets back to back, with light sources between the glass sheets to make the wall a brilliantly luminous panel.

In their asymmetrical, rectilinear composition, the walls of the Barcelona Pavilion looked in plan very much like a De Stijl painting. In the third dimension, the building had some of the sweep of Wright's Robie House. And the pedestal seemed reminiscent of [Karl Friedrich] Schinkel's neoclassicism. Yet, even if these influences were present (and they probably were), Mies improved upon each of them: [Theo] Van Doesburg never painted as beautiful a composition as the Barcelona plan; Schinkel never designed a pedestal more elegant than the travertine base that supported Mies's pavilion; and Wright never composed a more modern, more striking sweep of horizontals than those that gave the Barcelona Pavilion its significant verve.

At one end of the pavilion the green Tinian marble walls that enclosed the interior seemed to slide out, under, and beyond the roof plane to form an enclosed sculpture court whose floor was largely taken up by another reflecting pool, also lined with black glass. On a small base in this pool Mies placed a statue by Georg Kolbe, and the resulting composition had become a favorite example of those who advocate collaboration between architects on the one hand, and sculptors and painters on the other. The Kolbe did, indeed, look beautiful in this setting; but, while Mies always intended to put a figure into this little court, the idea that he collaborated with Kolbe in the design of this setting is, unfortunately, a myth. The truth is that Mies was very anxious to borrow a [Wilhelm] Lehmbruck figure for this spot; and when this proved to be impossible to arrange, he grabbed a taxi on one of his last days in Berlin before leaving for Barcelona, drove out to Kolbe's studio and borrowed the best substitute he could find. [...] Although the success of the Kolbe in this classic court does not prove that collaboration between artists and architects is unnecessary, it does suggest that there may be other and better ways toward integration of the arts. [...]

Unfortunately, the Barcelona Pavilion was dismantled at the close of the exhibition and shipped back to Germany in pieces. Where it ended up, Mies was never able to discover. Yet its influence upon modern architects the world over has been tremendous. Some of Wright's best Usonian houses of the late 1930s were quite clearly influenced by the grandiose simplicity of the Barcelona Pavilion—just as Mies had been influenced by the sweep of Wright's Robie House of 1908. But, quite apart from Wright (who, needless to say, never acknowledged any such influences), there were and are numerous others—especially among the younger generation of modern architects—who are unable to this day to escape the powerful impact of this jewel-like structure. Most of Paul Rudolph's early houses in Florida, in the late 1940s and early 1950s, were variations on the Barcelona theme; I. M. Pei's penthouse office for William Zeckendorf on a rooftop above Madison Avenue is in part almost a replica of the 1929 pavilion—as are some of the beautiful details of the plaza at the base of Pei's Mile-High Center in Denver, Colorado. In Los Angeles, of course, a highly successful firm of architects built a near-copy of the Barcelona Pavilion out of stucco and sheet aluminum and turned it into the firm's offices. From Tokyo to Stockholm the Barcelona Pavilion has been copied in large or small part, in cheap or precious materials, again and again. [...]

Mies's critics have pointed out, with some justification, that he is at his best when there are no serious functional problems to solve and when there are no budget limitations worth mentioning. They have said that Mies is really an architectural sculptor—admittedly a master at the manipulation of spaces and forms, materials and finishes—but that architecture is a mixture in equal parts of functions and aesthetics. Mies's answer to this is that buildings have a long life; that most of them outlive their original function and must adapt themselves to different uses; and that the only permanent ingredient a building can be expected to possess is beauty. History, of course, is on Mies's side; nobody remembers whether the Parthenon ever worked really well, but everyone remembers what Phidias did there for the eternal splendor and glory of architecture. By the same token, no one will long remember that the German Pavilion at Barcelona contained no exhibits— and could not have contained any exhibits—in the conventional sense; but history will record that in 1929, on a hill above Barcelona, Mies van der Rohe built the most beautiful structure of an era.

Peter Blake, *The Master Builders* (New York: Alfred A. Knopf, 1960), 208-12. The section on Mies van der Rohe was published separately as *Mies van der Rohe: Architecture and Structure* (Baltimore: MD: Penguin Books, 1964), 51-57.

Peter Blake (born Peter Jost Blach in Berlin, 1920-2006) was a German-born, American architect and critic. From 1948 to 1950 he was curator for architecture and design at the Museum of Modern Art, New York, and then from 1950 to 1972 was one of the key authors of the magazine *Architectural Forum*. Apart from polemical books, such as *God's Own Junkyard* (1964), he published monographs on Philip Johnson, Arthur Erickson, Edward Larrabee Barnes, Craig Ellwood, and Davis Brody.

LEONARDO BENEVOLO
The History of Modern Architecture

As vice president of the Werkbund, Mies was commissioned to design the settings for exhibits: the pavilion for the glass industry at the Stuttgart exhibition in 1927, the German pavilion at the international exhibition in Barcelona in 1929, and the model house at the *Bauausstellung* in Berlin in 1931.

In this subject—midway between a work of the imagination and a real building—he found an initial impulse for the realization of some of his finest images, whose value went far beyond their original starting point and stimulated much subsequent architectural thought.

Mies realized that an exhibition pavilion was not an ordinary building but something essentially different, which was to remain in existence only as long as it was going to be looked at and which was at the service of the public who was looking at it. For this reason he did not conceive of it as an enclosed building but as a collection of detached buildings, suited temporarily to defining a certain stretch of space (this was probably the link with earlier imaginative works, similarly destined to stimulate a public of visitors or readers).

The temporary nature and the fact that he was building—in Berlin—under cover of a hangar freed the artist from concern with any technical problems. In Barcelona the wealth of *aenas* enabled him to make use of precious materials such as marble, onyx, colored glass: thus there was nothing to prevent perfect finish or the completeness of the architectural result. We can get an idea of these works from photographs and the descriptions of contemporaries; like them, we are struck by the fact that there was apparently no wavering, in these buildings, between conception and execution, thought and reality. Profiting from the subject, Mies offered a sort of theoretical demonstration of the modern method of architectural planning. By breaking the construction down into its primary elements he dispelled all echoes and residues of former building habits, and space was once again clean, uniform, and blank, like the empty canvas of which Kandinsky[1] speaks; in this space simple geometrical prisms and pure materials gain extraordinary vibrancy, like the elementary forms and colors which peopled Kandinsky's canvas; marble partitions, gleaming columns, delicately poised roof slabs were set with absolute firmness in their uncluttered surroundings, qualifying them with terseness and discretion yet never enclosing them, suggesting an unbounded field of possible developments.

The distinction between technical and artistic values could be maintained only as a critical expedient, since constructional elements, simply in the way they were used, became expressive tools. Mies's handiwork was always recognizable, though not in any direct and particular way, since the extremely rigorous execution did not allow for any license, any wavering; the forms he designed had the value of prototypes, ready for industrial reproduction.

Leonardo Benevolo, *The History of Modern Architecture* (Cambridge, MA: MIT Press, 1977), 490.

Leonardo Benevolo (1923-2017) was an Italian architect, planner, and historian. He studied architecture in Rome and later taught architectural history at the universities of Rome, Florence, Venice, Palermo, and Mendrisio. Apart from his *History of Modern Architecture* (1960), he published *The Origins of Modern Town Planning* (1971), *The History of the City* (1980), and *The European City* (1995). Benevolo consistently emphasized the political and social conditions of architectural production. His training as an architect and interest in urban planning is reflected in his ample use of floor and site plans and many images with noncanonical views. By puncturing his interpretation of Mies's Barcelona Pavilion and House at the Berlin Building exposition with a footnote quoting Kandinsky's narcissistic and sexualized account of creating an abstract painting, Benevolo equated the pavilion with abstract sculpture, entirely untouched by structural, functional, representational ambitions, thus separating it from his core narrative about the modern movement.

1   The words of Kandinsky seem the most appropriate comment, although metaphorical, on the work of Mies: "[The empty canvas] apparently really empty, silent, indifferent, almost stupid. But actually full of tensions, with a thousand subdued voices, big with expectation. A little frightened, because it may be violated, but docile. It does what you ask of it, only it asks for mercy. It can receive everything, but it can't bear everything. The empty canvas is a marvelous thing, more beautiful than many paintings. Such simple elements. A straight line, a straight surface, slight, rigid, undaunted, affirming itself without scruples, apparently obvious, like a destiny already lived out. This way and no other. A free curve; vibrant, retiring, yielding, elastic, apparently indeterminate, like the destiny awaiting it. It could become something else but it doesn't. Hard and soft. A combination of both, infinite possibilities. Each line says: here I am! It proclaims itself, shows its expressive face: listen, listen to my mystery! A line is a marvel. A little dot, lots of little dots, here smaller, there slightly bigger. They've all dug themselves a hole but they remain soft, so many tensions constantly repeating, in chorus: listen, listen! Little messages gradually swelling into the great yes. A black circle, distant thunder, a world on its own apparently taking no notice of anything, wrapped up in itself, an instant conclusion. A: here I am, spoken slowly, coldly. A red circle, well-placed, proclaiming its position, leaning in on itself. But at the same time it is moving, because it would like to be everywhere at once, it spreads beyond all obstacles to the farthest corner. Thunder and lightning marvel. A: here I am, spoken passionately, the circle is a marvel. But the most marvelous thing of all is that all these voices together and so many more can still come together in a single voice, the whole painting has become a single: here I am!"

1960

REYNER BANHAM
Theory and Design in the First Machine Age

The German pavilion at the Barcelona Exhibition of 1929, a work of Mies van der Rohe [was] so purely symbolic in intention that the concept of functionalism would need to be stretched to the point of unrecognizability before it could be made to fit it—the more so since it is not easy to formulate in rational terms precisely what it was intended to symbolize. [...] Attention has been drawn to echoes of [Frank Lloyd] Wright, of De Stijl and the *Schinkelschüler* tradition in the pavilion, but its full richness is only apparent when these references are rendered precise. All three of these echoes are, in practice, summed up in a mode of occupying space which is strictly elementarist. Its horizontal planes, which have been likened to Wright, and its scattered vertical surfaces, whose distribution on plan has been referred to [Theo] van Doesburg, make out one of [László] Moholy [Nagy]'s "pieces of space" in such a way that a "full penetration with outer space" is effectively achieved. Further, the distribution of the columns which support the roof slab without assistance from the vertical planes is completely regular, and their spacing suggests the elementarist concept of space as a measurable continuum, irrespective of the objects it contains. And again, the podium on which the whole structure stands, in which Philip

Johnson has found "a touch of Schinkel," extending on one side a good way beyond the area covered by the roof slab, is also a composition in its own right in plan because of the two pools let into it, and thus resembles the patterned baseboards which form an active part in those abstract studies of volumetric relations that came from the [Nikolai] Ladowski-Lissitzky circle, and, like them, appears to symbolize "infinite space" as an active component of the whole design.

To this last effect the materials also contribute, since the marble floor of the podium, everywhere visible, or at least appreciable even where covered by carpeting, emphasizes the spatial continuity of the complete scheme. But this marble, and the marbling of the walls, has another level of meaning—the feeling of luxury it imparts sustains the idea of transition from quantity to quality of which Mies had spoken, and introduces further paradoxical echoes of both [Hendrik Petrus] Berlage and [Adolf] Loos. These walls are space-creators, in Berlage's sense and have been "let alone from floor to cornice" in the manner that Berlage admired in Wright; yet, if it be objected that the sheets of marble or onyx with which they are faced are "decoration hung on them" such as Berlage disapproved, one could properly counter that Adolf Loos, the enemy of decoration, was prepared to admit large areas of strongly patterned marble as wall-cladding in his interiors.

The continuity of the space is further demonstrated by the transparency of the glass walls that occur in various parts of the scheme, so that a visitor's eye might pass from space to space even where his foot could not. On the other hand the glass was tinted so that its materiality could also be appreciated, in the manner of Arthur Korn's "there and not there" paradox. The glass of these walls is framed in chromium glazing bars, and the chromium surface is repeated on the coverings of the cruciform columns. This confrontation of rich modern materials with the rich ancient material of the marble is a manifestation of that tradition of the parity of artistic and anti-artistic materials that runs back through Dadaism and Futurism to the *papier collé* of the Cubists.

One can also distinguish something faintly Dadaist and even anti-rationalist in the nonstructural parts of the pavilion. A Mondrianesque abstract logical consistency, for instance, would have dictated something other than the naturalistic nude statue by [Georg] Kolbe that stands in the smaller pool—in this architecture it has something of the incongruity of Duchamp's *Bottle Rack* in an art exhibition, though it lives happily enough with the marble wall that serves as a background to it. Again, the movable furniture and particularly the massive steel-framed chairs flout, consciously, one suspects, the canons of economy inherent in that rationalism that [Félix] del Marle had proposed as the motive force behind the employment of steel in chairs; they are rhetorically oversize, immensely heavy, and do not use the material in such a way as to extract maximum performance from it.

It is clear that even if it were profitable to apply strict standards of rationalist efficiency or functionalist formal determinism to such a structure, most of what makes it architecturally effective would go unnoted in such an analysis.

Reyner Banham, *Theory and Design in the First Machine Age* (London: Architectural Press, 1960), 321-23.

Peter Reyner Banham (1922-1988) was a British architectural critic and historian. His best-known work, *Theory and Design in the First Machine Age* (1960), was followed by a number of treatises that challenged and enhanced the field's methodology, such as *The New Brutalism* (1966), *The Architecture of the Well-Tempered Environment* (1969), *Los Angeles: The Architecture of Four Ecologies* (1971), *Megastructure* (1976), and *A Concrete Atlantis: US Industrial Building and European Modern Architecture* (1989).

1961

VINCENT SCULLY, JR.

Modern Architecture: The Architecture of Democracy

Other houses by Mies of the 1920s also show this attempt to reconcile the American compulsion toward movement with the European instinct for closed, bounded forms. In the German pavilion at Barcelona, of 1929, Mies was able to bring the opposites into harmony with each other. The building sits upon a platform, almost a classic podium, but one that is mounted from the side. The columns and slab of the structure are clearly separate from the asymmetrically placed planes of wall that lead the observer in a fluid, asymmetrical movement through space. But the road is contained on both ends of the platform by closed wall planes, recalling those of a European garden, which enclose two pools, like bounding seas. The building itself recalled the gleamingly machined, environmental and therefore not figurally active, forms of the Constructivist sculptors. It was thus purely spatial, its solids thinned and dispersed, but in the smaller pool stood the figure of a man [sic] by [Georg] Kolbe, balanced on a rock and gesturing with his outstretched arms. Toward this image the observer was led, seeing it first through the black glass, "darkly," and then coming out to it where its act was exposed to the sky and framed by the Constructivist planes. Now, however, its sudden, precarious gesture seemed to be creating the Constructivist environment around itself and, once seen, controlled the building completely. All the planes seemed to be deriving from it, positioned by it, even as its lifted arm could still be faintly perceived from the far end of the platform. Consequently, the union was optimistic and exact: mobility and enclosure were reconciled; the architecture of a precise but fluid environment was shown as created by the human act. The Barcelona Pavilion was thus the temple, perhaps appropriately temporary, of the International Style, and it embodied the ideal symbols of the European and American components which had gone into its creation.

Vincent Scully, Jr. Modern Architecture: The Architecture of Democracy (New York: George Braziller, 1961), 27.

Vincent Joseph Scully, Jr. (1920-2017) was a professor for the history of art and architecture at Yale University, where he taught from 1947 until his retirement in 2009, and one of the most important American architectural historians in the second half of the twentieth century. He published books on topics as diverse as the Shingle Style, the villas of Palladio, Frank Lloyd Wright, and Louis Kahn. In addition, he wrote many introductions to books of colleagues (notably Robert Venturi's *Complexity and Contradiction in Architecture*, see p. 177) and engaged in the contemporary architectural debate via countless articles in magazines.

1961

JAMES MARSTON FITCH
Mies van der Rohe and the Platonic Verities

Mies's fame was really founded on two buildings, both of them comparatively small, one of them so evanescent that it had come and gone before anyone had a chance fully to grasp its significance. These two buildings, the German pavilion at the Barcelona International Exposition of 1929, and the Tugendhat residence at Brno, Czechoslovakia, of 1930, proved to be two shots that would indeed be heard around the world.

Although both buildings played important roles in the battle for worldwide acceptance of the contemporary style, the pavilion was perhaps the most influential. This elegant little building lasted only a few months and few people who saw it appreciated its significance. Fortunately, it was photographed before it was dismantled, and through this medium it has survived to engrave its dazzling image on the modern retina. No other single building of the twentieth century was to do more in shaping the tastes of that era. It was one of those statements so rare in the world of art which established the artist at one stroke, imperishably. Mies could have died that summer, at the age of forty-three, and his position as a world historic figure in architecture would have been secure.

How was this possible? The building's success was certainly not due to its size, or to its cost or to its complexity. It was not due to any single innovation: both Wright and Le Corbusier had already employed the hovering roof, the nonstructural screen walls, the floor-to-ceiling glass. Nor was it because the building was especially advanced technically. Although it used chrome-sheathed columns, its marbles would have been familiar to the Romans.

The greatness of the pavilion lay in something far subtler. It lay in the fact that it managed to express, in the most exquisitely polished and exact terms, the highest aspiration of a Europe wracked by war and inflation. Here was that clarity of order and peace that Europe longed for. Here were noble spaces, unpolluted by any connection to a discredited, futile past. Here were fine materials, freed of decadent motifs and moldy symbolism, glowing with their own intrinsic beauties. Here was the catalytic image that was to clarify problems of design for whole generations of architects.

In this building Mies was able to dissolve the ordinary elements of enclosure—floors, walls, and ceilings—and magically to reconstitute them as abstract planes, divorced from structural function. Then, on a floor plan which might have well been a composition by his friend, the painter [Theo] van Doesburg, he has reassembled these planes, not to form box-like rooms, but to modulate a continuously flowing space. The elements are few and simple: an unbroken floor plane of creamy Roman travertine, a floating roof slab of immaculate plaster, and between these two, a series of vertical planes in green Tinian marble and gray and translucent glass which intersect or slide by one another as in a Cubist painting.

Aside from his own throne-like chairs of chrome and bond pigskin and two pools, one with a sculpture (and with his usual consummate taste, Mies had wanted a sculpture by his friend [Wilhelm] Lehmbruck, recently dead, but could not get it), aside from this, there was nothing else in the building—nothing else.

A statement of such shattering power and purity could have been possible only under the circumstances which surrounded its erection: a last-minute government decision to build a pavilion, a limited budget, no exhibit material, and no time to collect any.

"It is very curious how buildings come to pass," Mies said many years later when recalling this incident. "I was told, 'we need a pavilion—design it—and not too much glass.' I must say," Mies said, "it was the most difficult work which ever confronted me, because I was my own client. I could do what I liked but I did not know what a pavilion should be." In retrospect it is easy to see that the greatness of the pavilion stems precisely from the lack of program. It gave free rein to his authentically platonic ideals of architectural perfection, without so much as a travel poster or receptionist to complicate his design.

James Marston Fitch, "Mies van der Rohe and the Platonic Verities," in *Four Great Makers of Modern Architecture: A Verbatim Record of a Symposium Held at the School of Architecture at Columbia University from March to May 1961* (New York: Da Capo Press, 1963), 154-63.

James Marston Fitch (1909-2000), an architect, preservationist, and historian, was a professor at Columbia University from 1954 to 1977. Afterward he became director of historic preservation at the New York architectural office of Beyer, Blinder, Belle, supervised the renovation of Grand Central Terminal, and prevented a planned expressway through SoHo. Among his publications are *American Building: The Environmental Forces that Shape It* (1947, updated 1999) and *Historic Preservation: Curatorial Management of the Built World* (1982). His text on the Barcelona Pavilion was the verbatim record of a lecture he gave as part of a three-month-long symposium at Columbia University's School of Architecture on Wright, Le Corbusier, Gropius, and Mies—the "Four Great Makers of Modern Architecture."

ROBERT VENTURI
Complexity and Contradiction in Architecture

Mies's exquisite pavilions have had valuable implications for architecture, but their selectiveness of content and language is their limitation as well as their strength. I question the relevance of analogies between pavilions and houses. [...] Perhaps the boldest contribution of orthodox modern architecture was its so-called flowing space, which was used to achieve the continuity of inside and outside. The idea has been emphasized by historians ranging from Vincent Scully's discovery of its early evolution in Shingle Style interiors to its flowering in the Prairie House and its culmination in De Stijl and the Barcelona Pavilion. Flowing space produced an architecture of related horizontal and vertical planes. The visual independence of these uninterrupted planes was scored by connecting areas of plate glass: windows as holes in the wall disappeared and became, instead, interruptions of walls to be discounted by the eye as a positive element of the building. Such cornerless architecture implied an ultimate continuity of space. Its emphasis on the oneness of interior and exterior space was permitted by new mechanical equipment which for the first time made the inside thermally independent of the outside.

Robert Venturi, *Complexity and Contradiction in Architecture* (New York: Museum of Modern Art, 1966), 24-25, 71.

Robert Venturi (1925–2018) was an American architect and theorist, whose "gentle manifesto" of 1966, *Complexity and Contradiction in Architecture*, is considered something of a founding manifesto for the postmodern movement in architecture and for a more measured and critical approach to modern architecture. With his wife, Denise Scott Brown, he authored the equally influential *Learning from Las Vegas* (1972), which advocated an embrace of the commercial vernacular of the American main street, and their shared office, Venturi, Scott Brown, and Associates, in Philadelphia, has completed numerous institutional buildings in the US and abroad. Venturi famously responded to the apocryphal Miesian term, "Less is more," with his own, "Less is a bore," but would ultimately confess great admiration for Mies's work.

1968

BODO RASCH
Architecture - Research

Architecture means the art of building. Its realm is the defined space-contents, such as the choreographically defined functions, as well as the according space with its constructed and formed borders. Three different areas—function, space, border—each have their own rules. We consider architecture an art and separate its essence from economic and functional considerations. An important work of architecture can naturally fulfill its purpose perfectly and be designed and built in a very economic fashion. This, however, is not an indicator of its artistic value. On the other hand, a useless and expensive building can be a great work of art, such as: the Barcelona Pavilion.

1.
The function: man walks and rests—comes from zones of movement, from paths, to zones of calm—to places, he changes his direction of movement accordingly—and calmly assumes the direction intended by the artist—all in all a choreographic design of functions.

2.

The space in which the function happens is, in the case of the Barcelona Pavilion, a horizontal volume in the form of a rectangle, into which the function is placed in the most elegant fashion.

3.

This volume is mostly defined by the floor and ceiling plates. A layer results, which is limited vertically, but open to all sides. Horizontally, wall screens from different materials are placed, which create a spatial chain, limits through which the function is formed and defined. Mies called this principle "irrational space," in similar fashion the artistic contents is defined in the buildings of classical antiquity of sacred spaces and old city squares. The always existing four dimensionality of architecture arrives from the choreographic contents of its function: a measure of time, defined by the human gait. The formal creation of the edge itself—the designed structure which is important for the new approaches to building and materials, will be executed by the designer. The creative work of the architect is not rendered obsolete by that.

"Architektur - Forschung," *Arch+*, no. 1 (January 1968): S. 3-14; Bodo Rasch, 9-10.

The brothers **Heinz** (1902-1996) and **Bodo Rasch** (1903-1995) were part of Germany's avant garde in the 1920s and became well known through a number of visionary projects. They maintained an office for architecture, furniture and advertising in the 1920s and collaborated with Mies during the preparation of the Stuttgart Weissenhof Exhibition. The newly founded architecture magazine *Arch+* used its first issue in January 1968 to ask prominent German architects about their essential take on "contents and scope" of the term *architecture*. Two questions were asked, deliberately without prefacing them with a "thesis." 1. What, in your opinion is encompassed by the term architecture? 2. Do you think research in architecture is necessary?

1969

GIOVANNI KLAUS KOENIG
Gropius or Mies

Because of his stubborn obstinacy toward the few things in which he really believed, Mies went through Expressionism, Sachlichkeit, and Nazism without being affected by any of them. He designed the German pavilion at Barcelona—an unequalled classic of the "New Objectivity"—and the monument to Rosa Luxemburg and Karl Liebknecht—a paragon of new plasticism in an Expressionist version. Both of them were buildings without a "prime function"—pure symbols and therefore, as indicated by [Bruno] Zevi, pure poetry. But symbols of what, if they were not based on any semantic code, and—as any purely poetic work—they only reached their coherence and their meaning in their own formal structure? Symbols of architecture's symbolic nature, rather than emblems of any other thing extrinsic to architecture itself. In fact, one could replace the sickle and hammer for lictorian fasces, and the monument to the victims of Berlin would become an exhibit of the Fascist revolution. Or one could leave in place [Georg] Kolbe's sculpture at the Barcelona Pavilion, but hoist the Swastika on the mast; the absolute vacuity of Miesian space would symbolize the artistic emptiness of Nazi Germany even better than it did with regard to the artistically substantial Weimar Republic. All this is perfectly consistent; by rejecting any internal ideological commitment in the structure of the architectural image, the latter remained untouched by partisan politics.

Giovanni Klaus Koenig, "Gropius or Mies," *Casabella*, November 1969, 34-39.

Giovanni Klaus Koenig (1924-1989) was an Italian architect, vehicle designer (see Milan's *Jumbo Tram* of 1978), historian, and a professor at the architecture schools of Venice and Florence as well as coeditor of the magazines *Casabella* and *Parametro*. Among his publications are *L'invecchiamento dell'architettura moderna* (1963), *Architettura dell'Espressionismo* (1967), and *Architettura e comunicazione* (1970). Like several of his Italian colleagues, Koenig positioned Mies decisively and critically in the political context of his time.

1970

SERGIUS RUEGENBERG
Recollections of Work with Mies van der Rohe on the Barcelona Pavilion

I made a base from white plasticine in a scale of 1:50. Thus the model was about 1 meter long and ca. 0.6 meter wide. [...] I glued colorful Japan paper, which I had gotten especially from a store in Potsdamer Strasse, onto strips of cardboard, which had the height of the walls at 3 meters (6 centimeters in the model). [...] This paper also had a structured surface, so it seemed marbleized; that was the main condition, the walls should be marble. I chose Japanese red, a light yellow, and green for the colors. [...] I cut the strips to a length of 13.5–15 centimeters. We also needed glass strips, which I had made by a glazier. [...] Now the game could begin: since the base was soft, the walls remained standing. [...] Mies made small sketches the next day regarding the main entrance. The main purpose was to get up the stairs and onto the podium to turn around to get into the interior. That is what Le Corbusier supposedly did at the Weissenhof housing estate. [...] We moved the walls back and forth, and then there was the idea of lighting the room with a "luminous wall." Once the room had been defined by the position of the walls, the ceiling was applied in the form of a piece of cardboard. [...] A day later we had to sketch out the ideas for the load-bearing supports. Three different solutions were being considered. For Mies it was very important that very few posts supported the ceiling. I had cut 6-centimeter-tall pieces from nickel-plated wire, which one could easily press into the plasticine. We determined the final version. [...] Mies made a couple of sketches, squatting in front of the model. [...] Again and again we took off the roof in order to check on the relationship between the columns and walls. For the pools I put down a light green cardboard and for the smaller one a black cardboard (later to be made from black glass). The conversation with the structural engineer E. Walther (Moabit, Elberfelder Strasse) only happened after I had already drawn an elevation and a preliminary section; I was in the middle of drawing the grid (1.1 by 1.1 meters) onto the floor plan. For the section it was important to make the edge of the roof as thin as possible and not to show a gutter. Now Mies called in the engineer. His task was to make the cruciform columns as thin as possible, and the engineer brought them down to 18 by 18 centimeters with the attached cladding from nickel-plated sheet metal, and the reflection of the cladding would make the supports as invisible as possible. [...] Then Mies told me how he imagined the connection between the roof girders and the iron supports reaching up to them. He had drawn a freehand sketch of the plan and elevation of this detail. The engineer had suggested the draining of the roof in such a way that the full height of the ceiling was visible, and the bolted-on cantilevers only showed an edge of 24 centimeters. The rainwater was drained inside through several points into the walls, so that the zinc pipes had a flat oval form. [...] Now we also drew the details for the glass walls, also two details for the doors in front and back of the pavilion. I designed the handles for them (later, when the building was already standing, Mies had the doors removed).

Thus the principle of the free walls became more visible. [...] Then we looked for the material for the marble; the German offers [...] came from central Germany and from Silesia. [...] Only Roman travertine and marble from the French and Swiss Alps was acceptable. When Mr. Köster [the Berlin stone supplier] mentioned onyx in a conversation, we chose that material for the wall, where the actual representation was going to happen, at the very center of the house.

Typescript in the Berlinische Galerie Archive, quoted in Eva-Maria Amberger, *Sergius Ruegenberg* (Berlin: Berlinische Galerie, 2000), 78–81.

Sergius Ruegenberg (1903–1996, see also p. 248) worked with Mies van der Rohe for nine months in 1925–26 and again for a more extended period from 1928 to 1931. When he left, Mies confirmed in a letter of recommendation that Ruegenberg had been involved in both "design and execution of the representative pavilion for the German Reich in Barcelona" and "supervised its construction."[1] Ruegenberg also worked on the Tugendhat House in Brno and a number of competitions in Mies's office.

1 Letter of recommendation from Mies for Ruegenberg (undated, but after 1931), Eva-Maria Amberger, *Sergius Ruegenberg* (Berlin: Berlinische Galerie, 2000), 21.

WILLIAM H. JORDY
The Impact of European Modernism in the Mid-Twentieth Century

When Mies later returned to the project of 1923 (Brick Country House) in an actual building—the Barcelona Pavilion—he inevitably reduced somewhat its theoretical purity, and especially its expansiveness. Unlike the earlier project, the pavilion is confined to a near rectangle which the U-shape of a major segment of its wall semi-enclosed. The basic rectangularity of the organization of the pavilion substantially stabilizes the pinwheel dynamics of the 1923 scheme, and the raised platform further bounds the composition, much as the stylobate base delimits the classical temple. Amidst the planes, a rectangular roof slab supported on eight freestanding columns evokes the specter of a classical temple, giving a focus, however tenuous, to the composition. To this "temple" focus the planar wall elements are freely, but rigidly, related. (These wall elements are nonstructural, even though some of them may appear to assist the columns in supporting the roof plane.) In this conversion of the early scheme, Mies magnified, as he doubtless intended, the architectural image of support and supported, or structure and enclosure: but at some cost to the cosmic reach (whether consciously intended or not) of the project. It was precisely this skeletal image of

the rectangular *prisme pur* embedded in the open composition of the Barcelona Pavilion, and the docility with which the independent wall planes tended to echo this rectangle, that enabled Hitchcock and Johnson to overcome certain reservations and include it within the canon of the International Style. The Barcelona Pavilion can be seen in two ways: as a construction of discrete elements, or as light planes modulating a continuous space. Seen in the first way, the pavilion anticipates Mies's late work in the United States, where structure assumes visual dominance in his building. Seen in the second way, the pavilion is secured to the International Style.

William H. Jordy, *The Impact of European Modernism in the Mid-Twentieth Century*, vol. 5 of *American Buildings and Their Architects* (Oxford: Oxford University Press, 1972), 148–49.

William H. Jordy (1917–1997) was a leading American architectural historian. After receiving his PhD at Yale and teaching there for seven years, he became a professor at Brown University for the next three decades. Among his major publications are two volumes of the five-volume *American Buildings and Their Architects* (1972) and *Buildings of Rhode Island* (2004). His essays were published posthumously as *"Symbolic Essence" and Other Writings on Modern Architecture and American Culture* (2005).

NORBERT HUSE
Neues Bauen 1918-1933:
Modern Architecture during the
Weimar Republic

If we consider the pavilion as a house, which it clearly was by its typology and furnishings, and if we ask about its usability, the result will be less positive, as this building was designed merely for aesthetic contemplation during a temporary visit, not for a permanent stay. The auxiliary rooms relegated to a corner, which did not rule out the possibility of dwelling, were a concession. In reality, a statue by [Georg] Kolbe was the only inhabitant. The architecture represented itself, structurally as much as through its composition. Through their arrangement and the extraordinary rarity and expense of their materials the individual elements seemingly assumed the character of exhibited treasures. This is just as true for the separating walls inside as for the marble wall behind the small pool, whose main purpose was to reflect said marble wall. From the photographs we cannot tell how far this independence of its parts went. The danger within this architecture, however, its narcissism, is palpable even within the photographs. To which degree other elements might have counterbalanced this impression, we cannot tell.

Norbert Huse, *Neues Bauen 1918-1933: Moderne Architektur in der Weimarer Republik* (Munich: Moos, 1975), 80.

Norbert Huse (1941-2013) was a German art historian and critic whose work focused on the Venetian Renaissance and on questions of historical preservation, even though it was his 1975 book on modern architecture in the Weimar Republic that became a milestone in the period's critical evaluation in postwar Germany. A convinced opponent of the Barcelona Pavilion's 1986 replica, Huse completely ignored it in his 2008 *Geschichte der Architektur im 20 Jahrhundert*[1] (History of architecture in the twentieth century) and continued to base his evaluation on Sasha Stone's photographs.

1 Norbert Huse, *Geschichte der Architektur des 20. Jahrhunderts* (Munich: Beck, 2008), 37.

MANFREDO TAFURI AND FRANCESCO DAL CO
Contemporary Architecture

The German pavilion constructed by Mies for the International-al Exposition of 1929 in Barcelona is pure negative dialectic.[1] The edifice is a montage of parts, each speaking a different language specific to the materials used in it: the travertine of the pavements, the marble of the wall facings on the court, the chrome steel of the slender supports, the black and green glass windows and onyx surfaces underlining the spatial succession. The pure forms reveal an apparent spatial continuity; the transparencies become diaphragms. A labyrinth of signs that comes to rest in the metaphysical space of the indoor pool faced in black marble, which is given a note of life by a statue by Georg Kolbe, placed out of reach. The continuity between the involucrum and the spatial succession of the interior disappears under the thin, white roof, the sole and scarcely robust element of coordination.

Manfredo Tafuri and Francesco Dal Co, *Modern Architecture* (New York: Harry N. Abrams, 1979), 155.

Manfredo Tafuri (1935-1994), a Marxist Italian architectural historian and professor at the University of Venice, was one of the leading critical voices in the second half of the twentieth century. His 1980 volume, *The Sphere and the Labyrinth*, provided a deeply researched overview of architectural strands of thought since the eighteenth century, with a particular emphasis on the undercurrent of a moderate modernity in 1920s Germany. **Francesco Dal Co** (*1945) is an Italian historian of architecture. He is the director of the department of architecture at the University of Venice, editor of the magazine *Casabella*, and directs the architecture publications at Electa Editrice. He has published books on Kevin Roche (1985), Carlo Scarpa (1986, 1998), Tadao Ando (1995, 2010), and Frank Gehry (1998). By reading the pavilion as a "montage," Tafuri and Dal Co were the first to pick up Reyner Banham's suggestion in 1960 to see Mies in the context of the Dada movement and its provocative montages.

1 "Negative dialectic" is a reference to Theodor Adorno's eponymous *magnum opus* of 1966, which rejected the affirmative character of Hegel's dialectics and instead emphasized the lack of clarity regarding the identity of objects and the terms used to describe them. Theodor W. Adorno, Negative Dialectics (New York: Continuum, 1973). Originally published as *Negative Dialektik* (Frankfurt: Suhrkamp, 1966).

RUDOLF ARNHEIM
The Dynamics of Architectural Form

The central, symmetrical location of the equestrian statue of Marcus Aurelius on Michelangelo's Capitol Square in Rome is the most obvious example of a sculpture fully anchored in a highly defined space. A modern example that has assumed almost mythical qualities among students of architecture—especially since the building has been demolished—is the statue by Georg Kolbe placed by Mies van der Rohe in his German Pavilion for the International Exposition in Barcelona, 1929. The life-sized nude, conspicuous as the only organic shape in a building formed of rectangular slabs, stood in a corner that otherwise would have escaped the visitor's attention. It stood on a terrace in a small pool, which was visible through the glass partition of the large internal space, and it was backed by low walls. The sculpture pool was accessible through a narrow corridor that would have led pointlessly to an empty corner without the statue as its visual focus. By giving a special accent to the far corner of the building, the architect stressed the strongly confined rectangularity of the whole design and underscored the diagonal correspondence between the large pool paralleling the longer side of the building near the open entrance and the small, hidden pool marking the building's shortest side at the remote end.

As this example shows, not only does the setting determine the place of the object, but inversely the object also modifies the structure of the setting. Placed in the corner of a terrace, Kolbe's statue gives the rectangular shape of its more immediate environment an eccentric focus, which contrasts with the symmetry of the rectangular terrace. The resulting asymmetry creates a tension that must be justified and counterbalanced by the configuration of forces in the building as a whole.

Rudolf Arnheim, *The Dynamics of Architectural Form* (Berkeley: University of California Press, 1977), 22-24.

Rudolf Arnheim (1904–2007) was a German-born perceptual psychologist and theorist of art and film. He left Germany in 1933 and ended up in the US, teaching at Sarah Lawrence College, Harvard University, and the University of Michigan. His *Dynamics of Architectural Form* came on the heels of his most acclaimed publications *Art and Visual Perception* (1954) and *Visual Thinking* (1969), in which he explored the psychology of visual perception.

LUDWIG GLAESER
Mies van der Rohe: The Barcelona Pavilion

While there were already plans for official reception spaces, the decision to build a separate national pavilion was made as late as half a year before the opening. According to Mies, the pavilion was an afterthought prompted by the sudden appearance of other national pavilions. Designed in what was for Mies an unusually short time, then delayed by budget cuts and logistical problems, the pavilion was assembled in Barcelona in a record two months. With a delay of only eight days, it opened to the public on May 27. As it was a temporary addition to the fairgrounds, the Germans were required to dismantle the pavilion after the exposition closed in January of 1930. Faced with the usual deficit and the beginning of the Depression, they decided to sell all recoverable materials back to the suppliers in Germany.

The extreme brevity of its existence contributed much to the almost mythical aura that the pavilion acquired a generation later. By then it was generally regarded as the culmination of Mies's work in Germany if not as "one of the few buildings by which the twentieth century might wish to be measured against the great ages of the past."[1] From the vantage point of his contemporaries, such claims were hardly to be expected, and whether Mies himself believed the pavilion to be his masterpiece is uncertain. Some of the basic ideas were probably first conceived in connection with the Tugendhat House, which he was designing at the same time. It was, however, the formulation of these ideas in the pavilion that recurred in his work of the 1930s, in particular the many court-house studies. […]

The way Mies accommodated the public and ceremonial functions suggests analogies with a Romanesque church plan: the open part of the pavilion representing the atrium, the roofed part the basilica replete with nave and aisles, and the end walls the apse formed by the walls around the small pool. It even had a monumental altarpiece in the golden onyx wall which, although shifted perpendicularly out of axis, clearly marked the Pavilion's ritual center. The secular celebration Mies must have had in mind for his part of the Pavilion was the inaugural reception at which King Alfonso XIII was to sign his name into a "golden book" placed on a table next to the onyx wall. To further demarcate the ceremonial area, a black carpet covered the floor between the onyx wall and the glass partition opposite, which could be closed off with a red curtain. While the combination of black, red, and gold may have had a symbolic reference to the colors of the German Republic, more explicit political logos such as a large German eagle are known to have been rejected by Mies. […]

Traditionally, European pavilion architecture had an oriental component, and the Barcelona Pavilion is no exception with its strong Japanese influence. It is as noticeable in the building's transparency and proportions as in the contemplative nature of the space, which seems to tolerate but one silent viewer.

The much discussed influence of De Stijl, which pervades Mies's entire work of the 1920s, is particularly apparent in the pavilion plan with its asymmetrical, parallel, or perpendicular placement of freestanding wall elements and their extension beyond horizontal delimitations. Moreover, the first of the preliminary plans, which envisaged a more complex solution for the unroofed area, indicates Mies's intentional use of De Stijl methods. This first plan also implies that Mies originally intended the walls to support the roof and only after an intermediate stage where both walls and columns shared the load did he divide and identify the functions of both elements by placing the columns in front of the wall. The freestanding wall elements probably originated in the exhibition installations Mies designed in connection with the 1927 Weissenhof exhibition. There, in the glass industry display, plate glass was shown in the form of freestanding partitions reaching up to a hung ceiling of tautly stretched muslin, which, in turn, may have established the image of the ceiling as a continuous floating horizontal plane.

Ludwig Glaeser, Mies van der Rohe: *The Barcelona Pavilion, 50th Anniversary* (Friends of the Mies van der Rohe Archive in connection with the exhibition, Mies van der Rohe: The Barcelona Pavilion, National Gallery of Art, Washington, DC, October 14–December 2, 1979).

Ludwig Glaeser (1937–2006) studied architecture in Berlin before arriving at the Museum of Modern Art in 1963. After Mies's drawings had been given to the Museum in 1969, Glaeser published *Ludwig Mies van der Rohe: Drawings in the Collection of The Museum of Modern Art*. He was curator of the Mies van der Rohe Archive from 1972 to 1980 and catalogued its 20,000 documents. In 1979 he organized an exhibition at the National Gallery of Art in Washington to celebrate the fiftieth anniversary of the pavilion's construction. The show toured to several cities, among them Barcelona, helping to refuel interest in the building.[2] Glaeser's comparison of the pavilion with a Romanesque church plan has remained unique in the building's long reception history. The slim exhibition brochure was designed by Massimo Vignelli (1931–2014), famous for the New York City subway map,

the architectural journal *Oppositions*, and many corporate logos. He arranged the contents sideways in such a way that the fold fell right in the
middle of Stone's iconic photographs—exactly along the central horizon line
where Stone had aligned his camera with the joint between marble slabs.

1   Editors' note: Without naming the source, Glaeser cited here Henry-Russell Hitchcock; see
    Henry-Russell Hitchcock, *19th- and 20th-Century Architecture* (Harmondsworth: Penguin Books,
    1958), 376.
2   Franz Schulze, "The Barcelona Pavilion Returns," *Art in America* 67, no. 7 (1979): 98–103.

KENNETH FRAMPTON
Modern Architecture: A Critical History

Despite the classical associations of its regular eight-column grid and its liberal use of traditional materials, the Barcelona Pavilion was undeniably a Suprematist-Elementarist composition (compare with [Kazimir] Malevich's *Future Planets for Earth Dwellers* of 1924 and the work of his indirect pupil Ivan Leonidov). Contemporary photographs reveal the ambivalent and ineffable quality of its spatial and material form. From these records we may see that certain displacements in its volume were brought about by illusory surface readings such as that effected by the use of green and tinted glass screens, to emerge as the mirror equivalents of the main bounding planes. These planes, faced in polished green marble, in their turn reflected the highlights of the chromium vertical glazing bars holding the glass in place. A comparable play in terms of texture and color was effected by the contrast between the internal core plane of polished onyx (the equivalent of Wright's centrally placed chimney core) and the long travertine wall that flanked the main terrace with its large reflecting pool. Here, bounded by travertine and agitated by the wind, the broken surface of the water distorted the mirror image of the building. In contrast to this, the internal space of the pavilion, modulated by columns and mullions, terminated in an enclosed court, containing a reflecting pool lined with black glass. Above and in this implacable, perfect mirror, there stood the frozen form and image of Georg Kolbe's *Dancer*. Yet despite all these dedicated aesthetic contrasts the building was simply structured about eight freestanding cruciform columns that supported its flat roof. The regularity of the structure and the solidity of its matt travertine base evoked the *Schinkelschüler* tradition to which Mies was to return.

Kenneth Frampton, *Modern Architecture: A Critical History* (London: Thames and Hudson, 1980), 164–65.

Kenneth Frampton (*1930) is a British architect and historian, was trained at the Architectural Association School of Architecture in London, and has taught at Columbia University since 1977. Among his many publications are monographs on Le Corbusier and Alvaro Siza and his survey *Modern Architecture: A Critical History*, which has seen several editions since 1980 and been translated into all major languages. At the time of this text, Frampton was, together with Peter Eisenman, Manfredo Tafuri, and Rem Koolhaas, a fellow at the Institute for Architecture and Urban Studies (I.A.U.S.) in New York. They all shared an interest in Russian Constructivism and abstract compositional strategies. Tafuri's influence is palpable in Frampton's emphasis on the pavilion's "illusory surfaces." Six years later, his view had markedly changed (p. 264).

MANFREDO TAFURI
The Sphere and the Labyrinth

The theatre dreamed of by Appia for a community that needs no theatres to realize itself was to have, however, another fleeting expression. In 1929 in the Barcelona Pavilion, Mies van der Rohe constructed a scenic space whose neutrality shares profound similarities with that of the rhythmical geometries of the sets of Appia and Craig. In that space, a place of absence, empty, conscious of the impossibility of restoring "synthesis" once the "negative" of the metropolis has been understood, man, the spectator of a spectacle that is really "total" because it is nonexistent, is obliged to perform a pantomime that reproduces the wandering in the urban labyrinth of sign-beings among signs having no sense, a pantomime that he must attempt daily. In the absoluteness of silence, the audience of the Barcelona Pavilion can thus be "reintegrated" with that absence.[1] No more attempts at synthesis between the "grease paint and the soul." In a place that refuses to present itself as space and that is destined to vanish like a circus tent, Mies gives life to a language composed of empty and isolated signifiers, in which things are portrayed as mute events. The sorcery of the theatre of the avant-garde dies out in the wandering without exits of the spectator of Mies's pavilion, within the forest of pure "data." The liberating laugh

freezes at the perception of a new "duty." The utopia no longer resides in the city, nor does its spectacular metaphor, except as a game or a productive structure disguised as the imaginary.

Manfredo Tafuri, *The Sphere and the Labyrinth: Avant-Gardes and Architecture from Piranesi to the 1970s* (Cambridge, MA: MIT Press, 1987), 111–12.

Four years after his reading of the Barcelona Pavilion as a "montage of parts," Italian critic Manfredo Tafuri suggested a new, more complex reading of the pavilion in the context of the work of Adolphe Appia and Gordon Craig at the Reform Stage in Hellerau near Dresden before the war. Appia's evocative sketches of almost abstract stage configurations consisting merely of stairs and platforms (which Mies might have known from his visits to his fiancée Ada Bruhn in Hellerau), inspired Tafuri's new reading of the pavilion as a stage, a "scenic space."

1 The "metaphysical" character of the Barcelona Pavilion as a place of the exposition of nothing was perceptively grasped in N. M. Rubio Tuduri's article, "Le Pavillon d'Allemagne à l'Exposition de Barcelone par Mies van der Rohe," *Cahiers d'Art* 4 (19299): 408–11. (See pp. 78–80.) Despite the impressive bibliography compiled, it does not seem that the significance of Mies's work has been captured by Juan Pablo Bonta's *An Anatomy of Architectural Interpretation: A Semiotic Review of Mies van der Rohe's Barcelona Pavilion* (Barcelona: Gustavo Gili, 1975).

1980

JOSEP QUETGLAS
Loss of Synthesis: Mies's Pavilion

In the pavilion, the plane that separates the ground and contains the space is formed by the rectangular travertine platform, more than a meter in height. It is a base that hides, to whomever approaches the pavilion from the front, the way to climb up to it: the eight stairs have been hidden behind the piece that serves as a baseboard, at the same level as the platform.

This segregation of the platform still remains reinforced by the very placement of the pavilion in the space of the exhibition: opposite the gigantic colonnade at the end of the transversal avenue. The first image of the pavilion was always one of a solitary object placed behind this fragment of a virtual peristyle, of a cage formed by columns and the unending blind wall of the Victoria Eugenia Palace. The visitor had to leave behind the site of the exposition and cross the threshold in order to reach the pavilion.

If the platform is enough to define the space of the pavilion as different, to segregate it as a stage separated from the ground that the public of the exposition walks on, the plane defined by the two covers, reduced to a sheet, will serve to transform this space, not only into something different, but into something enclosed, into an interior. [...]

What is it that grows, develops, flows, and spills over toward the exterior in Mies's project? Space? No. What grows are the walls: exactly the opposite of space. In Mies's project, spaces remain perfectly defined, static once they have reached their form, in contact with each other but not in contagion. Only that which is not space, or the space where we will never be able to penetrate, space that we are denied—that is to say, the solidness of the wall—shows its capacity to unfold, to organically meld itself with the forceful lines of the exterior world. [...]

[The mirrors of the pavilion reflect] our gaze without permitting it to penetrate, returning back to us our image always placed outside of the pavilion. To look into the pavilion is to find oneself excluded. [...] A house without doors, closed, where every visitor is excluded; a house formed by spaces that are impermeable to one another; these are the materials of the pavilion.

Josep Quetglas, "Loss of Synthesis: Mies's Pavilion," in *Architecture Theory Since 1968*, ed. K. Michael Hayes, trans. Luis E. Carranza (Cambridge, MA: MIT Press, 1998), 384–91. Originally published as "Pérdida de la síntesis: el Pabellón de Mies," *Carrer de la Ciutat* 11 (April 1980): 17-21, 23-26.

Josep Quetglas Riusech (*1946), a Catalan architect and historian, studied under Rafael Moneo at the Architecture School of Barcelona, and from 1988 taught the history of art, modern and contemporary architecture at the Polytechnic University of Catalonia. He has published widely on Spanish and European modern architecture. His first essay about the Barcelona Pavilion appeared in 1980 in the journal *Carrer de la Ciutat* (founded by Beatriz Colomina, Juan José Lahuerta, Helio Pinon, and Josep Maria Rovira in 1977, two years after Franco's death, as an alternative to established academic journals). Quetglas's title was adopted from Manfredo Tafuri's statement about the pavilion as lacking a "synthesis" in his *The Sphere and the Labyrinth* of the same year. He was the first to include the colonnade across from the pavilion in his interpretation, which deliberately and convincingly challenges established tropes.

1981

WOLF TEGETHOFF
Mies van der Rohe: The Villas and Country Houses

The pavilion was erected above a foundation sheathed in square slabs of travertine. This platform rose along the front to a height of 1.2 meters above the level of the street, and was therefore clearly perceived as a podium. The walls rising above it on that side were set back from the front edge of the platform by the width of one grid unit, so that the podium appeared as an independent, three-dimensional solid. At the narrower ends of the building, however, the foundation abruptly ended; the walls rose directly up from the ground with no transition of any kind. To be sure, the podium did not end at the point where the front wall surface did, but was continued far enough around each of the corners to produce an effective tie between the lower structure and the upper one. The slightly rising terrain approaching the slope behind the building was built up to the height of the platform. In this way an area was created level with the garden that was outlined by a double row of semicircular hedges at the foot of the slope.

For the relationship between the structure and the exterior space, the foundation proved to be of decisive importance. In its specific character, thanks to its considerable height and its block-like massiveness, it was reminiscent of the podium of a Roman temple. As a result of the abrupt transition between the horizontal and vertical surfaces, as well as the hidden placement of the stairs when viewed from the plaza, its effect was even stronger than that of its Roman prototype. The building thus appeared to be set apart, separated from the earth on which it stood. Instead, it rested on the podium as though on an independent base, a relationship expressed above all in the quadratic network of lines on the platform. But this network was not, as has been frequently assumed, to be thought of as some kind of module that provided a binding measurement for the proportions and the arrangement of the walls and supports. Rather it stood for a geometric but by no means "cosmic" system, providing a place of order in the face of the countless arbitrary details of the site—a system which can, however, adapt itself to the individual architectural situation wherever necessary.

The impression of the building's inaccessibility and remoteness is enhanced by the fact that the platform could only be approached by turning toward its northern edge. (By contrast, Mies arrived at a very different solution in the case of the plaza of the Seagram Building and the terrace of the National Gallery in Berlin.) The completely open design of the building stood in direct contradiction to the monumental barrier that was the podium. The wide opening of the building itself, only appreciated visually, thus completely contradicted the initial impression of remoteness and inaccessibility suggested by the podium.

At the narrow ends, however, this relationship was reversed. There the pavilion was firmly anchored in the ground, appearing from without as a compact, closed solid. The shrubbery reaching clear up to the end walls strengthened the impression of the building's being rooted to the ground. Moreover, flower boxes planted with vines were set along the top edge of the south end wall, and in time these vines ranged luxuriously down along the flat surfaces. Nature here extended almost symbolically onto the structure itself, causing the boundaries to blur even further. A similar effect was created on the north side because of the natural structure of the marble, the coloring of which was matched in the outer layer of plaster. The dark green veining of the Tinos marble blended visually with the surrounding cypresses and conifers, appearing to be the architectural crystallization of their organic forms. In the surviving photographs this is particularly apparent from the way in which the plants on the shadowed north side can scarcely be distinguished from the wall. The placement of the steps in the indentation of the podium must also be interpreted in connection with this particular point. Although the approach to the platform was located on the street side of the pavilion, it could only be seen from the north. Toward the east, where the central axis of the plaza represented the prime point of view, it was screened by the projecting side wall that was formed by a continuation of the front edge of the podium. Approach to the building was thus accomplished at a diagonal, along an ideal middle line between the two so different sides, which had to present itself as the only possible solution. The staircase thereby came to be placed precisely in the border zone between the north flank, "tugged to the earth" but completely closed off, and the wide-open front of the building, which yet appeared to have no direct access. At the same time, the foundation, breaking off just around the corner, modifies the motif of the podium, decreasing its importance and hierarchical prominence and making it seem less of a barrier. The approach led along the closed Tinos wall, and with each stope one came to see more of the out-side terrace and the large pool, while the immediately adja-cent wall of clear glass provided a first glance into the interior of the pavilion. The step-by-step unfolding of the structure prevented a premature deviation from the path by increas-ingly attracting the visitor's attention.

The only side of which one can speak with a certain justifica-tion of a continuous transition between interior and exterior space was the back of the pavilion. There the platform ended at a level with the built-up garden area. The offset placement of the freestanding wall elements and the resulting multitude of views to the outside and along the length of the building would seem to make any clear division line impossible. None-theless, the concept of "open space" should only be used here with considerable reservations: the wall sections all ran longitudinally, and with the exception of the open middle axis they were placed quite close to the edge of the platform. In this way they completely screened the interior of the pavil-ion from the garden. Narrow, perpendicular passageways on the front and back sides formed the only access, and could be closed off at night by means of glass doors that were removed during the day. As the arrangement of the seating area in front of the onyx wall reveals, the real center of the building was moreover oriented to the front. The garden itself, with its semicircular boundary of hedges, focused on the pavilion as well, and was spatially confined by the adjacent slope to the west. Comparable in this regard to the separated areas of the later Country Houses designs, it functioned more as an open extension belonging to the pavilion than as a section of un-limited exterior space.

Wolf Tegethoff, *Mies van der Rohe: The Villas and Country Houses,* (New York: Museum of Modern Art, 1985), 87–88.

Wolf Tegethoff (*1953) is a German art historian and was, from 1991 to 2016, director of the Zentralinstitut für Kunstgeschichte, Munich. His publication *Mies van der Rohe: The Villas and Country Houses* (English edition, 1985) was the first in-depth analysis of the material in the Mies Archives at the Museum of Modern Art and the Library of Congress. He has also published two monographs on the Tugendhat House: *Brennpunkt der Moderne: Mies van der Rohe und das Haus Tugendhat in Brünn* (1998) and *Ludwig Mies van der Rohe: The Tugendhat House* (2000).

MICHAEL GRAVES
A Case for Figurative Architecture

If we compare the understanding of the exterior of the building to that of its interior volume, another dimension of figurative architecture arises. A freestanding building such as Palladio's Villa Rotonda is comprehensible in its objecthood.
Furthermore, its interior volume can be read similarly—not as
a figural object but as a figural void. A comparison between
such an "object building" and a building of the modern movement, such as Mies van der Rohe's Barcelona Pavilion, allows
us to see how the abstract character of Mies's building dissolves any reference to or understanding of figural void or
space. We cannot charge Mies with failing to offer us figurative architecture, for this is clearly not his intention. However,
we can say that, without the sense of enclosure that the Palladio example offers us, we have a much thinner palette than
if we allow the possibility of both the ephemeral space of
modern architecture and the enclosure of traditional architecture. It could be contended that amorphic or continuous
space, as understood in the Barcelona Pavilion, is oblivious to
bodily or totemic reference, and we therefore always find ourselves unable to feel centered in such a space. This lack of
figural reference ultimately contributes to a feeling of alienation in buildings based on such singular propositions.

Michael Graves, "A Case for Figurative Architecture," in *Michael Graves: Buildings and Projects 1966-1981*, ed. Karen Vogel Wheeler, Peter Arnell, and Ted Bickford (New York: Rizzoli, 1982), 11-13.

Michael Graves (1934–2015) was an American architect and educator. He was trained at the University of Cincinnati and at the Harvard Graduate School of Design, and won the Rome Prize of the American Academy in 1960, where he spent the next two years. In 1962 he assumed a professorship at Princeton University, which he held for thirty-nine years. After his early membership in the New York Five group (with Peter Eisenman, Richard Meier, Charles Gwathmey, and John Hejduk), which represented a radical neomodern aesthetic and ideology, his architectural and design practice ultimately became best known for key examples of postmodern architecture, such as the Portland Building in Portland, Oregon (1982), and the Humana Building in Louisville, Kentucky (1985).

JUAN NAVARRO BALDEWEG
The Limit of Principles in the Architecture of Mies van der Rohe

Surely Mies was chosen to design the Barcelona pavilion because of his experience in exhibition installations, which also helps us to understand how he was able to meet the given condition of "not too much glass." He naturally resorted to his habit of thinking in terms of symmetry. And so he had only to substitute the white linoleum for a more durable material such as travertine, and the black linoleum with another material, such as marble; or (in the case of the central zone) with the onyx, a more expensive type of stone that provides the unique accent in this game of symmetries inside the pavilion. The glass seems to require the counterweight of a material just as rich in reflections and luminosity, which excluded the brick which Mies was so good at handling. Its use would have been a point of incongruity with respect to the visual richness of the glass and steel, the pond with its shimmer of water and the sunlight reflected on floor and ceiling. One of the preparatory drawings captures this visual complexity and the desire for equivalence. The only thing that may visually distinguish the Barcelona pavilion from the Stuttgart *Glasraum* is the vertical element, the totem, the pillar inside. Determining the structural sign would eventually represent the greatest challenge for Mies van der Rohe during the conception of his work. But there are the brightnesses, the transparencies, the games, the reflexes, that is to say, the diverse and balanced language that Mies wanted to employ. When studying the complexities of the Barcelona Pavilion, one must take into account another source of stimuli and reminiscences: the brick houses that Mies is projecting and building between 1927 and 1930. [...] The desire for abstraction requires careful attention to the edges: hence, the problems of topological development of an architectural type such as the exhibition pavilion, which involves creating a homogeneous space, are greatly complicated. This is one of the reasons why in the pavilion the platform advances more than in a house, which we imagine having glass panels from the ground to the first floor. Obtaining a homogeneous space requires, as we have said, creating a labyrinth with clearly defined limits, which implies, at the same time, a principle of order. This, in the case of the pavilion, is located on the platform in the form of the precise series of cruciform pillars inside (a structural element which here Mies does not seem to emphasize, but about which he will obsess over the length of his career). Mies tended, therefore, to approximate his professional activity (in the most conventional sense of the word) to the world of installations or exhibitions. In this way, it ultimately extended the horizons of architecture by moving it to a territory where there are no uses, where activities are left undefined because what matters most is the location and the highlighting of specificity of the materials. And this leads Mies to systematically transform the more conventional floors of the rooms, even though they always present certain small spills into the fluid spaces (those double-walled walls that are beyond the limits required by their function). And he translates them into that language of the free panel: the most suitable for the work to be manifested, when the different elements are deployed in degrees of equivalence, of equality. I want to go further and go back to the origin of this way of conceiving or creating enclosures that are, on the one hand, biased, equivalent, that present those inputs in excess, all of which makes them resistant to the viewer; while, on the other hand, they are visually determined.

This text is based on a lecture that Juan Navarro Baldeweg gave in 1983 at the Collegi d'Arquitectes de Catalunya (COAC). It was included in his collection of essays *La Habitación Vacante: Pre-Textos de Arquitectura*, ed. José Muñoz Millanes (Madrid: COAC/T. G. Ripoll, 1999), 77-92.

Juan Navarro Baldeweg (*1939) is a modernist Spanish architect and former professor at the Superior Technical School of Architecture of Madrid (ETSAM). He has built conference centers in Salamanca (1985), Cádiz (1988), Salzburg (1992), and Benidorm (1997) as well as theaters and museums. In Rome, he was responsible for the redesign and restoration of the Bibliotheca Hertziana, the German Institute for Art History (1995).

1984

K. MICHAEL HAYS
Critical Architecture: Between
Culture and Form

The pavilion has been highly regarded as the most immaculate transcription of the modern spatial conception: a synthesis of Wright's horizontal planes and the abstract composi-
tions of the Suprematist-Elementarists; with honorific nods to
the walls of [Hendrik Petrus] Berlage ("let alone from floor to
cornice"), the materials of [Adolf] Loos, and the podium and
columns of [Karl Friedrich] Schinkel; all processed through
the spatial conceptions of De Stijl. This seems to claim for the
Pavilion a rarefied spatial order that presents itself as an a pri-
ori mental construct rather than a palpable worldly object.
However, this is precisely not the order of Mies: "The idealis-
tic principle of order [...] with its overemphasis on the ideal
and formal, satisfies neither our interest in simple reality nor
our practical commonsense."[1]
The Barcelona Pavilion begins with a horizontally extended
space which is described by the uninterrupted roof slab, its
relation to the columns and walls, and the corresponding
constancy of section and volume implied by the floor plane.
Space is, quite literally, continuous between the pavilion and
the plaza in front of the Palace Victoria Eugenie. The pavilion
more specifically engages its site through the building, but

the limpid harmony of the exterior is confounded in the experience of the spatial succession of the interior.

There is no prescribed logic of passage; the composition is neither a relational hierarchy of component parts nor a series of identical units repeated in a potentially endless chain. What is presented instead is an assemblage of different parts of disparate materials: the travertine pavement and walls surrounding the large pool, the marble walls facing the court, tinted glass diaphragms, the onyx slab and light wall, the chromium columns and glazing bars. The relationships among these parts are in constant flux as one moves through the building. Because there is no conceptual center to organize the parts or transcend our perception of them, the particular quality of each material is registered as a kind of absolute; space itself becomes a function of the specificities of the materials.

The normal system of expectations about materials, however, is quickly shattered as materials begin to contradict their own nature. Supporting columns dissolve in an invasion of light on their surfaces; the highly polished green Tinian marble reflects the highlights of the chromium glazing bars and seems to become transparent, as does the onyx slab; the green-tinted glass, in turn, becomes an insuperable mirrored screen; the pool in the small court—shielded from the wind and lined in black glass—is a perfect mirror, in which stands Georg Kolbe's *Dancer*. The fragmentation and distortion of the space is total. Any transcendent order of space and time that would confer an overarching unity onto this assemblage is systematically and utterly dispersed. Mies has constructed a labyrinth that denies us access to the ideal moment of organization lying beyond the actual experience of this montage of contradictory, perceptual facts. The work itself is an event with temporal duration, whose actual existence is continually being produced.

A brief analogy will perhaps afford these points added clarity. In 1929 Max Ernst published his pictorial novel, *La Femme 100 Têtes (The Hundred Headless Woman)*, a purely metropolitan inspiration comprising a series of collages made from scenes gathered from popular nineteenth-century illustrated books and magazines onto which Ernst grafted objects or occupants foreign to them. What results in such collages as *Tous les vendredis, les Titans parcourront nos buanderie (Every Friday, Titans will invade our laundries)* is a laconic display of two incommensurable experiences interlocked across the surface of the work. Like Ernst, Mies was able to see his constructions as the place in which the motivated, the planned, and the rational are brought together with the contingent, the unpredictable, and the inexplicable.

K. Michael Hays, "Critical Architecture: Between Culture and Form," *Perspecta* 21 (1984): 14–29.

Kenneth Michael Hays (*1952) is an American architectural historian who trained at Georgia Tech and MIT before being appointed as a professor at Harvard's Graduate School of Design in 1995. Among his publications are monographs on Hannes Meyer, John Hejduk, Diller & Scofidio, and Bernard Tschumi, as well as his anthology of critical texts, *Architecture Theory Since 1968* (2000). Hays resolutely contradicts the common narrative of Mies's dependence on earlier and contemporary colleagues, and echoes Manfredo Tafuri's analysis of the pavilion as a "labyrinth" and a montage of fractured and contradictory elements. Tafuri's reference to Dada is replaced with one to Max Ernst's Surrealism. Hays's reference to the "temporal duration" of any encounter with the pavilion harks back to debates about the pavilion in the context of the space-time continuum in the 1930s and 1940s.

1   Philip Johnson, *Mies van der Rohe* (New York: Museum of Modern Art, 1947), 194.

GEOFFREY BROADBENT
On Reading Architectural Space

It so happens that Mies van der Rohe provided us with a splendid taxonomy of spatial division, real and implied, in the Barcelona Pavilion of 1929. [...] There is more to the manipulation of space than simply putting four walls, a ceiling, and a floor around it!

If we look at Mies's plan then the walls labeled *a* were solid; probably brick—no one seems to know—and covered with onyx. His Pavilion indeed was a decorated shed.[1] Solid walls clearly provide the ultimate separation between spaces [...] clear and unequivocal. Nothing can pass through them, not even light. Separation is absolute.

The walls labeled *b* were translucent, however. They let through light but you couldn't actually see through them, nor could anyone pass through.

The walls labeled *c* were made of clear glass, held in place by floor-to-ceiling mullions. One could see through them, but one could not pass through them. The mullions too implied a vertical plane which one could have walked through if the glass had not been there.

The rows of columns too, labeled *d*, also implied vertical planes, although not so distinctly as the mullions did; they were further apart and therefore the implied division of spaces was more tenuous.

After that it was a matter of edges. The line *e*, which looks so solid on plan, actually represents the line of the roof above, carried by the columns and probably by the walls, again no one seems to know. As a horizontal slab supported above and parallel to the floor slab, it helped to "clamp" a horizontal slice of space which was then subdivided by the various kinds of wall and other implied vertical space dividers.

Certainly, as a slab, the roof separated the spaces below from the infinite space above, but its edges worked rather differently. For the vertical eaves, as physical things, in themselves, implied planes of spatial division extended upward into infinite space and downwards to the floor slab.

There were similar implied vertical dividers at the edges of the floor slab itself (labeled *f*). No one could fail to read those, for indeed if anyone tried to step through them, he would have fallen off the edge.

Lastly there were edges to the pool (labeled *g*) and again, anyone who failed to read those would have fallen into the pool. The change of surface—and the change of level from paving to water—was a fairly drastic one. But vertical dividers of this kind are implied wherever there are changes of material, of color or of texture within a horizontal surface, from paving stones to cobbles, and so on.

So more than any other architect, in any other circumstances, Mies provided in the Barcelona Pavilion a taxonomy of space-divider types. All architects use some of these whenever they design, although rarely so many, so starkly juxtaposed.

Geoffrey Broadbent, "On Reading Architectural Space," *Expaces et Sociétés* 47 (1985): 99-143.

Geoffrey Haigh Broadbent (*1929) is a British architect and educator, a professor at Portsmouth University from 1967 to 1994, and a faculty member at the British School in Rome since 1981. One of the key figures to introduce semiotics into architectural interpretation in the 1970s, he contributed an essay to Charles Jencks's and George Baird's *Meaning in Architecture* (London: Barrie & Rockliff the Cresset P., 1969), and took part in the symposium *Architecture, History and Theory of Signs* at Castelldefels in 1972. He is the author of *Design in Architecture: Architecture and the Human Sciences* (1973) and *Emerging Concepts in Urban Space Design* (1996). In this essay, Broadbent presents the Barcelona Pavilion as a taxonomy of spatial divisions.

1   The term *decorated shed* was introduced by Robert Venturi, Denise Scott Brown, and Steven Izenour in their 1972 book *Learning from Las Vegas*, where they distinguished between simple boxes whose function is advertised via a sign or decoration outside, and a "duck," a building whose overall form is designed to be expressive.

1985

FRANZ SCHULZE
Mies van der Rohe: A Critical Biography

The Barcelona Pavilion is Mies's European masterpiece and quite possibly the capstone of his life's work. Its consequence to the New Architecture has been often and amply demonstrated; that it belongs among a select few works of the modern movement to stand comparison with the greatest architecture of the past is a judgment of comparable historical accord. […] The foundation of the pavilion seen from its axial approach had the effect of a Roman podium, so that the horizontally oriented, flat-roofed structure it supported might have seemed the counterpart of a Roman temple were it not for the asymmetry of the freestanding walls beneath the roof—marble and glass planes that appeared to slide past each other, under and out from under the roof, in an altogether unclassical kind of movement. Moreover, rising from the south end of the podium was another section of wall in travertine, again an element with no classical counterpart. Only by making a further unclassical gesture of his own, by departing from the axis to his right, could the visitor see that that wall turned the corner as if to enclose the podium at the southern end. He now also perceived that the front of the podium was recessed to the west and that from the jog forming the recess, a staircase rose. To ascend the eight steps thus required another turn, 180 degrees to the left. Bit by bit a travertine terrace and a large reflecting pool lined in green glass came into view directly before him. It was this open area that the tall travertine wall enclosed. As he mounted the stairs, however, his attention was also drawn to his right, where he could make out an interior space beneath the roof, revealed yet closed off by a transparent glass wall.

Access to the interior required still another 180-degree turn to the right. As he entered he may have noticed amid the prevailing asymmetry one feature of striking regularity: in front of the vert antique wall leading inside, a row of slender, X-sectioned chrome-plated columns, equidistantly placed like ceremonial guards attending the sarabande of the wall planes. Proceeding deeper into the roofed area, he might easily have forgotten to inquire the function of these columns as he found himself in a central space dominated by a single element: a freestanding wall roughly ten feet high and eighteen feet wide made of a ravishing and rare marble called onyx dorée, golden, with a venation that ranged from dark gold to white. To the left of the onyx wall as he faced it was a milk-glass wall lit from within; in front of the onyx, a table that bore the king's golden book and to the right of it, a pair of metal-framed lounge chairs set side by side, each with rectangular cushions in white kid leather.

These materials all around the visitor, not least among them the black carpet on which he was standing and the scarlet drapery that covered a portion of the glass wall behind him, were without exception sumptuous. Thus to the physical impression of free-flowing space was added the visual sensation of rich color and opulent surface, plus another, deriving from the dazzling play of reflections given off by the polished marbles and the glass. The reflections shifted as he moved,

mirroring what he had seen or adding to the promise of something yet to come. Through the bottle-green glass wall behind the chairs he could make out the standing bronze figure of a woman, reachable by a left turn behind the green glass to a platform at the edge of a second pool, smaller than the first and lined with black glass. The figure, *Evening*, by Mies's contemporary Georg Kolbe, seemed to rise out of the water at the far end, thus encouraging the visitor to advance toward it, laterally across the pavilion. The Tinian marble wall enclosing the pool slides out from under the roof and acted like a clamp to the whole north end of the structure, informally balancing the travertine wall at the south end. Following this Tinian wall the visitor made his way back again, southward, along the west side of the pavilion, whence he could either reenter the central space past and around the rear of the onyx wall or continue, between a dark gray glass plane and a small garden immediately to the west of the podium, into the terraced area. Or he could simply exit onto the garden path and follow a staircase upward to the Spanish Village. No matter how he visited the pavilion and even if he bypassed the central space, he was obliged to describe a circuitous route.

Thus movement was a factor central to the concept of form and space in the Barcelona Pavilion. All that Mies had postulated in the Brick Country House about the dynamic interaction of inner and outer space was now fulfilled, moreover in a built work. His debts to both Frank Lloyd Wright and Theo van Doesburg were manifest in his union of the American's concept of free-flowing interior space with the De Stijl precedent of sliding geometric planes. A passionate feeling for materials was traceable to his own family's craft tradition. Other influences were at work as well: from Reich, the bold color scheme, from Le Corbusier—specifically from the entry to the first floor of the single-family house at Weissenhof—the device of the revelatory 180-degree turn at the top of the staircase. Indeed, in that same passage there was a reverberation of Schinkel's use of a parallel exterior staircase in the Gardener's Cottage at Charlottenhof.

The podium itself has been cited as a further reflection of the old Prussian master's classicism, yet the pavilion as a whole owes more to Schinkel, the child of early Romanticism. The freedom with which Mies organized spaces at Barcelona brings Charlottenhof to mind, as if he had abstracted the forms of the Gardener's Cottage, then exploded them.

But he rang in a containing element: the columns, eight of them, ranged quite formally in longitudinal rows of four. Part of their purpose was to hold up the roof independent of the walls, which, unlike those in the Brick Country House, were now freed of this assignment. For the first time Mies separated the function of support in a building from the definition of space. He had something else in mind as well. Frank Lloyd Wright, who greatly admired the pavilion, once declared, "Someday, let's persuade Mies to get rid of those damned little steel posts that look so dangerous and interfering in his lovely designs." Wright recognized that Mies could have achieved the same spatial flow by requiring the walls to support the roof; doing so would not have relieved the walls of their space-defining role or deprived the pavilion of its spatial dynamism. However, Mies' intention for the columns was not the functional use of structure but rather the expressive use of ordered structure. In the Barcelona Pavilion the contention of objective and subjective orders was held in equipoise.

Franz Schulze, *Mies van der Rohe: A Critical Biography* (Chicago: University of Chicago Press, 1985), 155–58.

Franz Schulze (1927–2019) was the Betty Jane Schultz Hollender Professor of Art Emeritus at Lake Forest College, where he taught from 1952 to 1991. Among his publications is a biography of Philip Johnson (1996) and a 2012 revised edition of his 1985 Mies biography, coauthored with Edward Windhorst. Franz Schulze provided a sumptuous and detailed description of a visitor's path through the Barcelona Pavilion, which was based entirely on Sasha Stone's photographs, as the replica had not been completed.[1]

1 In the revised edition of 2012, this part was decisively (and inelegantly) shortened, while Schulze's central analysis of movement as "a factor central to the concept of form and space" was eliminated altogether.

DAVID SPAETH
Mies van der Rohe

The few contemporary descriptions of the pavilion focus more attention on Mies's use of marble, onyx, and travertine than on the space he created. For many critics his use of traditional building materials appeared to be a rejection of the aesthetic with which the modern movement was identified. But such an attitude reduces modern architecture to white walls with unadorned surfaces using reinforced concrete or steel—especially chrome-plated steel—for its structure. Modern architecture was and remains much more than that.

Other critics found in Mies's skillful handling of traditional and new materials an attempt by a "modern" architect to develop an architecture which appealed to the senses, especially the eyes, as well as the intellect. But few went beyond this to understand that the conceptual originality of the space and the tension created by the placement of load-bearing and non-load-bearing elements were more important than the materials Mies used to create space. [...] Mies's use of materials was based on their appropriateness to function and on aesthetics rather than their properties in a polemic. Thus freed from short-lived social or political considerations, his work addressed questions of a more general and timeless nature.

Because the pavilion was conceived as a continuum, it transcended the physical limitations of its site as well as the physical definition of space which walls, floors, and roof planes traditionally made. There was no inside to this building. There was only the phenomenon of a more defined outside. The space Mies created had the characteristic of a Möbius strip in that, as one moved through it, what was first perceived as inside was, in actuality, outside. Mies was clearly aware of this ambiguity. Mies had two pairs of doors, traditional architectural elements used to help define inside from outside, removed for the official photographs. Only the surface-mounted hinges in the floor and ceiling betrayed the doors' existence.

David Spaeth, *Mies van der Rohe* (New York: Rizzoli, 1985), 66–68.

David Spaeth (1941–1995) was an architect and architectural historian who was trained under Mies van der Rohe and Ludwig Hilberseimer at the Illinois Institute of Technology and became a professor at the University of Kentucky in 1969, where he taught architectural and urban design. He practiced architecture in Lexington and Louisville. David Spaeth published *Ludwig Mies van der Rohe: An Annotated Bibliography and Chronology* (1979) and an illustrated biography, *Mies van der Rohe* (1985). Spaeth's analysis is remarkable for the evocative image of the Möbius strip that similarly turns space inside out.

ROBERTO SEGRE
History of Architecture and Urbanism in the Developed Countries, Nineteenth and Twentieth Centuries

The importance given to the German pavilion at the International Exhibition of Barcelona (1929) is symptomatic of the value scheme applied by bourgeois criticism. Built by the architect Ludwig Mies van der Rohe (1886–1969), it is one of the most fleeting works of the modern movement, but it has become a classic reference model. This demonstrates the primacy of formal codes over functional, technical, or symbolic-expressive codes. For although the pavilion represents a subtle application of the precepts of rationalism, it is at the same time a denial of its essential contents. The work is world-renowned because it brings to a maximum synthesis the treatment of the differentiated planes—floor, ceiling, and dividing walls—the total separation of the steel load-bearing structure from the enclosure and the definition of spaces, characterized by fragmentary indications, that allow its continuous articulation: this is produced by means of the variation of the materials—steel, glass, travertine, onyx—and the architectural determinants. A mirror of water, a platform, and a bench delimit the outer space; the continuous cantilevered slab indicates the interior; the marble or glass slabs define the internal environments, characterized in turn by the furniture.

What do we mean by the negation of the essential contents of rationalism? This movement is characterized by the elaboration of formal and functional typologies that cover a wide range of social needs. However, the pavilion does not fulfill any specific function: in its interior there are no exhibited products nor advertising messages; it is only an architectural symbol of the presence of Germany in the Exposition. In this sense, Mies's assertion about the premises set forth in it is refuted by his own work: "Only if the central problem of our time—the intensification of life—becomes the content of the exhibition will they find meaning and justification."[1]

In what terms was life supposedly intensified? What contents should be expressed by a Germany that was oscillating between progressive and reactionary forces, with an increasing political dominance of the latter? It is evident that the form evades the progressive commitment and opts for the search for a transcription in current codes of German "classicism," evidenced through the cold and timeless presence of precious materials—ancient and modern: the new image given by the chromed steel lining of the profile columns in dialogue with the onyx marble panels. We share the interpretation of an Italian critic (Koenig, 1969), referring to the ideological meaning of the pavilion: "the absolute emptiness of the Miesian space would simulate the artistic emptiness of Nazi Germany far better than the artistically so substantial Republic of Weimar." Finally, more evidence of the conservative and elitist character of Mies's work appears in the small furniture designed for the pavilion. While the concept of spatial continuity also implies adaptability and variability to the requirements of the functions, in this case, the so-called spatial fluency of the building is foreign to the free decision of the users, as if it were a sculpture. And this is corroborated by the immobility of furniture, in particular the Barcelona chair, designed for this occasion and symbol of the rigid organization of the space established by Mies. The chair is, in short, the modern transcription of the luxurious eclectic armchair enthroned in bourgeois rooms. Its excessive weight, which makes it practically immobile, and its craftsmanship—camouflaged by its image of high technology—constitutes the antithesis of the economical furniture series of the Bauhaus, true answer of design to the needs of the community.

Roberto Segre, *Historia de la arquitectura y del urbanismo: Paises desarrollados, siglos XIX y XX* (Madrid: Instituto de Estudios de Administracion Local, 1985), 185-86. The same text appeared in Roberto Segre, *Arquitectura y urbanismo modernos: Capitalismo y socialismo* (Havana: Editorial Arte y Literatura, 1988), 184-85.

Roberto Segre (1934-2013) was an Italian-Cuban historian of architecture whose family fled Fascist Italy in the late 1930s and settled in Buenos Aires, where Segre graduated from architecture school in 1960. Fascinated by the Cuban Revolution, he moved to Havana in 1963, where he joined the faculty of the School of Architecture and Urbanism. He taught there for the next three decades before accepting a teaching position at the University of Rio de Janeiro in 1994. Among his publications are several books about Cuban and Latin American architecture. His is the most outspokenly Marxist critique of the Barcelona Pavilion.

1   Segre paraphrased a 1928 text by Mies about exhibitions: "Only if the central problem of our time—the intensification of life—becomes the content of the exhibition will they find meaning and justification." Mies van der Rohe, "On the Theme: Exhibitions," *Die Form* 3, no. 4 (1928): 121. Quoted from Fritz Neumeyer, *The Artless Word, trans.* Mark Jarzombek (Cambridge: MIT Press, 1986), 304.

ALISON AND PETER SMITHSON
Notes on the Barcelona Pavilion

The first impression upon entering the Barcelona Pavilion while under reconstruction is that it is all one-third larger than the pavilion-image that the photographs formed in one's mind. That the majority of these photographs are doctored—their backgrounds' whited-out—has possibly contributed to this loss of scale in the image of the myth.

In the reconstruction, this apparent increase in scale, the travertine expanse—formally accepted as descendant of the Germanic neoclassical tradition—becomes, because of its color, some sort of desert; which I connect to the idyll of Saint Jerome's restorative "place apart." The Mies pavilion offers the possibilities: in the open, of Saint Jerome in the desert: under cover, of Saint Jerome in his study. For one can add to those instinctive reasons for accepting the Barcelona Pavilion as myth, an inheritance, by osmosis of this western idyll.

The old photographs of the Barcelona Pavilion were, naturally enough, black and white, but so were all the photographs of our youth. Our generation was in no doubt as to the nature of the materials—(green) marbles or (golden) onyx. In fact, directed by the photographs, our myth image is nearer to what they were than the reconstruction is. Yet, because mythical qualities are of their nature somewhat vaporous—and deliberately kept so, that they might continue to inhabit the peaks of one's mental landscape—the information gained from captions to the black-and-white photographs was not so detailed for us to know that two sources were used for the green marbles: Aosta, Italy; and Larissa, Greece.

Marble always engages our consideration because of its surprising composite quality working with the variations of stresses in the depth of its make-up. The pellucid greens; the unforeseen portions of apple green; the semilucent darkness that requires study to be sure it is still green; an undersea or much wetter green. Yet in considering these reconstructed qualities—as Mies might have stared into their composition—part of our consciousness is always aware it is not the same marble as made the myth.

What could not be appreciated before the colored reality was the forest connection. I find in the Mies building the travertine-contained space becomes a sunlit clearing, the green marbles perform as the forest frame, while the shaft of light beamed down from the slot falls into its new role as a signal of forest and the light-barred metal frames act under their top cover as if they were birch saplings. [...]

During reconstruction of the Barcelona Pavilion, my eyes having been conditioned by the photographs, the enclosed tank of water called for its surfaces to be made black [...] is its progenitor the Landwehrkanal, Berlin?[1]

The long travertine bench we supposed generated by von Klenze's tufa bench in the Königsplatz, Munich.

Our generation cannot think in terms of literal connections; probably that was the lesson from the Heroic Period.

Mies as a choirboy in the Dom, Aachen, probably saw a shaft of light falling into the Romanesque grove; possibly also gained affection for onyx there. Through being a boy in the mason's yard of his father and uncle, he could probably recognize the quality of a block of marble in its raw state. Real experience, observations, the considerations of the inventive mind.

The Barcelona Pavilion stood for difference that risked the neck. The achievement of its happening, that its fabrication became a milestone in many minds.

The myth is of that leap from the Silk Exhibition, from the Otterlo mock-up, into the minds of generations.

Alison and Peter Smithson, *Changing the Art of Inhabitation* (London: Artemis, 1994), 35–46.

1985

PETER SMITHSON
All that Travertine

But for a later generation, familiar through republication with all that travertine in Nazi architecture and who have been born since Europe has been colonized by Hilton International; can the pavilion be mythical to them? Rebuilt as a facsimile, can it still carry the smell of its revolutionary intent?

Alison (1928–1993) and **Peter Smithson** (1923–2003) rank among the most influential British architects of the twentieth century. Both had studied architecture at the University of Durham. Their 1953 Hunstanton School made them instantly famous, as it applied the language of Mies van der Rohe in an economic fashion, using mass-produced parts with rough finishes. Their work stood for the early application of the term *new brutalism*. They were also part of Team 10, which was in charge of preparing the tenth CIAM *(Congrès International d'Architecture Moderne)* conference and ultimately succeeded this organization. Their observations in 1985 and 1986 were made during several visits for lectures and a seminar in Barcelona, and published after Alison's death by Peter Smithson.

1 Editors' note: Alison and Peter Smithson's reference to the Landwehrkanal hints at the infamous location where the body of Communist agitator Rosa Luxemburg was deposed after she had been murdered by a right-wing militia in 1919. She and Karl Liebknecht, who was executed the same night, were later buried and commemorated at Friedrichsfelde Cemetery, where Ludwig Mies van der Rohe designed a monument for them in 1926 (destroyed by the National Socialists in 1935).

JOSEP QUETGLAS
From Mies's Pavilion to the Pavilion of the Mies Foundation

No one can reject the rebuilding of the Mies pavilion, because the Mies pavilion has not been rebuilt, and it cannot be rebuilt in its architecture, that is, in its reasoning and its theoretical, cultural, artistic, and visual implications in the presence of its author. […] The foundation's pavilion cannot be confused with the Mies pavilion. And consequently, no one, if he appreciates Mies, can be irritated by the construction of the pavilion of the foundation. Of course, the material reconstruction of the pavilion could have been of interest, but only if it had been possible to put all the elements of the 1929 building back into place. […] Let us forget Mies for a moment and assume that the architects of the foundation "set the tone" just for the sake of argument, rather than from conviction. We might find the same colors, the same sizes and motifs of stones and windows—very well; the same vegetation surrounding it—yes; but we also want the same atmosphere: the traffic on the Avenue of the Marquis de Comillas would have to have as many and the same cars as in 1929; we would approach the pavilion with the same gestures and in the same clothes; the gravel would crush just the same under our shoe soles of the same leather; the freshness and the smell of the air of Barcelona would have to be the same as in 1929 and especially that we, the visitors, would have to come with the same frame of mind as in 1929, that is to say that the foundation would have to reconstruct the sight, hearing, and smell that we all had in 1929. Do we really see a chrome pillar or a dark crystal moon with the same ebullient excitement, with the same eyes as the provincial Barcelonans of 1929? If not, the building is not the same. And that is not the case. The pavilion cannot be the same, cannot be rebuilt, just as we cannot reconstruct the Acropolis of Athens or the Pyramids of Egypt.

We do not see the Mies pavilion, because the pavilion of the foundation has hidden and destroyed the void it left and because no one has rebuilt what existed in 1929. What do we see today in Montjuïc? We see something that has as much to do with Mies as the Caravelle of Columbus—currently in the harbor of Barcelona[1]—has to do with Columbus or the Pueblo Espanol of Montjuïc has to do with the popular architecture and material culture of our country: what we see is a parody. If there are people who like this, and if they become culturally enriched by contemplating stainless steel, Klein curtain rails, ostensibly concealed electrical outlets, onyx veneer joined with silicone, ingenious air outlets, rational water droplet profiles, adjusted wall distances, recalculated roof cuts and slopes [...] then so be it. There is no reason to blame them. But in all honesty, it cannot be called "Mies." Those who respect Mies will continue to prefer the living mystery of the old photographs of the pavilion, the old drawings of the master.

Josep Quetglas, "Du Pavillon de Mies au Pavillon de la Fondation Mies," *Criticat* no. 5 (March 2010): 84-91, https://issuu.com/criticat/docs/criticat05/93.

Josep Quetglas Riusech (*1946), a Catalan architect and historian, studied under Rafael Moneo at the Architecture School of Barcelona, and from 1988 taught the history of art, modern and contemporary architecture at the Polytechnic University of Catalonia. He has published widely on Spanish and European modern architecture. He has written with particular intensity about the cultural context of the Barcelona Pavillon (see p. 206, 284) and had substantial reservations about its reconstruction.

1 For many years a supposed replica of Columbus's ship Maria anchored in the harbor of Barcelona. It had been constructed (historically inaccurately) for a movie production and left there as a tourist attraction. On May 23, 1990, it was destroyed by the Catalan Separatist organization "Terra Lluire."

1986

REM KOOLHAAS/OMA
Less Is More

In 1985 we were invited to participate in the Milan Triennale; the Palazzo della Triennale, subdivided neatly into rooms, had all the deadlines/charm of the treasure chamber of a belated pyramid. (Were we all slaves, carrying our wares to its vaults only to be taken into the grave by a nonexistent pharaoh–the public?)

OMA's room, projected in the curved exedra of the fascist Triennale building, was deformed–another misfit.

By then, phobic about the duty to reveal, we decided to embody our resistance in an exhibit about exhibition. At the time, a clone of Mies's pavilion was being built in Barcelona. How fundamentally did it differ from Disney?

In the name of a higher authenticity, we researched the true history of the pavilion after the closing of the 1929 world's fair and collected whatever archaeological remnants it had left across Europe on its return journey. Like a Pompeian villa, these fragments were reassembled as far as possible to suggest the former whole, but with one inevitable inaccuracy: since our "site" was curved, the pavilion had to be "bent."

The crowds had gone. The king and queen had signed the book. The pools were emptied. Unlike the other temporary pavilions, which looked more like buildings, the German pavilion was too heavy to be moved easily. Since Germany was in a state of confusion, it was decided to leave the pavilion on loan to Spain until a decision could be made. So it stood, a gothic outpost in the land of the Moors. Meanwhile, the political situation in Spain became tense and the pavilion was forgotten as other problems became more pressing. Bombs exploded nearby. For a few days it served as the headquarters for the Anarchists, but they quarreled about the use of the spaces. One of them made a plan so ridiculous, with such an absurd profusion of desks, cabinets, and chairs, that the result was catastrophic. Because of this experience the Anarchists were the first to declare that modern architecture didn't work, and once again the pavilion was abandoned. Later it was badly damaged, becoming the first architectural ruin, but no one noticed. The new regime was determined to resolve the question of the pavilion. They disliked the fact that it had been the Anarchists' headquarters and so, being on good terms with the new government of its Heimat, they decided, as a friendly gesture, on its repatriation. The train journey was complicated. The railway tracks of each country were of different widths; many transfers were needed. After long delays the pavilion finally arrived in Berlin. It was now an architectural orphan; its creator had just left for the USA. The new government was against modernism and hardly even bothered to open the crates containing the pavilion. But its unacceptable modernity was a matter of context, and the marble slabs could serve other purposes. First they were used on the set of a propaganda film aimed at homesick soldiers scattered around the world. With the precious stone as a pompous background, a voluptuous blonde sang a sentimental aria. As décor (to soften the contours of the marble slabs and improve the acoustics), they were draped with purple satin, yellow silk, and red velvet. Next the marble was incorporated in the construction of a ministry, where it became the floor of the service entrance. The war grew more intense. Berlin was bombed and the ministry was hit many times. A few days before the city was liberated the marble slabs cracked. The ministry became an improvised hospital and camp. In the euphoric time that followed the liberation, it was sometimes the scene of wild parties. After the liberation, Europe had to be rebuilt. Each fragment, each particle of the pavilion was reused. The ministry was dismantled and the marble preserved. The other crates containing the pavilion were finally unpacked. First the planners of the east side of the city suggested reassembling the entire pavilion as a gas station, for the time when each worker would own a car. But the dimensions and the hidden module of the structure prevented that or any other use. Eventually it became the locker room for a gigantic sports complex planned for the 1952 Olympic Games. The games were intended to promote friendship among all European countries, but only the locker room had been built when they fell victim to the Cold War. It was left standing on abandoned ground, visited only by soccer fanatics and passersby, until one day a scientist from the West, who was investigating the rebirth of classicism in Eastern Europe, saw a fragment that seemed vaguely familiar. He entered the showers, which smelled like the inside of the pyramids, and found more. He became convinced that he had discovered the remnants of the mythical pavilion. Negotiations were initiated by his party, and ten years later, within the context of a cultural exchange, the fragments were exported in return for one medium-sized computer and a secret design for a new machine gun.

Office for Metropolitan Architecture, "La Casa Palestra," *AA Files* 13 (Autumn 1986): 8–12. Also published as "Less is More," in OMA, *S,M,L,XL* (New York: Monacelli Press, 1995), 48–61.

Rem Koolhaas (*1944) is a Dutch architect, theorist, and urban designer. He is a founding partner of the Office of Metropolitan Architecture (OMA), winner of the 2000 Pritzker Prize, and is considered one of the most important contemporary architectural thinkers and urbanists. His firm has completed commissions around the world, and among his most important publications are *Delirious New York* (1978), *S,M,L,XL* (1995), *The Harvard Design School Guide to Shopping* (2002), *The Great Leap Forward* (2002) and *Countryside, A Report* (2020). Koolhaas responded to the fiction of the new pavilion with a fiction of his own, namely the story of the pavilion after the exhibition, in the form of a photo novella.

1986

SERGIUS RUEGENBERG
A Conversation

Frobenius had an exhibition in Berlin about his African research. Mies was very interested in the [...] culture of North
Africa and its buildings. There are already freestanding walls
without supports inside the houses, mostly for cult purposes.
On the walls some signs are symmetrically applied and cultural artifacts are placed in front of them. We can see that
Mies has realized similar walls as well, for example with the
onyx wall in the pavilion and later in America. But it is always
clear that it wasn't the walls themselves that interested him,
but in particular their special function as a focal point for communication or the meeting of people. There was always a table and chairs, one would write or talk with each other. Those
were all inspirations which came from [Hugo] Häring, sugges-
tions of a purely intellectual kind. [...] Le Corbusier's influence
was different. The first book which we had of Le Corbusier,
Mies had had translated. He was very impressed by these
great and new ideas, for example by a small house on concrete piers, whose rooms one could furnish one way or another. A little later Mies returns from the Weissenhof estate and
immediately talks about his impressions—as was typical of
him. He is enthused about a single room. Everything else
does not matter. This one room Le Corbusier had built: you

came up a staircase, had to turn 180 degrees to get into the room, and you would see a wall in the middle. That marked the center, while on the other side at the front, there was a "green wall," a huge window with plants in front of it. This experience Mies took as a basis for the Barcelona Pavilion, although he would place the walls there with more freedom and worked with much larger panes of glass.

Günther Kühne, "Der Skelettbau ist keine Teigware: Sergius Ruegenberg berichtet von Mies van der Rohes Berliner Zeit," *Bauwelt* 11 (February 28, 1986): 346-51.

In this interview, the eighty-three-year-old **Ruegenberg** (biography see p.186) placed Mies's design into the architectural context of its time. He emphasized the important influence of the radiating floor plan for Frank Lloyd Wright's Avery Coonley House of 1908, which, as he recalled, Mies had copied with his help from the Dutch journal *Wendingen* in 1925.

1986

JORGE NUDELMAN AND JORDI ROIG
Construct in 53 × 17

The construction of an imaginary universe, a theme that travels through the popular literature of illustration, marks the beginning of a new sensibility, one that resorts to the primitive, the past, the original, the first version, the return to limit situations. The recovery of the Homeric epics, archaeology, the invention of Eldoradas, islands of Robinson, of unreachable Atlantis, and therefore ideal, unverifiable, will become part of children's libraries, a logical encounter between ideas and minds without limits. Who has not imagined, heart pounding, hidden in a closet, in the dark, in silence, to be in the belly of a motionless wooden horse? Who has not traveled secret passages, has not flown in the middle of the blizzard? We recreated these spaces in games where we only needed the vignette of a storybook or old illustrations of magazines accumulated in the attic.

Now, as then, it is not a question of constructing a scene. We are not willing to show an image, but want to live a reality that no longer exists. We need to live the epic, conclude the adventure. How many imagined, desired architectures, because they are part of what we now do, have we actually lived in?

How many times have we regretted the destruction of the Crystal Palace? Are we able to imagine Melnikov's Pavilion of

1925, eaten by woodworms and inhabited by spiders? Or the pavilion of l'Esprit Nouveau, also constructed of wood? [...] Emblematic architectures, converted into landmarks, references, dreams. Gardens of Babylon in the middle of the desert. "Darkroom" movie architectures, destined for dioramas, perhaps to fade. That is why, when you assure us that you are building Mies's pavilion, right here, in Barcelona at the same place where it was once raised, the desire excites us.

At last we can see it, walk it, reflect on it, play, leave our mark. We quickly review the photographs. We get emotional. We look at them again and again. The proportions, the space, the light, are perfect, almost sublime. The reflections, the shadows, the transparencies, the shades of the stone, its vein, the glitter of the metals, the glasses, and the water. And the sculpture of Georg Kolbe, seen from the right places, immovable, but we can glimpse it from the inside through the dark glass. Everything is clear and precise. We play then, we enter the tunnel of time, we return to the inauguration of the exhibition, we participate in an imaginary debate on this new architecture or we are indignant at the almost general indifference. We are dreaming, and in the dream, as always, everything is gray. The sky is white and the earth is black. The rest, shades of gray, shiny, silky, flat, veined. The people are gray, the trees, the flags, the shadows.

We get carried away by nostalgia. We idealize those past times, clean them from roughness, and suddenly, building what had disappeared, we change the course of history. Now we can. Now the story is something malleable, usable, flexible. In earlier times the past was part of the present. In the Renaissance, a certain past is brought to the present, consciously, calculated. But it is only with Romanticism, Hegel, the modern movement, and others close to us, that art, architecture, will begin to correspond to something, to seek the never seen, to belong only to its present, or, at any rate, to the future.

Tired perhaps, weak after so much struggle, or dizzy after so much floating in the void created by themselves, the architects lie on the branches of memories, recovering temples and offices, in the name of the postmodern. Within this tailor's box are all the stylistic recoveries, decontextualized and inexpressive despite, of course, their expressive anxiety. We began by longing for the shape of the gothic streets, the great avenues, the pagan temples, and the Christians.

Then dust off the manuals: the historical form becomes ahistorical, but the houses are still houses. New historicism becomes avant-garde, modern in tradition, and as in dreams, we condense time, nostalgia follows nostalgia. It's the fashion.

The story will surely be written again. The ephemeral casual pavilion will have become perennial, will age and we will see it darken. Perhaps it will become a monument, a stone that is still. Commemorative plaques, flowers, crowns, and occasionally some candles are likely to be placed.

It is also likely that, as in dreams, we not only recover the site, but the place, we reconstruct the exhibition of 29, and why not, the Barcelona of 29.

Only in that contrasting world of dreams is it possible to understand the pavilion as a monument, and rescue it for the good memory of its promoters.

Thank you very much.

P.S. Almost as a game we wrote a letter—in the most provocative way possible—to a number of architectural professionals, some of whose answers are discussed below. The issues we raised could be summarized as follows:

The German pavilion at the 1929 exhibition has been considered as a masterpiece of twentieth-century art. Will the unique and unrepeatable character of a work of art be contaminated by successive adaptations and interpretations of the original? The "postmodern" movement has embraced historicist features: archaeology, reconstruction, ruins, and monuments. [...] Do you think this reconstruction is part of this spirit?

Also, this movement has been understood as the expression of the crises of modern architecture. Could the reconstruction of the Mies pavilion lead to a reaffirmation or reassurance of the principles of the modern movement?

Would Mies build the pavilion in the same way he built it in 1929?

Alison and Peter Smithson

A & P Smithson returned a photocopy of our letter, with the following question highlighted in red and answering with a curt "yes." At the end they added a phrase that we dare not interpret.

"The postmodern movement has been" stained "with historicist characteristics: archaeology, reconstruction of ruins and monuments ... Do you think this reconstruction can be included in this spirit?"

"Yes."

"An 'ordinary' house for a liberal Spain (Catalonia) should be built by a new Mies."

Manfredo Tafuri

Dear friends,

I have received your letter of 12 March and I answer to your questions:

a) The reconstruction of Mies's pavilion cannot be considered more than a romantic gesture. The reconstructed pavilion will, however, be seen as a true, necessarily approximate, model of the 1929 work, and will thus be useful to anyone who studies the history of architecture of the 1920s. But extrapolated attention from his context runs the risk of becoming a fetish. Its original meaning lay in its appearance among the chaos of the Exhibition of 1929, to demonstrate "nothingness" in those years and its own disappearance. In no way will its reconstruction be loaded with "other" meanings.

b) There is no "postmodern movement." There is only a group of lousy architects who seek to emphasize the invention of associative formulas and draw on lousy historians (Jencks, Stern, Portoghesi). In parenthesis: whoever calls himself postmodern demonstrates an astonishing and offensive ignorance of history—the history they embarrassingly declare to love is a history they themselves made up.

c) Similarly, there are no "principles of the modern movement," unless this phrase does not intend to speak of the CIAM formulas: they are only a minimal and perhaps a secondary part of the history of contemporary architecture. As I have tried to show on other occasions—most recently in *The Sphere and the Labyrinth* (1984)—the "fable" of the modern movement is only a historiographical construct, one, which, by the way, has long run its course.

d) To know how Mies would rebuild his pavilion would require a spiritistic session.

To conclude: I think you are attaching too much importance to a marginal issue. I do not think that a debate on this subject helps us to understand our situation. We need deeper historical research and in general it is essential not to remain continuously immersed in the discipline of architecture.

Sincerely,

Manfredo Tafuri

Robert Venturi

Thank you for your kind letter of May 12 explaining your project to rebuild the Barcelona Pavilion. This is to express my unequivocal enthusiasm for your idea. It is a tragedy that a building as significant as this in the history of art of the twentieth century did not survive and it would be a very significant, appropriate, and magnificent gesture if it could be rebuilt. It is not wrong to correctly reconstruct a great work of art archaeologically to remain a model for the future and a monument of the past. This can work particularly well because the technology of this building, by its very nature, can be accurately reproduced today. You have my most sincere support for our important project.

Sincerely,

Robert Venturi

Kenneth Frampton

It is difficult to answer all your questions. But let's go in parts. Of course the unique quality of a work of art is compromised by any form of reconstruction. On the other hand, a work as canonical as Mies's Barcelona Pavilion, which no living person has seen, surely deserves to be rebuilt, especially when this reconstruction is taking place in the same place. It is a very different case, for example, with the reconstruction of the Pavilion of L'Esprit Nouveau in Bologna. Of course our whole period is "dyed" by nostalgia, but I find it hard to believe that this necessarily makes the Pavilion of Barcelona a typical "postmodern" work of archaeology. Personally I have the impression that it is rather part of the reconstruction of the modern movement at a deeper level. It is quite unlikely that Mies would have allowed himself to be involved in the reconstruction of a facsimile of his early work.

Yours sincerely,

Kenneth Frampton

Arthur Drexler

Gentlemen,

Please forgive my delay in replying to your letter of 12 May. As you may know, this museum was reopened to the public that month, after a long period of construction and renovation. The following comments may arrive a bit late to be useful for your series, but I still respond because I find your questions interesting and serious. You ask how the unique character of the German pavilion could be "contaminated by the successive adaptations and interpretations of the original." As far as I know, there have been no adaptations and interpretations. Since 1929 the building has never been rebuilt. The present project in Barcelona is the first one that is being carried out. More general adaptations, using the open Miesian plan, play a very small role in modern architecture (ah!) and they certainly have not devalued the Barcelona Pavilion. Since Mies himself agreed to rebuild it in 1959, one must acknowledge that he was not opposed to this project. At what point he would have made changes or not remains a matter of speculation. In my opinion he would not have made any significant changes in the appearance of the building, and certainly would not have made them inside. I think he would have completed the sides of the podium, which were not finished in 1929 due to economic reasons.

The historicist tendencies of postmodernism have not really taken much interest in the great achievements of the early modern movement. (I wish it were the opposite.)

On the other hand, it is certainly true that a more sympathetic response to the past does make people more curious about episodes in the history of modernism that have long been judged irrelevant by current opinions. I can well imagine that the reconstructed German pavilion, visited by students of architecture from around the world, could indeed reaffirm two aspects of Mies's contribution: one, the exquisite beauty of this particular building and two, the timelessness of an aesthetic which, however, Mies himself was not prepared to sustain indefinitely.

As you know, 1986 will be the year of the centenary of the birth of Mies. During this year, the Museum of Modern Art will present a great program of exhibitions with Mies's architectural and furniture designs. The exhibition will include several hundred drawings from the Mies van der Rohe Archive and will be accompanied by several publications. This ample exhibition and the reconstruction of the pavilion of Barcelona will undoubtedly renew the professional interest in the ideas of Mies. How useful these will appear now is something that I cannot predict. But I can say that we, all of us, are the heirs to the problems that Mies himself helped to create. One of the questions that the exposition will have to ask is the extent to which there are possible solutions to those problems to be drawn from Mies's own philosophy.

Sincerely yours,

Arthur Drexler

Jorge Nudelman and Jordi Roig, "Construir en 53 x 17," el Croquis (October 1986 6): 6-9.

Jorge Nudelman Blejwas (*1955) is a professor at the Instituto de Historia de la Arquitectura, Universidad de la República, Uruguay. He was born in Montevideo, where he studied architecture before moving to Madrid to complete his PhD, and from 1986 on taught at the Escuela Técnica Superior de Arquitectura de Barcelona. He contributed an essay on Uruguayan architecture to the 2015 Museum of Modern Art exhibition, *Latin America in Construction: Architecture 1955–1980*. **Jordi Roig** (*1955) is an architect and professor at the ETSAB de la Universidad Politécnica de Cataluña. In the spring of 1984, when the rebuilding of the pavilion began, the two young architects sent a questionnaire about the project to a handful of prominent architects and historians. The results were published on the occasion of the opening in the journal *El Croquis*.

PETER EISENMAN
miMISes READING; does not
mean A THING

The Brick and Concrete Country House projects were followed by the Barcelona Pavilion and Tugendhat House, which
exemplify the next period of Mies's work. In the Barcelona
Pavilion, particularly, one can discern an important stage in
Mies's ongoing confrontation with the classical notion of enclosure and the enclosing wall. Here Mies converts two additional architectural elements into textual counters: the column and the roof. Though the theme is the court house type,
Mies instead of enclosing a court, breaks it open to reveal the
column and the roof. The two elements previously employed
textually, the wall and the podium, operate in the same way.
Again, the wall is not the wall of finitude—the wall that makes
space and symbolizes the classical relationship between man
and object. These walls cleave space; they begin and end in
response to no greater order: rather, they obey only their own
mute existence.

The podium in the Barcelona Pavilion, as in both of the earlier
houses, is not entered axially. (As will be seen, axial entry will
become a textual counter when classical elements become
embedded in Mies's work.) In fact, the early schemes in many
of Mies's projects have a formalist bias. These are then worked

through until they ultimately become textual. In the early studies of the Barcelona Pavilion there are further tentative gestures toward what might be termed a "latent classicality," for example, the alignment of the pool with the main podium. This alignment would have caused the direction of the main entry to be reinforced by the line of the podium and the pool, thus erecting a virtual barrier between the outside and the inside. In the realized project, the pool is pushed out into the landscape, up against the corner of the wall. It is no longer framed by a terrace, but now penetrates the wall, seeming to intrude from the outside. In the early schemes the entire podium except for the small utility pavilion was enclosed by an uninterrupted perimeter rectangle. In the realized scheme, this perimeter is fractured at every corner, almost imperceptibly but enough to engender instability. The principal motive for the fracturing is to disengage the roof plane formally from the floor plane, and then to engage it as a signifier, that is, as another textual encounter. The condition of the roof plane in the Barcelona Pavilion is in opposition to Le Corbusier's *Maison Dom-ino*, where the stature and status of man is symbolized by the roof plane/podium as coupled horizontal datums. With the Barcelona Pavilion, the hovering roof, formerly a symbol of shelter and enclosure, is stripped of this meaning. It hovers, but symbolically shelters and encloses nothing—it is extracted from its former symbolic presence and recast as a sign. Indeed, there is no interior space in the pavilion; its symbolic presence is one of spatial continuity and the denial of usable interior space.

The Barcelona Pavilion is the first use of the column in Mies's work; it, too, becomes a notational device. For Le Corbusier the column was the quintessential symbol of the new architecture. His columns were typically round and set back from

the facade, creating the canonical "free plan" and "free facade" that were to become trademarks of modernist architecture. For Mies, the column is employed as a sign, not a symbol. In the Barcelona Pavilion, the columns, though detached
from the walls, are set forward rather than back; because of
their cruciform shape they seem intended to define the corners of an en-suite sequence of square bays. But, in fact, they
signify the absence of corners. This is emphasized by Mies's
use of reflective stainless steel, which causes the columns to
mirror and double their own infinitude—their absent presences. When the corners disappear, the negative space is
read as presence (even though void). The glass planes further
mirror and enforce these voids as presences (echoing the
roof's function—to shelter nothing), thus becoming the signs
of absent enclosure. (In fact, the glass doors were intended to
be taken down every day and only put up for security at
night.) The stainless steel mullions that divide and frame the
glass also provide yet another level of optical self-reference
and the signification of absence—they seem as absences in a
present glass screen.

Peter Eisenman, "miMISes READING; does not mean A THING." in *Mies Reconsidered: His Career,
Legacy, and Disciples*, ed. John Zukowsky (Chicago: Art Institute of Chicago; New York: Rizzoli,
1986), 86-98.

Peter Eisenman (*1932) is an architect, theoretician and theoretician and
professor at the Yale School of Architecture. His critical writings have appeared in a series of volumes, such as *House of Cards* (1987), *Diagram Dia-
ries* (1999), *Inside Out* (2004), and *Ten Canonical Buildings* (2008). In 1967
he founded the Institute of Architecture and Urban Studies (IAUS) in New
York City, which became, with its journal *Oppositions* since 1973, one of the
key voices for avant-garde thought in American architecture and urbanism.
In 1972 Eisenman had participated in an international conference about
architectural semiotics together with Charles Jencks, Juan Pablo Bonta,
Geoffrey Broadbent, and Alan Colquoun.[1] It profoundly influenced his ap-

proach to architectural interpretation, as evidenced in this piece. Eisenmann contradicted here Manfredo Tafuri's pessimistic observation of "empty and isolated signifiers" at the pavilion (see p. 203).

1   Tomás Llorens, *Arquitectura, historia y teoría de los signos: El simposio de Castelldefels* (Barcelona: La Gay Ceincia, 1974).

1986

KENNETH FRAMPTON
Modernism and Tradition in the Work of Mies van der Rohe

An analysis of the Barcelona Pavilion must always commence with the eight freestanding columns, which, together with the freestanding asymmetrical planes, constitute the most active spatial elements of the composition. Already we can see how certain classical and vernacular metaphors are latent in what is normally regarded as a quintessential modern work. The eight columns, regularly spaced on a square grid and symmetrical with regard to the flat slab they support, may be read as a metaphor for a classical belvedere, while the spatial figure implied by the asymmetrical freestanding walls and glass screens may be read as a reference to the compressed and elongated Arts and Crafts house, as exemplified by Frank Lloyd Wright's Robie House, built in 1908 in Chicago, with which Mies was certainly familiar.

A referential complexity of this order demands that such generalized categories as *modernism* and *traditionalism* be broken down into their specific syntactic and semantic referents if we are to arrive at a more precise understanding of Mies's unique sensibility. In this light, it is possible to regard the Barcelona Pavilion as a proliferation of a number of complementary opposites: columnar versus planar, tectonic versus atectonic, opaque versus translucent, still versus agitated, open versus closed, and, even, architecture versus building. The first opposition is largely formal and virtually self-evident. The fourth and fifth are best described by the nature of the water's surface, ruffled where open and absolutely flat where enclosed. The last opposition may be said to derive from the fact that the "classical" cruciform columns imply *architecture*, whereas the pin-wheeling, planar space-form implies *building* by recalling the organic nature of the vernacular.[1]

A detailed analysis of the cruciform steel column of the Barcelona Pavilion indicates that the modernist/traditionalist opposition manifests itself in Mies's work as much at the level of detail as in the constitution of the whole. Cruciform in plan and clad in chromium, this dematerialized column could hardly be more modernist, particularly when compared to Le Corbusier's cylindrical white *piloti* of the same date, a form of column which Mies employed, presumably a demonstration of a more normative architecture, for the 1931 Berlin Building Exposition. While Mies's Barcelona column is, like any column, essentially a point support, it is also by virtue of its cruciform section, paradoxically planar.

Nothing could be more modernist than this dematerialized, partially planar column clad in a shimmering reflective surface; yet at the level of cultural memory, what do these serried vertical highlights of varying width remind us of, if not the perceptually varying flute-widths of classical columns? What is mnemonic in the case of the columns is equally so in the case of the freestanding space dividers, faced here in polished onyx and marble. Again, nothing could be more abstract and avant-garde than these mysteriously suspended wall planes; but they once again recall classical form in the nature of the associations aroused by their stone-veneered surfaces. What is true of the columns and walls is also true, in a different way, of the planes of the raised floor and the ceiling where the former is a travertine podium and, hence, by definition classical, its planar counterpart, the continuous white plastered ceiling, could hardly be more modernist and abstract. And yet the fact that the chromium columns lack any kind of conceptual fixity in relation to the floor and the ceiling (there is not even a vestigial capital or base) establishes a strange state of equivalence between those two parallel layers, despite their superficial differences. The volume contained between them becomes a seemingly unlimited expanse of abstract, universal space. This modernist space field is at once checked and terminated by traditional elements: marble-clad walls, a reflecting pool, and a figurative sculpture by Georg Kolbe. In the floor and ceiling of the Barcelona Pavilion, we can see how the poles of the modernist/traditionalist opposition gravitate, in expressive terms, to fundamentally different architectural elements: to the ceiling in the first instance and to the floor in the second.

Kenneth Frampton, "Modernism and Tradition in the Work of Mies van der Rohe," in *Mies Reconsidered: His Career, Legacy, and Disciples,* ed. John Zukowsky (Chicago: Art Institute of Chicago, 1986), 35-53.

Kennneth Frampton's (biography see p. 202) view shifted markedly from his stance in 1980 after he had seen the reconstruction and his interests and allegiances had shifted as well. The I.A.U.S. in New York had closed in 1984, at the height of discussions about postmodernism in architecture and its rediscovery of a "presence of the past." Frampton had developed an interest in what he termed "critical regionalism"[2] as an antidote to the globalizing and superficial tendencies of postmodern architecture by embracing local vernacular.

1   Most Arts and Crafts houses were typologically related to the English yeoman farmhouse, which grew organically in a pin-wheeling U- or L-formation, with the great hall at the head and the farm sheds and outhouses at the tail. This was, of course, a vernacular form.

2   Kenneth Frampton, "Towards a Critical Regionalism: Six Points for an Architecture of Resistance," in Hal Foster (Ed.), *The Anti-Aesthetic: Essays on Postmodern Culture* (Seattle: Bay Press, 1983), 16-30.

1986

FRITZ NEUMEYER
The Artless Word–Mies van der Rohe on the Building Art

In particular in regard to the Barcelona Pavilion, the planning phase of which fell into the year 1928, the proximity of philosophy to architecture becomes difficult to ignore. This was a display structure the function of which was to point to itself as objective meaning. Regardless of the external impetus–the listing of the Spanish royal couple in the Golden Book–there were no concrete functions to be fulfilled that could have disturbed the impression of an ideal Platonic object. With this building Mies had the opportunity to deliver a similarly confessional testimony for a new, non-unilateral modernism, this time using the language of architecture. [...] With this building Mies could deliver an architectonic example of that "totally new power ... that new dynamic" that, according to [Romano] Guardini, was called for so that the aspects of modern man's reality can be "seen in tandem." [...] The spatial discipline of the northern Italian villa, emphatically described by Guardini, conveys the idea of an ideal existence to which he thought modern man should become receptive. It is not inappropriate to glance at the Barcelona Pavilion with Guardini's descriptions in mind and to ask whether Mies might not have been guided by quite similar motives when he placed this building, reduced to a minimum of restrictive materials, like a transparent gate symbolically in the way of the visitor to the world's fair. [...] The pavilion revealed an ideal world of opposites and a gradation of value. An order of becoming took up its position on the pedestal, the spiritual principles of which rested visibly on Platonic thinking. Plato's position in humanistic thought was transcribed by Mies into architectonic terms. The grid of slender pillars followed the geometrical net drawn by the seams of the travertine slabs. Their cruciform pattern demarcated the coordinates at which the concrete and the dematerialized orders interlock. The grid of pillars was not so much a statically required support system as a measured mediator of the infinite. In this order was placed a rhythmical sequence of wall panels that might answer to Siegfried Ebeling's demand for a Dionysian reevaluation of space. [...]

The architectonics of the pavilion demonstrate Guardini's "double way into the intrinsic" by idealizing in both directions: the pedestal conveys the belief in an ideal past rooted in the eternal; the artfully arranged dynamic balance of the freestanding wall panels of the pavilion announce faith in an ideal future in which all opportunities stand open. Origin and utopia, myth and idea fused in Mies's spatial poetry.

The broad strong wall panels of onyx and vert antique and the glass walls embody substance in an exemplary fashion. Out of them Mies erected an open, one is tempted to say, neoplastic, cella that permitted, much as in classical space, a view over the pedestal, framed by the supports. This cell, by the abolition of limits, is transformed into a place of the universal, an order that lies beyond its confines. Much as in Guardini's philosophy, the subjective is affirmed but oriented to an objective order. The freedom gained by the new technological space dynamics has been reevaluated by Mies in the spirit of the infinite. Instead of erecting his walls with lightweight, prefabricated wall segments, which could have been fitted into the support structure—as would have been in keeping with such a temporary structure—Mies decided on onyx blocks that formed in their heaviness a gravitational counterweight to the grid of lightweight supports. [...]

The steel supports also, to which Mies had given the profile of an even-armed cross, were related to an elemental form that could be viewed as the mystical symbol of all building. Encased in a garment of nickel, they remotely recalled gothic pillars but also Greek columns with flutings. Furthermore, the shining skin imparted a dematerialized look that did not disrupt the unification of the space. The sky, the ultimate symbol of the yearning for infinity, was reflected in their polished surface. [...]

In Barcelona Mies made experienceable by artistic means that metaphysical space that resides behind all empirical space, so that men who crossed this frame would feel the possibilities of a hidden life, both in themselves and in their epoch.

Fritz Neumeyer, *The Artless Word: Mies van der Rohe on the Building Art*, trans. Mark Jarzombek (Cambridge, MA: MIT Press, 1991), 211-15.

Fritz Neumeyer (*1946) was a professor for architectural theory at the Technical University of Berlin from 1993 to 2014. Among his publications are *The Artless Word: Mies van der Rohe on the Building Art* (1986), *Ludwig Mies van der Rohe: Hochhaus am Bahnhof Friedrichstraße* (1992), *Friedrich Gilly 1772-1800: Essays on Architecture* (1994), *Der Klang der Steine: Nietzsches Architekturen* (2001), and *Quellenschriften zur Architekturtheorie: Bauen beim Wort genommen* (2002).

WINFRIED NERDINGER
Afterthoughts on the Centenary:
New Literature about Mies van der Rohe

Neumeyer also wants to explain Mies's architecture with the help of his freewheeling associations, despite Mies's frequent assurances that "a building is not a thought," and that he was interested in the art of building and not in theories. The main space in the Villa Tugendhat is, according to Neumeyer, naturally characterized by "an absolute ability to concentrate" and a "Dionysian urgency for life"—Dionysian!—while every item was fixed in its position precisely down to a millimeter! As to be expected, the Barcelona Pavilion is then being presented as a "platonic object." Neumeyer is not interested in the fact that the building evolved genetically from the Krefeld Villas and the variable spaces in the Weissenhof apartment block, rather than having fallen from the platonic firmament of ideas after a reading experience of [Romano] Guardini. Without any analysis of the pavilion's floor plan, of the direction of movement, of spatial impressions thanks to precisely guided viewing angles, of spatial definitions, of its structure or the appearance of materials, we are presented with a rhetorical construct fixed in literature: "On a classical base an order of becoming assumed its position, whose principals were visibly [!] based on the fundamentals of platonic thought. Plato's position in the emergence of humanistic education was represented by Mies with the tools of architectural disposition." The construction of a plinth, the geometric grid lines of the floor plates, and eight columns that don't fit precisely into this grid, turn, according to Neumeyer, the building into a built history of philosophy and supposedly illustrate the position of the most influential philosopher in the humanities. But this is not enough, into this assumed platonic order a "rhythmic sequence of wall plates is placed, which could be the equivalent of a Dionysian reorientation of the space for which Siegfried Ebeling argued." The Barcelona Pavilion as an intersection of Plato, Humanism, and Nietzsche, as well as an illustration of books by Guardini and Ebeling. [...] If one continues to argue along those lines, one can decipher Karl Marx's *Kapital* in each factory and Heidegger's *Being and Time* in each humble abode in the Schwarzwald.

Winfried Nerdinger, "Nachlese zum 100: Geburtstag: Neue Literature zu Mies van der Rohe," *Kunstchronik* 41, no. 8 (August 1988): 419–29.

Winfried Nerdinger (*1944) is a professor emeritus at the Technical University in Munich and former director of its Architecture Museum. Among his numerous publications are: *Theodor Fischer* (1989), *Das Bauhaus* (2018), *Walter Gropius* (2019), and many edited volumes, for example *Rekonstruktion der Geschichte, Geschichte der Rekonstruktion* (2010). On the occasion of Mies's centenary Nerdinger looked at a number of new publications about Mies. His most spirited critique was leveled at Fritz Neumeyer's *The Artless Word*.

PAUL RUDOLPH
Conversation at 23 Beekman Place

Peter Blake: So there we have it: site, space, scale, structure, function, and spirit. Have you noticed every time you talk about one of those things, you seem to touch upon or refer to Mies's Barcelona Pavilion in one way or another? Why is that?

Paul Rudolph: To me, the Barcelona Pavilion is Mies's greatest building. It is one of the most human buildings I can think of—a rarity in the twentieth century. It is really fascinating to me to see the tentative nature of the Barcelona Pavilion. I am glad that Mies really wasn't able to make up his mind about a lot of things—alignments in the marble panels, or the mullions, or the joints in the paving. Nothing quite lines up, all for very good reasons. It really humanizes the building. [...] The courtyards and the interior space cast a spell on you which you will remember forever.

PB: If you were to put your finger on it, what do you think you learned from the Barcelona Pavilion?

PR: I made a few sketches that are meant to illustrate the impact of the actual building (as rebuilt in 1992 [*sic*] on the same site as the original 1929 Pavilion), which is very different from drawings, photos, etc. The Barcelona Pavilion is religious in its nature and is primarily a spatial experience. We have no accepted way of indicating space, and therefore the sketches made are very inadequate. One is drawn by the sequence of space through it. Multiple reflections of the twentieth century modify the architecture of light and shadow in a manner that no other building can equal. Twentieth-century concepts have affected all of the past. Reflections are organized so that shadows are lit and become spatial ornamentation for the whole. These shadows and reflections are most intense at crucial junctures, such as the principal entrances or turning points in the circulation. For instance, a forest is created via reflections and refractions in the marble and glass surrounding you. This multiplicity of reflections unites the exterior and interior but also helps to explain the mystery of the whole. I think it is simply unprecedented in architecture and the greatest of all of Mies's buildings. [...]

PR: The circulation from the east leads you up a flight of steps that leads to the platform on which the pavilion stands. This flight of stairs is spatially compressed, and when you reach the top of the platform, the pool causes you to turn 180 degrees. This turn prepares you for the compressed entry with a glass wall on the right and the green Tinian marble wall on the left, all modified by reflected trees. This squeezed space leads directly into the larger dominating space that contains the major function of the Pavilion. This flow of space continues all the way through the building in a highly disciplined way; nothing is left to chance. In my diagram the compressed space, the liberated space, the movement of space diagonally, vertically, and curved space modify the rectangular plan in a very clear and surprising fashion. The space is revealed but also hidden. The density of space is greater as it approaches the defining planes that form the Pavilion. This inward pull to the defining planes is offset by the reflective surfaces, so that most of the surfaces vibrate. I have tried to define the essential fluidity of these spaces and the interconnection of the inside and the outside. This highly disciplined flow of space is all-pervasive—a natural constriction and release of space that leads you on, on, on; everything is in motion, and you are carried along almost by unseen but felt forces.

PB: How does it work?

PR: The space becomes more dense the closer it comes to the walls and more fluid as it approaches the center. My second drawing is an attempt to illustrate this. The diagram indicates the way one follows the prescribed path in and out of the building. The angle of vision as it meets the wall surface is similar to the angle of reflection. Byzantine structures, with their curved and reflective surfaces, approached by the same effect, but this is very different because the universe is also reflected. Reflections in the Barcelona Pavilion augment and embellish the spatial organization and never contradict the thrust of the whole, for it is integral to the whole.

PB: Your third drawing describes the circulation through the Pavilion in still another way.

PR: The dots represent the natural places where you might pause, where you might stop, and turn, and look around. Everyone sees the world through a 22.5-degree cone of vision around a horizontal line about five feet four inches above the ground. I think Mies studied these angles of vision very carefully. Nothing has been left to chance, for at each turn the clarity of composition remains composed and its fluidity and its interrelationships remain intact. By the way, the importance of the 22.5 degrees of the angle of vision as a method of organizing and moving through space is not really a twentieth-century discovery. The Acropolis, I believe, was organized much in the same way, for it utilized the universal angle of vision, lending coherence to the elaborate and unparalleled organization of its sequence of space. In fact, I think the organization of great European urban spaces show that this angle of vision must have been understood. [...]

PB: Did you ever talk to Mies about these things?

PR: No, but I believe the reason the Barcelona Pavilion seems so serene, so logical, so peaceful, so spiritual is due to Mies's interest in movement, in space, in his interlocking spaces and his analysis of seeing.

PB: In your fourth drawing you seem to have concentrated on the ends of walls, the sharp edges that are a characteristic of a freestanding wall panel of the sort employed by Mies in this pavilion. What are you trying to say?

PR: The revealed ends of the walls, the edges, are a method of leading you in a very logical way to investigate what is behind and beyond this screen. It also celebrates the clarity of structure juxtaposed with a non-load-bearing wall or screen. The idea that is implied in all these spaces in the Barcelona Pavilion is one of the reasons for its power. The sketch suggests that curved space and diagonal space is implied in spite of the literal geometry. The seemingly haphazard arrangement of divisions of space in the building follows a very consistent pattern. Planes in space—as opposed to traditional walls with holes for light and access cut into them—make clear the essential method of twentieth-century building. However, planes in space at the pavilion are spatially much more important, because the mirrorlike finish of the columns reflects what is near, and columns do not count for very much.

PB: It seems to me that you are always conscious of another space and then another beyond those walls and that you are drawn from one to the next.

PR: I should say that all these things are related one to the other. The invisible, diagonal, radiating planes from the ends of the walls—planes that don't really exist at all but are implied everywhere—are a profound contribution to the spatial fluidity of the pavilion.

Paul Rudolph, "Conversation at 23 Beekman Place." Interview with Peter Blake (1986), in Roberto de Alba, *Paul Rudolph: The Late Work* (New York: Princeton Architectural Press, 2003), 203-17.

Paul Marvin Rudolph (1918-1997) was an American architect and chair of the architecture school at Yale University. His architecture is known for its use of exposed concrete and complex spatial configurations. Among his most famous works are the Yale Art and Architecture Building in New Haven (1958-63) and the campus of the University of Massachusetts at Dartmouth (1963-69). His friend **Peter Blake** (1920-2006) was an architect and writer (see p. 160). While Rudolph's early houses in Florida had been influenced by the Barcelona Pavilion, his search for more spatial complexity had turned him into an admirer of Wright and dismissive of Mies. "Mies didn't use space psychologically at all," he said. Mies's notion of space was "always a regular series of columns in a series of horizontal planes [...] horizontal flowing of space." Asked in 1986 about the reconstructed pavilion, Rudolph conceded wearily: "I will make a special trip, if necessary, to see the Barcelona Pavilion, but I wouldn't go very far to look at another Mies office building." Rudolph went as soon as it opened and had an epiphany. Back home, he created seven color diagrams, drawn into the pavilion's floor plan, examining "circulation," "spatial organization," "cones of vision," "clarity of structure," "flow of movement," and "light and shade." They looked like scientific recordings of energy fields but, according to Rudolph, "hardly did the building justice."

1987

PAUL GOLDBERGER
Architecture: Mies Masterpiece's New Incarnation

It is an extraordinary building, but as remarkable as the structure itself is the curious sense it engenders. The crowds wander through it as if it were some sort of archaeological artifact, recently unearthed, and in a sense that is what it is—not uncovered, of course, but rediscovered just as completely. Most demolished buildings slip away from the public consciousness after they are torn down; the pavilion, however, only grew in stature. Writers, historians, critics and architects acclaimed the original pavilion as one of the seminal buildings of the modern age; virtually none of them had ever seen it, of course, but that did not stem their enthusiasm for the building, and their determination to confer upon it legendary status. […] So, there is reason to believe that the experience of visiting this new pavilion is fairly close to what it must have felt like in 1929. Indeed, what is most astonishing is how new and fresh the pavilion feels, even though its image is now familiar and the radical rethinking of architectural space that it represented is no longer anything new or startling. But so perfect is Mies's art that we feel in 1987 as if we were seeing all of this open, flowing space for the first time—as if we, like the visitors to the original pavilion in 1929, had known only tight, overstuffed rooms and were having our first breath of modernist fresh air. [...]

In a sense [...] the pavilion was always a kind of folly—an unreal building for an unreal purpose. But this makes it no less extraordinary, and it makes the extent to which many of its architectural motifs have become commonplace no less appropriate. For we can now understand, as we could never have understood in the days when the pavilion existed only in photographs, how truly sublime this building is. Most important, we can sense what is like to move through the pavilion, something still photographs could never tell us: the truth is that it is like walking through a dream of spatial perfection. From almost every vantage point the pavilion makes a superb backdrop for the human figure, but more exciting still is to see it alive with constant movement—what an extraordinary place this would be to choreograph a dance piece, for example.

Some Mies purists have complained that some of the glass as well as the onyx used on one of the interior walls is not precisely like the original, but these things matter little in the face of the nearly perfect level of execution here. The only real problem with this recreation is that the 1986 pavilion has one neighbor that the 1929 pavilion did not—a dreadful building of concrete that looks like a parking garage and in fact houses offices for the upcoming Olympics in Barcelona.

The greatest service the City of Barcelona, which has already done much for architecture by rebuilding the Mies pavilion, could perform now would be to demolish this structure, which squats in front of the Mies pavilion, squeezing it and clamoring for attention. For it is worse than a vulgar intrusion—beside Mies van der Rohe it becomes a living demonstration of how far down modern architecture has come since 1929.

Paul Goldberger, "Architecture: Mies Masterpiece's New Incarnation," *New York Times* (March 26, 1987), C 22.

Paul Goldberger (*1950) is an architectural critic and educator. He has written architectural criticism for *The New York Times*, the *New Yorker* and *Vanity Fair* magazine. He is also a professor (and former dean) at the Parsons School of Design. Among his book publications are *Ballpark* (2019), *Building Art: The Life and Work of Frank Gehry* (2015), *Why Architecture Matters* (2009), and *Up from Zero: Politics, Architecture, and the Rebuilding of New York* (2004). Goldberger's perceptive account of his visit to the rebuilt pavilion ends with a plea to demolish the 3000m^2 brutalist exhibition hall by the architects Juan Paradinas, Luis Garcia-German, and Jose Ignacio Casanova Fernandez, which had stood across from the pavilion's site since 1973. It was, indeed, taken down in 1993.

HUBERT DAMISCH
La plus petite différence

There is no history of architecture, no matter how critical, that does not give the Barcelona Pavilion a special place, value, and significance as an example to be followed. [...] The so-called identical reconstruction of the Barcelona Pavilion easily looks like a parable. Now reproduced, the model has lost its value as a monument and become nothing more than a double or doublet, one of a pair, a life-size maquette, something like the Esprit Nouveau Pavilion perhaps, reconstructed a long way from Paris on the outskirts of Boulogne [*sic*][1] or, if the project goes ahead, Melnikov's pavilion among the "follies" of La Villette: curios at worst; museum pieces at best (and are things any different—and in what context!—with the restored Villa Savoye?). The parable (which means comparison, parabola) shows us that despite its repetitive appearances, Mies's work does not lend itself to reproduction, in the strict sense of the term, and that if there is a series there, then its generative principle is to be found not in repetition or some recurring typology but in the patient, obstinate, methodical search for the minimal deviation, the minimum perceptible difference between two individuals that all the signs suggest merge, and in which precisely lies the difference eliminated by reproduction. But that would still count for little if the difference were reduced to a simple variation. Difference, in Mies, was the object of real labor, prompted by an intention, if not a concerted calculation. It fabricated a story, a story that was exclusively architectural, so that we are entitled to speak of the labor of the work—the very labor of which the reconstructed Barcelona Pavilion is today like the recovered emblem, the recaptured trophy. [...] The reconstruction of the Barcelona Pavilion will be justified when the Catalan capital becomes one of the obligatory stops on a pilgrimage that starts in Berlin and leads, via New York, to Chicago, justified for all those who do not confuse history with the cult of relics or ruins, who are not easily taken in and can claim to have seen with their own eyes, touched, and explored the monuments of a modernity captured at the very real moment of its difference.

Hubert Damisch, "La plus petite difference," in *Noah's Ark: Essays on Architecture*, ed. Anthony Vidler (Cambridge, MA: MIT Press, 2016), 212–28. First published in: *Mies: Sa carrière, son heritage et ses disciples* (Paris: Centre Pompidou, 1987), 14–18.

Hubert Damisch (1928–2017) was a French philosopher, art historian and, from 1975 to 1996, professor at the École des Hautes Études en Sciences Sociales in Paris. He wrote extensively on the history and theory of architecture, painting, theater, photography, and film. Major works include *The Origin of Perspective* (1995) and *Skyline: The Narcissistic City* (2002). This essay appeared first in the exhibition catalogue of the 1987 exhibition, *Mies: Sa carrière, son heritage et ses disciples* at the Centre Pompidou in Paris (based on the 1986 exhibition at the Art Institute of Chicago, called *The Unknown Mies van der Rohe and His Disciples of Modernism*).

1   Editors' note: The reconstructed *Pavilion de L'Esprit Nouveau* stands in the outskirts of Bologna, Italy, not Boulogne-sur-Seine, France.

1988

JOSEP QUETGLAS
Fear of Glass: The Barcelona Pavilion

The final metaphor of discontinuity in Mies's temple comes to
us as a piece of collage: the colonnade, by provenance the
work of a mediocre local architect, is already erect when Mies
selects his site.[1] After all, did not Mies demonstrate throughout his life a taste for collage, for the interaction between het-
erogeneous pieces deriving from diverse materials and different formal contexts? From his years as an apprentice in the
office of Peter Behrens, when he pasted behind a window the
cropped photograph of a zeppelin, making it appear to be
aloft in the skies of Berlin, to his drawings incorporating photographs of works by Maillol, Rodin, and Picasso, there is in
Mies a constant taste for difference, for the discontinuous
landscape, for insertions.

The German pavilion is one of these collages constructed. In
fact, one could make a representation of it as such. In the lower left foreground of the kit would be the cutout of the colonnade; in a corner to the right, the cutout of the statue by Kolbe; in the center, between the parenthesis of both these
presences, some vague indications in pencil of vertical planes
and columns. An inked grid would be the floor.

One must insist on the colonnade as an integral component of the pavilion. Cornered on a slope of the site, hidden on three sides by a tall, blind wall and vegetation, the pavilion is solely seen from the avenue at whose extreme end it is located and which it closes—always on the other side of the strange vigil kept by the colonnade. [...] Why is it the colonnade that confronts the visitor, separating him from the pavilion? In the end, the question can be asked in the following manner: we already know the function the colonnade serves, but what is, who is, the line of columns?

The answer can be found in a book well known to any cultured young German at the turn of the century, *The Birth of Tragedy*. Here Nietzsche establishes, in one of the first chapters, the precise origins of tragedy, namely the chorus. What is the chorus, however, and what is its role? [...]

The chorus is like a living wall, a wall of people, a line made up of petrified people—of columns. The colonnade is a chorus—and the pavilion as such, is not just scenography but a theatrical representation. What is proof? Let us assemble the pieces: the pavilion is the modern house and the pavilion is the representation of tragedy. The pavilion is the tragic representation of the modern house.

Josep Quetglas, "Fear of Glass: The Barcelona Pavilion," in *Architectureproduction*, ed. Beatriz Colomina (New York: Princeton Architectural Press, 1988), 123-51.

Josep Quetglas Riusech (*1946) (biography see p. 210, texts 209, 244) studied architecture and architectural history under Rafael Moneo at the Architecture School of Barcelona, where he received his PhD in 1980. He taught there from 1974-1988 and then became professor for the history of art, modern and contemporary architecture at the Polytechnic University of Catalonia. He has published widely on Spanish and European modern architecture, in particular on Le Corbusier and on the Barcelona Pavilion (*Der*

gläserne Schrecken: Mies van der Rohes Pavillon in Barcelona. [2001]).
Quetglas adopts Manfredo Tafuri's (text p. 207) idea of the pavilion as a
collage as well as that of a stage set and develops them further.

1 Sometime in late 1928, screens of eight freestanding Ionic columns had been erected on the
   eastern and western sides of the Plaza de Bellas Artes, in front of Mies's future site and of the
   pavilion of the City of Barcelona. Apparently, parts from four columns in the center of the
   plaza (built by Josep Puig i Cadafalch in 1919) were reused. They represented the four stripes
   on the Catalan flag and had been demolished under dictator Primo de Rivera earlier that
   year as a symbol of Catalan independence. (The eight columns in front of Mies's pavilion were
   demolished after the Second World War; the four columns in the center were recreated in 2010.)

MASSIMO CACCIARI
Mies's Classics

While much has been said about the Miesian *Raum ohne Eigenschaften*, the root of the expression has been little understood. It would be more helpful to speak of a space free of qualities. In other words, the space-rhythm reflection-of-light does not fit the dimension of a specific intention or will to a purpose or specific quality. It has no goal. Qualities distinguish light functionally, imprisoning and walling it in, directing its rhythms one way. They are therefore contingent, and insofar as they are, they fall absolutely short of reflecting the *Wesen* of construction. In speaking of *ohne Eigenschaften*, there is a tendency to confuse two metaphysically opposed planes—quality and value—as though "without qualities" meant *Entwertung*. Space-rhythm must be utterly freed of qualities in order that it may express itself as value. The spirit of value's freedom, the issue of value, opposes the spirit of the quality, which is the spirit of the fixed letter, of the specific function that is the prison of contingency. [...] The Barcelona Pavilion is the most startling evidence of this entire problematic, specifically that of the appearance of value only after we have completely emptied the work of qualities, after we have utterly removed it from contingent qualification. [...] Only when construction is emptied of quality's "what" will it be possible to indicate *Das Wesen des Bauens*—the expression itself states this. It is *Erinnerung*—an authentic self-penetration—in the direction of construction's light, which comes before any determined building. In this sense, I would say that each element (glass, marble, water) is more intuited than worked on or treated. It is as though every element were intuited the way ideas are, purely in the mind, each in its essence as *kalón* [ideal, perfect beauty] stripped of any determined function, any specific goal. Every element carries out a service, but it services the *ergon* [work] which transcends any *Zielsetzung*.

Massimo Cacciari, "Mies's Classics," *RES: Anthropology and Aesthetics*, no. 16 (Autumn 1988): 9-16.

Massimo Cacciari (*1944) is an Italian philosopher and politician. He received his PhD from the University of Padua with a thesis on Immanuel Kant's *Critique of Judgment* and in 1985 became professor of aesthetics at the Architecture Institute of Venice under the directorship of Manfredo Tafuri, before founding the department of philosophy at the University of Milan in 2002. For many years a member of the Italian Communist Party, he was elected into the Italian parliament in 1976. From 1993 to 2000 and again from 2005 to 2010, Cacciari served as the mayor of Venice. In this essay from 1988, he addresses the implications of the Barcelona Pavilion's lack of function as a precondition for its role as a perfect embodiment of beauty within the framework of the modern movement.

ROBIN EVANS
Mies van der Rohe's Paradoxical Symmetries

Perusing the slides I had taken of the reconstructed pavilion, I found it difficult to decide which way up they went—an artifact of photography, no doubt. Then I changed my mind. It was not an artifact of photography, but a property of the pavilion itself, a property of which I had not been conscious while there. The photographs had made it easier to discern. Soon after, I was looking at some student sketches of the pavilion, and I discovered that someone else had experienced the same difficulty. He had inadvertently begun to caption his drawing the wrong way up.

Disclosed in our pictures of the pavilion was something quite different from the effect noticed by Kandinsky and exploited by cartoonists ever since, that nonfigurative forms have no privileged orientation. At Barcelona the reversibility derives from the most unlikely source: symmetry. It is unexpected because Mies had gotten rid of bilateral symmetry (the kind we expect) making a conspicuous show of its absence. He then reintroduced it, in quantity, in another dimension, where no one would think of looking for it: horizontally. [...] Although incomplete, the horizontal symmetry of the Barcelona Pavilion is very powerful. Its overwhelming strength is attributable to one simple fact: the plane of symmetry is very close to eye level. For a person of average height, the dividing line between the onyx panels is indistinguishable from the horizon line. [...] In Mies's pavilion the plane of symmetry is almost impossible to escape. The eyes are delivered into it by virtue of normal ambulant posture, and so the retinal images of the lower and upper halves are rendered equal. The only way to avoid this is to stoop, sit, or squat. I have since looked at as many photographs as I could find of both the original and the reconstructed pavilion. They show that, although nobody ever mentions this commanding plane, most people (and their cameras) occupy it. If the photographs contain figures, notice how their eyes hover around the horizontal joint between the onyx slabs. If not, notice, first, how many elements reflect across this line, then look at the receding contours of obliquely viewed surfaces and notice how nearly identical are the angles from floor and ceiling to the horizon—a property of all perpendicular, rectangular planes in perspective, viewed from mid-height. Notice the difficulty of distinguishing the travertine floor, which reflects the light, from the plaster ceiling, which receives it. If the floor and the ceiling had been of the same material, the difference in brightness would have been greater. Here, Mies used material asymmetry to create optical symmetry, rebounding the natural light in order to make the ceiling more sky-like and the ambience more expansive. [...]

First, symmetry is eliminated (in the composition of plan and elevation), then it is smuggled in sideways as an optically constructed symmetry between floor and ceiling, and finally it is readmitted in its normal orientation as a family of fictions (in reflections). Mies did not dispense with symmetry in his radical European works, only to restore it later in the USA. Symmetries were never present in greater strength and numbers than they were in the Barcelona Pavilion, which turns out to be a veritable Trojan horse filled with them. [...] According to Tafuri and Hays, Miesian reflections are a way of breaking things up; according to me, a way of creating coherence.

Robin Evans, "Mies van der Rohe's Paradoxical Symmetries," *AA Files* 19 (Spring 1990): 56-68.

Robin Evans (1944–1993) was a British architect, teacher, and historian. His essay on the Barcelona Pavilion responds to Manfredo Tafuri, Michael Hays, and Josep Quetglas's contention that the reflections and distortions in the pavilion are a central key to its understanding, as "reflections break up the calm and isotropic space of ordinary perception," relating via their critical distance to the precariousness of its times. (See pp. 207, 218, 284.) Evans's argument centers on his discovery of the pavilion's symmetries, "of an entirely different order to those of monumental classicism." They provided an aesthetic distance, an "architecture of forgetting," whose beauty distracted from the surrounding "politics and violence" of the 1920s.

1990

CAROLINE CONSTANT
The Barcelona Pavilion as Landscape Garden: Modernity and the Picturesque

Early plans indicate Mies's explicit use of picturesque devices. He distributed three pedestals for statues throughout the pavilion, each positioned to provide a focal point at the end of a major viewing axis. The sequence is analogous to the eighteenth-century pictorial circuit—a series of points at which a view is contrived to arrest the progress of the observer. Moreover, these moments of stasis punctuate the experience and accentuate the discontinuities between sculpture and architecture, reflecting those between architecture and landscape in the earliest English landscape gardens. Ultimately, Mies reduced the number of statues to one, that in the inner court, to increase the continuity of the sequence. There is only one relative point of stasis, and it focuses not on the statue but on a wall of onyx dorée, which Mies from the early conceptual stages endowed with iconic value. By eliminating these sculptural focal points, he rejected pictorial means and overcame a tendency common to the early picturesque garden, that of focusing attention on objects rather than the landscape. This momentary pause relies not on the contrast between architecture and sculpture but between elements conceived as part of an architectural system and an isolated architectural element, elevated, like the single column in the Temple of Apollo at Bassae, to the level of the sacred. [...] Mies's desire to control the visual sequence, evident in his preliminary sketches, was to remain the pavilion's spatial leitmotif. The site offered the possibility of an extended view in only one direction, that of the approach, yet Mies thwarted any such extension by devising a series of nonaligned transverse walls in order to limit visual expansion to the pavilion's longitudinal dimension, which he bracketed with end walls. For Mies the walls were the primary agents in the spatial sequence, unlike Le Corbusier, whose concept of the free plan relied on the structural and conceptual primacy of the columns. Mies's columns, introduced at a later stage in the design, remained structurally ambiguous. His later recollection of the project reflects this difference: "One evening, as I was working late on the building, I made a sketch of a freestanding wall and I gave myself a shock. I knew it was a new principle." [...]

Mies used the paving grid to provide visual rather than mathematical order, adjusting the dimensions of the travertine blocks to align with the joints in the vertical surfaces. The spatial continuity is perceptual. The result is not "universal" space, but space as a palpable entity, a conceit that relies on separation rather than unity. [...] The podium and columnar grid are frequently cited as evidence of Mies's tendency to resort to classicism. Yet neither is perceived as a whole: the end walls and reflecting pools interrupt the podium surface, while the spurious reading of the columns as a classical colonnade is possible only in plan. As Josep Quetglas has noted, each column exists in a distinct spatial context. Mies's shimmering cruciform columns support a similar contradiction: their formal precision dissolves under the visual distortion of their polished steel surfaces. Rather than refer to some external reality, these elements all serve, like the partitions or roof slab, as mute testimony to the symbolic essence of architecture. In its silence Mies's architecture is cacophonous. The pavilion is a montage of independent systems: travertine slab and plaster ceiling, chromium columns and marble partitions (of travertine, Tinian, verde antique and onyx dorée), together with various tints of glass (brown, green, milk, blue, and black), all colliding visually in the polished, reflective surfaces. The precision of the materials contrasts with their perceptual instability. [...] Critics have persisted in interpreting the onyx wall as the heart of the composition. Curiously, however, there has been little mention of an equally significant phenomenon: the luminous volume that lies closer to the pavilion's geometric center. It appears only peripherally in the published photographs; moreover, its sensual qualities seem to elude photographic representation. This inaccessible void bounded by etched glass was the only building element that Mies adjusted to conform to the paving grid. Originally conceived as a thin, wall-like element, it was ultimately realized as a volume of light. Embodying an element of nature, it has certain attributes of a courtyard but, like the entry court and the inner sculpture court, it can be occupied only in the imagination. A comparable luminosity in the inner court, which is continually bathed in sunlight, is visible upon mounting the podium and serves to draw the spectator in. In contrast, the ineffable qualities of the luminous wall can be perceived only from within. Its end walls of verde antique marble and black glass render it invisible from the entry stair or rear garden, while the sunlight of the outer court counteracts its phenomenal presence from that direction. [...]

Charged with designing a German *Repräsentationsraum*, with implications for serving formal or ceremonial rather than utilitarian purposes, he rejected emblematic motifs or signs. The architecture alone expresses the Pavilion's role as a symbol of the modern, progressive state of Germany, represented internationally for the first time in Barcelona. Two flags flanking the entrance were its sole representational devices. There is another, more immediate parallel to Mies's use of materials: the Italian grotto as a conspectus of natural and artificial wonders had a counterpart in the *Wunderkammer*. The collection was seen as a metaphor for the world. Its underlying order, like that of the pavilion, was based on aesthetic rather than scientific criteria, with objects grouped according to material, for example. The Barcelona Pavilion shares with the *Wunderkammer* the aim of epitomizing a sense of mystery and wonder rather than offering rational explication. Where the cabinet of curiosities originated in response to the crisis of values following the breakdown of Renaissance certainties, Mies's pavilion reflects a comparable phenomenon during the post-Enlightenment era.

Caroline Constant, "The Barcelona Pavilion as Landscape Garden: Modernity and the Picturesque," *AA Files* 20 (Fall 1990): 46–54.

Caroline Constant (*1944) is a landscape and architectural historian and professor emerita of architecture at the University of Michigan. She is the author of *The Modern Architectural Landscape* (2012), *Eileen Gray* (2000), *The Woodland Cemetery: Toward a Spiritual Landscape* (1994), and *The Palladio Guide* (1985), as well as numerous articles in books and professional journals.
Constant's idea of the pavilion as a picturesque garden folly picked up on similar ideas by Raymond McGrath and Vincent Scully in the 1930s and 1960s (see p. 124, 172). She agreed with Tafuri on the pavilion's montage of independent elements (see p. 207) and the perceptual instability of its reflective surfaces and attempted a new reading of the pavilion as "epitomizing a sense of mystery and wonder" just like a cabinet of curiosities, a *Wunderkammer*.

1993

IGNASI DE SOLÀ-MORALES, CHRISTIAN CIRICI, AND FERNAND RAMOS
Mies van der Rohe: Barcelona Pavilion

The building which we had seen reproduced dozens of times in all the major books on the history of art and architecture, whose simple plan we had studied on so many occasions without entirely grasping the distance between the clear order it seemed to reveal to us and the intellectual tension of the displaced elements, was an icon which for more than fifty years had been generating an intense energy, as a presence confined to the pages of books and magazines. To reconstruct the pavilion was, in these circumstances, a traumatic undertaking. On the one hand it meant entering into that Duchampesque perspective in which we had to accept, *helas!*, a certain inanity in our aesthetic operations. [...] Yet there was still a sense of daring in resolving to undertake the challenge of recreating before our very eyes in the three dimensions of physical space, what had for so long been essentially a graphic reference. [...] We have no doubt that all those of us who played some part in this undertaking are conscious of the distance that exists between the original and its replica. Because every replica is, indisputably, a reinterpretation. But it allows us again to walk amidst and see the startling contrast between the building and its surroundings, to let your gaze be drawn into the calligraphy of the patterned marble and its kaleidoscopic figures, to feel yourself enmeshed in a system of planes in stone, glass, and water that envelops and moves you through space, and contemplate the hard emphatic play of Kolbe's bronze dancer over the water. This is what we have tried to achieve and to offer to the sensibility and the culture of our time.

Ignasi de Solà-Morales, Christian Cirici, and Fernando Ramos, *Mies van der Rohe: Barcelona Pavilion* (Barcelona: Gustavo Gili, 1993), 39.

Ignasi de Solà-Morales, Christian Cirici, and **Fernand Ramos** were the architects in charge of the reconstruction of the Barcelona Pavilion in 1986. Ignasi de Solà-Morales (1942-2001) was a Catalan architect, historian, and professor at the Barcelona School of Architecture. He coined the term *terrain vague* for abandoned, obsolete, and unproductive areas in a city. Cristian Cirici (*1941) is a Catalan architect who was trained at the Architecture School of Barcelona. He won the Barcelona Prize for Architecture and Urbanism in 1997. Fernando Ramos Galino (*1944) is an architect in Barcelona and professor at the Universitat Politècnica de Catalunya, Barcelona. Among his buildings are collaborations in Barcelona with Richard Meier and Gae Aulenti.

1994

ROSALIND KRAUSS
The Grid, the /Cloud/, and the Detail

As I was reading some of the recent literature on Mies van der Rohe, I encountered a phenomenon I had not known until then: I came across the politically correct Mies, the post-structuralist Mies, almost, we could say, the postmodernist Mies. [... Mies] insists that an order is immanent [only] in the surfaces itself and that the order is continuous with and dependent upon the world in which the viewer actually moves. This sense of surface and volume, severed from the knowledge of an internal order or a unifying logic, is enough to wrench the building from the atemporal, idealized realm of autonomous form and install it in a specific situation in the real world of experienced time, open to the chance and uncertainty of life in the metropolis. [...] Indeed, in one description after another of the Barcelona Pavilion (by Robin Evans and Josep Quetglas, for example) the emphasis had shifted entirely away from the kind of contrapuntal but nevertheless classical logic of plan and elevation to which I had been introduced back when Mies was seen as the very epitome of the International Style, and instead what I was now being shown was a structure committed to illusionism, with every material assuming, chameleon-like, the attributes of something not itself—columns dissolving into bars of light, or glass walls becoming opaque and marble ones appearing transparent due to their reflectivity—but even more importantly, with a mysteriousness built into the plan such that the building is constructed without an approachable or knowable center and is in fact experienced as (to use these authors' word) a labyrinth.

Rosalind Krauss, "The Grid, the /Cloud/, and the Detail," in *The Presence of Mies*, ed. Detlef Mertins (New York: Princeton Architectural Press, 1994), 133.

Rosalind Epstein Krauss (*1941) is an art critic and professor at Columbia University. Her scholarship has mostly dealt with painting, sculpture, and photography in the twentieth century. She was an associate editor of the journal *Art Forum* in the early 1970s and then cofounded the journal *October* in 1976. This excerpt is from a paper she delivered at a 1992 symposium under the title *The Presence of Mies* in Toronto. While initially considering Mies (see texts by Hays and Evans on p. 218, 289) the bulk of her paper dealt with the painter Agnes Martin and the minimalism of her grids.

1997

TOYO ITO
Tarzans in the Media Forest

Mies's Barcelona Pavilion (1928–29) stands out as the most remarkable of all twentieth-century works of architecture. This is overwhelmingly true even in relation to all of the same architect's subsequent works. Nowhere else do we find a space filled with such "fluidity."

Although the structure is a combination of steel, glass, and stone, it does not imply the hardness of these materials. The glass and stone are merely the flat and simple, planar components of the space. Spaces created by the combination of abstract, horizontal planes have an infinite extension, described by Sigfried Giedion as a mutual interpenetration of interior and exterior spaces. Similar effects can be found in works of that time by Frank Lloyd Wright and architects belonging to the De Stijl school, but none of them produces as strong a sense of fluidity as the pavilion in Barcelona. This is not simply because of its spatial composition, but owes a great deal to the brilliance of the materials. Everything, from glass to the stone and metal, appears to fuse and flow out into the space. All the elements interact and create an atmosphere of eroticism within the space by their reverberation with the nearby surface of the water. The sensation created by the space is not the lightness of flowing air but the thickness of molten liquid.

In the early 1920s, Mies made several drawings of skyscrapers. His later works, such as the Seagram Building and the Lake Shore Drive apartment houses, are generally considered to represent his idea of a high-rise. Personally, I think it is the pavilion in Barcelona that best embodies the image presented in those drawings. The space composed of glass is given no distinct structure but stands like a pillar made of ice, beginning to melt in the air. It is an architecture born out of images alone and does not yet have a definite form. Of course the pavilion in Barcelona has a structure and a form as it stands on the ground, but the original image of the glass architecture contemplated by Mies in his earliest days is brought vividly to life. This is a work of architecture in which the architectural style is not yet manifest.

Mies is said to be a proponent of the "universal space" which swept through twentieth-century cities: a space created by a homogeneous continuum of grids extending both vertically and horizontally. True, Mies was one of the very first architects to come up with a skyscraper supported by a glass-and-steel curtain wall. And yet the image of a skyscraper that looks like a pillar of ice or the space embodied by the Barcelona Pavilion appears to differ considerably from the transparent office buildings that fill contemporary cities. The transparency of Mies's space seems to be entirely different from that of other modern architecture. [...] But the transparency of the Barcelona Pavilion is not that of clear air. Rather, it makes us feel as if we are looking at things deep underwater, and would better be described as translucent. The infinite fluidity we sense in the pavilion must arise from this translucent, liquid-like space. What we experience here is not the flow of air but the sense of wandering and drifting gently underwater. It is this sensation that makes the space distinct and unique.

The simultaneous fluidity and density of the Barcelona Pavilion gradually disappeared even from Mies's own architecture. Its place was soon taken by architectural formalism instead. The once fluid space was lost, as if a liquid had been turned into a solid. And as we await the arrival of the twenty-first century, we are once again in search of an erotic architecture that fuses with the environment.

Toyo Ito, "Tarzans in the Media Forest," *2G* (January 2, 1997): 121-44, quoted from: Toyo Ito, *Tarzans in the Media Forest* (London: Architectural Association, 2011), 115-24, quote in introduction above, 118. Translation by Thomas Daniell.

Toyo Ito (*1941) is a Japanese architect who won the Pritzker Prize in 2013. His work stands out for its variety and continuous stylistic and structural innovation. When writing this essay Ito was working on the Sendai Mediatheque, where, as he put it, the "columns were conceived as structures that sway and dance like seaweed in the water." Similar to Rem Koolhaas, Frank Gehry, and others, his view of the Barcelona Pavilion reflected and legitimized his current work.

GEORGE DODDS
Body in Pieces: Desiring the Barcelona Pavilion

The sedimentation of mythology built up around the Barcelona Pavilion during the past seventy years has resulted in a virtual labyrinth of interpretations. Each of these attempt in some way to codify the Bild-Bericht[1] images, often bolstering polemical readings of not only Mies's oeuvre, but the foundations of the International Style and the modern movement. This accumulated scholarship often reads like an oscillating field of disparate and at times mutually exclusive propositions. [...] For some, the pavilion is one of the most contextual and site-specific of Mies's European buildings. Others have argued with equal persuasiveness that it was a placeless and autonomous object and that its reconstruction could be sited anywhere in that the original was unfettered by distinctions of place. [...] Although it was the vanguard of what Hitchcock and Johnson called the International Style, it is also characterized as a critique of the foundations upon which that movement was based. It is both the emblem of Germany's postwar appeasement and the foreshadowing of Nazi totalitarianism. [...] There are some issues about which most authors agree. Perhaps the most pervasive of these is an emphasis on what is absent from, rather than what is present in, the pavilion.

Centers, edges, stairs, doors, exits, curtains, shadows, and even bodies—in all of these accounts, something invariably seems to be missing—but the bodies are, perhaps, the most troubling. While architectural photographers typically shoot their subjects empty, in the Bild-Bericht photographs the absence of human figures is almost palpable. Built "in the form of a house," these photographs show no trace of domesticity. The Kolbe sculpture of the female nude notwithstanding, this is a house where nobody ever seems to be home.

George Dodds, "Body in Pieces: Desiring the Barcelona Pavilion," *RES: Anthropology and Aesthetics* 39 (Spring 2001): 168–91.

George Dodds (*1958), a professor of architecture at the University of Tennessee in Knoxville, was the first since Juan Pablo Bonta in 1975 to look closely at the Barcelona Pavilion's reception history. He expanded his 2001 article into a book-length study in 2005 titled *Building Desire*.[2] His main concern in this piece is the lacuna between image and building, and its consequential impact in the case of the pavilion, where the original photographs became primary source material for its reconstruction.

1   Editors' note: The photos of the pavilion taken by Sasha Stone in June 1929 were distributed by the picture agency Berliner Bild-Bericht.
2   George Dodds, *Building Desire: On the Barcelona Pavilion* (London: Routledge, 2005).

DETLEF MERTINS
Architectures of Becoming: Mies van der Rohe and the Avant-Garde

Like the Glass Room, the German pavilion should be included among [Mies's] experiments with materials, although in this context it might more appropriately be called the Marble Pavilion, or even the Mixed Media Pavilion.

In the Glass Room, walls, ceilings, and floors had become abstract surfaces. Stretched white fabric sheets, colored linoleum, and plate glass had been made into transparent, translucent, and tinted rectangles of color, as thin as a sheet or a strip of film. The German pavilion by contrast reclaims flesh, staging a transformation of matter into spirit. [...] Everywhere the signs of fabrication are suppressed so that matter itself can assume the appearance of its underlying form–sharp, precise, mathematical. Where the planes of the Glass Room lacked depth, in Barcelona the eye sinks into the walls and floors. The observer dwells in the hollow interior of matter. The travertine plinth provides a geometrized ground whose thickness is apparent not only from outside but from within, in two pools of water. The surfaces of these basins may be as taut and slick as a mirror, but they are the outer membranes of deep dark pools, whose uncertain depth and viscosity draw the viewer in. The travertine is naturally pockmarked and flecked with holes, allowing us to see, even feel its substance. The pull is even stronger with the onyx wall, a honey-colored ocean enticing the eye to swim, get lost, dissolve.

Against their dark and variegated green ground, the white veins of the Tinos marble are mesmerizing, enveloping like the living walls of a garden frozen in a photograph—an image that threatens to come alive at any moment. Against the leaves of the trees that rustle above the wall, the stillness of the marble, the water and the bronze figure create mystery. The pattern of the marble might also suggest a photographic enlargement of the skin of an animal, the weave of a fabric, or even the texture of cellular tissue. Its materiality is paradoxically immediate yet distanced; its tactility is mediated by vision, more precisely by the new optics of photography, film, microscopes, and telescopes. The haptic is subsumed into the optic, nature into culture. [...]

Mies creates a rich interplay of closed and open, interior and exterior, transparent and opaque. Without absolute boundaries, the experience of the pavilion has no clear beginning or end.

Stepping up onto the podium, one is removed from the surrounding city. Thrown back into it on leaving one has been immersed in an extraordinary new beauty—a pocket of transcendent aesthetic experience, at once magical and existential. This is a space of solitude and self-reflection but also of connectivity. It offers no resistance yet slows the pace, to promote self-discovery not from within as much as in relation to the milieu. One's effortless glide through its interwoven complex of rooms, terraces, passages, and alcoves—rich and larger than life—sharpens the senses and expands the horizon of experience. Awareness is heightened to the point of expectancy. A space without hierarchy, center, or narrative, it is a labyrinth in which to search and discover, to wander and wonder and be struck with wonder. Both sacred and profane, this is a house of the gods that mortals can enter and experience—rich yet poor, full yet empty, austere yet magical, a space of transformation.

As in [Hans] Richter's films, the elements and spaces assume coherence and unity through the rhythm with which they move the observer through and around them. Yet at the same time, something of [Theo] van Doesburg's simultaneity also remains in effect—combining synchronic and diachronic conceptions of rhythm and unity. Reflections on the marble, glass, and water intensify the ambiguity between inside and out, up and down, reinforcing the cohesion of the whole by folding the parts onto themselves—establishing identity while precluding any stable image. If one looks along the dark glass wall that separates the sculpture court from the reception space inside, the court appears doubled onto the interior, the dark pool outside mapping almost perfectly onto the black carpet inside. Georg Kolbe's *Dawn* can be seen reflected not only in the pool but in the walls behind it and in the glass panels in front of it. Again and again from different vantage points, the statue is multiplied and dislocated, a symbol and symptom of the ongoing fracturing and recombination of identity feared in Expressionism and then celebrated in Dada and Surrealism.

The pavilion engenders a kind of timeless perpetual motion, both physically and psychically. It places the observer in a state of suspended animation and reverie that is nonetheless marked by movement, and by a combination of self-estrangement and self-integration. For Bergson and later philosophers of life, it was precisely this combination that underpinned life's endless process of becoming. [...] Mies's pavilion provided a setting for the active yet listless drama of becoming, offering its visitors not a blueprint for the future but a piece of it, proleptically achieved as a threshold and transformer. It reformulated the mission of glass architecture: to transform humanity by participating in its natural evolution, overcoming anthropomorphism and the problems of modernization in a new stage of development, a biocentric age of harmony and tranquility. By the late 1920s, as Mies absorbed the theories of historical change proffered by Guardini and his architect colleague Rudolf Schwarz, these aims became conflated with the task of creating the conditions for spirit within a secular, materialist, and industrial society, a society of the masses of mass production and mass media. While Richter made films like *Vormittagsspuk* (*Ghosts Before Breakfast*) of 1928, in which cinematic techniques were exploited to make miracles and epiphanies a part of everyday life, Mies's pavilion staged a similar cinematic *poeisis* in which visitors participated in a performance of self-estrangement and rediscovery on a higher plane of existence. They found themselves wandering effortlessly and aimlessly in a rich and dazzling milieu of almost pure abstraction—an immersive, labyrinthine environment in which matter had been formed into polished rectangles of varied colors, textures, and transparencies, and assembled into an open construct that was both finite and infinite. Suspended in a state between reality and delirium, liquefaction and crystallization, visitors experienced themselves and their world in a way that was both detached and connected, their identity now contingent on their multiple and fluid relationship to the context. While abstraction and alienation were understood to be problematic effects of instrumental rationality and industrial capitalism, here they were harnessed precisely to overcome these problems and usher in a new stage of modernity. In fusing the technological and the artistic means of the age, Mies produced a space for going beyond it, a space of expectancy and emergence.

Detlef Mertins, "Architectures of Becoming: Mies van der Rohe and the Avant-Garde," in *Mies in Berlin*, ed. Terence Riley and Barry Bergdoll (New York: Museum of Modern Art, 2001), 107-33.

Detlef Mertins (1954–2011) was an architectural historian who taught at the University of Toronto and, from 2002 to 2007, as chair of the department of architecture at the University of Pennsylvania. In his scholarly work, he returned again and again to the work of Mies van der Rohe. After his untimely death, a small group of scholars oversaw the publication of his major biography, *Mies* (2014). In 1994 he had edited a collection of essays, *The Presence of Mies*, and in 2010, together with Michael Jennings, edited a volume about the magazine *G*, in which Mies published several of his projects and which he helped to fund (*G: An Avant-Garde Journal of Art, Architecture, Design, and Film, 1923-1926*). A selection of his essays appeared as *Modernity Unbound* in 2011.

2001

BARRY BERGDOLL
The Nature of Mies's Space

Mies seized the opportunity of a commission virtually free of programmatic demands to craft a new paradigm for design as a structuring of the world that humanity can create. And as in Behrens's earlier exhibition pavilions and gardens, the German pavilion is at once a building and a landscape, a house and a temple, a measuring of space and an expansion of consciousness. Destroyed in 1930, it was recreated on the same site in 1981–86, and insofar as its experiential complexities have since then sponsored diverse interpretations, it has fulfilled just what Mies intended: a place in which the capacities of the new architecture opened new horizons of thought. Nor was this lost on visitors at the time, even if the interpretation of the building as a demonstration of the rational architecture made possible by new technological capacities was rapidly made dominant by powerful critics like [Henry-Russell] Hitchcock and [Philip] Johnson—neither of whom had seen the pavilion. One reviewer admired Mies's invitation of the visitor "to some shorter or longer period of rest and contemplation" in the only space in the fairgrounds where emptiness and quiet replaced a cornucopia of displays and new techniques of recorded sound and images. [...] In the German pavilion Mies defined two building blocks for an architecture understood as constructing a reality parallel to but separate from nature: the freestanding wall and the freestanding column. In effect, he set free two elements that the Renaissance architect Leon Battista Alberti had considered intimately related. He married this innovation with a renewal of the experiment in forming space out of panels of transparent and colored glass that he had first essayed in the Glass Room two years earlier, where he had given physical form to Ebeling's call for "spaces as membrane." Both the Glass Room and the pavilion were ambiguously structure and space, for like the reflective surfaces of the walls, they could oscillate perceptually between those roles. While the freestanding wall channeled and directed space, the cruciform columns provided a palpable reading, a gauge or measure of space.

The evolution of the design demonstrates that the grid was not a generative force, as it had been earlier for Behrens; indeed Sergius Ruegenberg recalled that the design was studied principally in a plasticine base in which the walls could be moved at will. Instead the grid was a late addition, a fine-tuning of visual experience: recorded insistently on the travertine surface of the podium shared by house and garden, it is an aesthetic and optical device to anchor the eye as it scans space. The walls do much of the work of carrying the roof, but they too serve as measures and anchors of space, both guiding the body in motion, through their famous sliding compositional relations, and anchoring the body in stasis by channeling views through various glass filters to the garden, the exposition, and even the city beyond, whose traffic often reflects on the glass walls with the movement of the sun. As Ruegenberg recalled in both sketches and an unpublished memoir, Mies insisted that the greatest difference between his own and Le Corbusier's staging of a prospect through expanses of glass was the use of a spatial grounding that could be felt bodily, even when it was outside the eye's peripheral field. "I must have a wall behind me," Mies is said to have explained, in one of his most telling extensions of the German tradition of empathetic analysis of the psychology of space.[1] The spatial paradigm of the pavilion is indeed new, but many of Mies's clients of the 1920s would recognize elements of their homes in what [Raymond] McGrath called, quite unself-consciously, a "garden house." In the earliest plan, a space for this experiment in shifting planes and viewpoints is carved out of the site by a hedge, a wavy line on the plan. Although Mies replaced the hedge, instead relying on the architectural (and instant rather than slow-growing) means of freestanding walls of glass, marble, and travertine, the link with nature—and with the origins of these walls in the garden devices of his earlier career—was reinforced by incorporating planters for vines into the very structure of the travertine walls partially enclosing the larger pool, which was itself planted with water lilies. [...]

The path describes an itinerary but the endpoints are multiple: the pool with Georg Kolbe's figure *Dawn*, set in a pool bathed in early light; the path leading axially to the grove behind the pavilion, which turns out to be centered on the podium and thus on the exhibition's cross-axis, previously so emphatically denied; or the terrace, with its long travertine bench overlooking a shallow pool that reflects both the setting sun and the pavilion itself. The hinge space between them all, at precisely the center of the rectangular podium—a space neither wholly indoors nor wholly outdoors, under the protective canopy of the cantilevered roof, and free of membranes to the outside world—is clearly the descendant of the outdoor dining areas in most of Mies's earlier garden houses.

As in Krefeld, a translucent wall provides soft, glowing illumination both here and inside the pavilion, where it is seen in counterpoint to the great object of display, a stunning warm-rose onyx wall.

The pavilion has a formal front facade and a more reserved back garden, but Mies—having arranged his sliding planes directly across a secondary entrance to the fair, and on the short route to the popular Pueblo Español, the Spanish village display—realized from the first that his building would be encountered from both sides. In fact he blocked the simple path through with a deep green wall of marble, so that moving in either direction would require a detour into the spaces of contemplation, whether roofed or open air. Mies's construction staged a heightened "world in itself"—the very demand Behrens had made of the architectonic garden. Set among the fair's abundant icons of historicist culture, the pavilion, a modernist propylaeum, was a place of transition between worlds.

Barry Bergdoll, "The Nature of Mies' Space," in *Mies in Berlin*, ed. Terence Riley and Barry Bergdoll (New York: Museum of Modern Art, 2001), 67–105.

Barry Bergdoll (*1955), the Meyer Schapiro Professor of Art History and Archaeology in Columbia University's School of the Arts and Sciences, was the Philip Johnson Chief Curator at the Museum of Modern Art in New York from 2007 to 2013. During this time, he organized a series of major exhibitions and edited or coedited their catalogues, among them *Latin America in Construction* (2015), *Partners in Design* (2015), *Home Delivery* (2008), *Le Corbusier: An Atlas of Modern Landscapes* (2013), *Bauhaus 1919-1933* (2009), *Henry Labrouste* (2013), and *Rising Currents* (2011). Among his numerous publications are *Mies in Berlin* (2001), *European Architecture 1750-1890* (2000), *Léon Vaudoyer: Historicism in the Age of Industry* (1994), and *Karl Friedrich Schinkel: An Architecture for Prussia* (1994).

1 See Eva-Maria Amberger, *Sergius Ruegenberg* (Berlin: Berlinische Galerie, 2000), 55. There is a copy of Ruegenberg's memoir, "Mies van der Rohe, Entwürfe und Bauten von 1908 bis 1939" in the collection of the Berlinische Galerie, BG-AS 3.80.

2002

REM KOOLHAAS
Miesunderstandings

Loyalty

Can respect kill? Mies has to be protected against his cham-
pions. In the year 1986, the Barcelona Pavilion was reconstructed in color. The resurrection destroyed its aura. (In architectural history it is still, obstinately, being presented in black
and white.) The mid-eighties also saw an apotheosis of the
market economy. Coincidence? Was Mies exploited in the
name of city marketing? From homage to insult, in the name
of memory and respect. In the market economy, shopping is
the live elixir of the urban environment. Today a big part of
the pavilion serves as a souvenir shop. "How did one treat
Mies, everywhere in the world? The Barcelona-Pavilion [...]
was rebuilt and has become a true magnet for the public in
the meantime." (John Vinci, the most vehement critic of the
OMA design, in an open letter to the IIT, in which he called for
the "defense" of the Commons.)

Rem Koolhaas, "Miesverständnisse," *Arch+* 161 (June 2002): 78-83.

Rem Koolhaas poured his frustration with the public approval process of
his design for Chicago's Illinois Institute of Technology (IIT) Campus, a student center that intersected with Mies's existing student center and refecto-
ry ("The Commons") into a short essay for Swiss magazine *Arch+*. By (false-
ly) claiming that a gift shop occupied a "big part" of the rebuilt Barcelona

Pavilion, Koolhaas seems to suggest that if Mies's masterpiece is soiled by commercialism, a contemporary addition to the IIT student center should not present a problem.

HAJIME YATSUKA
Mies and Japan

The flowing spaces that became paradigmatic of early modern architecture, seen in Wright or in Mies's early work, were not related to structural invention but were rather purely aesthetic inventions. For this reason, the resemblance between Katsura Villa's[1] plan and something like the Brick Country House project is merely a matter of appearance. However, after Mies introduced freestanding columns in the Barcelona Pavilion, the situation changed drastically. Although most of Mies's biographers describe this introduction as the result of the architect's coherent development of an integrated and rational approach to structure, I assume that it was rather an ad-hoc invention that came late in the pavilion's design. In his earlier perspective sketches, where walls were in a different position than the final plan, Mies did not draw columns. Even after the wall positions were fixed, there is a plan with no columns or with only six of them, instead of the eventual eight. Unlike the successive Tugendhat House (1930) and his model house for the Berlin Building Exhibition (1931), the walls of the Barcelona Pavilion stood close to the columns, in positions that appear quite convenient to support the roof. This suggests that Mies's original idea was to support the roof with the walls, and he changed his mind after he fixed the location of the walls. Far from being coherent and rational, this was rather a tour de force. For instance, the working drawings done and signed by his chief assistant Sergius Ruegenberg,[2] a copied set of which is now preserved in Tokyo University, recorded the indication of supporting steel structure in the walls that must have worked as supplementary structures to compensate for the insufficiency of the abruptly introduced column system. Further, whether the steel structure in the roof slab was originally designed as it was eventually built or not is uncertain. The aforementioned working drawings showed different dimensions for the beams, as we can see in construction photos of the time. But in either case, the roof was not so thin, as we see from photos taken at the ground level. The beams were taller in the center and were shorter toward the periphery. Together with reported practical shortcomings related to the transformation of the roof and the eventual leaks, it seems certain that Mies dared to take on this tour-de-force in spite of a lot of problems generated by a lack of preparation. [...]

In photographs the building looks perfect: Mies seems to have succeeded in dealing with the idea of freestanding columns as if they were intended from the beginning. However, Mies was certainly faced with what was to him a totally new problem, but one that is routine in wooden-frame structure: regularity and structural purity. The post-and-lintel structure is, of course also traditional in the West, but in masonry buildings, the choice of walls or columns does not make a critical difference in that both can work as bearing structures. And yet, if my hypothesis is correct, the basic structural conception of the Barcelona Pavilion was fundamentally changed after the introduction of steel columns. Along the same lines, the walls were not masonry either, but sliced veneers put over a hidden supporting structure. The building ceased to be masonry. There is no documentation regarding how the architect saw this problem. Frank Lloyd Wright might have grasped the potential in this problem when he stated that he found the pavilion fascinating but that only these columns irritated him.[3] For some time, walls and columns coexisted in the two realized houses mentioned above and in a series of exploratory court house projects that Mies produced from the end of his time in Germany through his early North American work. Even if he solved the practical problems of the pavilion, the dialectics of two elements remained: columns represented a basic systematic regularity, while walls represented spatial freedom. One may argue that this dialectic was what made these buildings exciting but from the pure viewpoint of critics considering structural logic, the ambiguity of the walls was never solved. For instance, the walls of the upper floor of the slightly later Tugendhat House contained steel structure at the request of the Tugendhats. In Mies's later North American works, furthermore, this dialectic was replaced by the dominance of columns. The flowing space that was preserved in the court house projects, if within the limit of the rectangular contours, was abandoned in later projects such as the Resor House (especially its idealized version used in publications), where the interiors were reduced to a single rectangular space and the walls did not extend to the ceiling. A flowing (irregular) space gave way to a rectangular (regular) space. The logic of the structural system and its correspondence with spatial limits (the envelope) reached their culmination in the Farnsworth House (1951). In this masterpiece, everything exists only for the epiphany of the single, simplest order.

Hajime Yatsuka, "Mies and Japan," *Cornell Journal of Architecture* 7 (2003): 52–62, https://issuu.com/cornellaap/docs/cja007-opt/9.

Hajime Yatsuka (*1948) is a Japanese architect and critic. He studied architecture at the University of Tokyo under Kenzō Tange and Sachio Ōtani. After graduation he worked for five years for Arata Isozaki and established his own office in Tokyo in 1984. He is a professor of architecture at the Shibaura Institute of Technology, a private university in Tokyo. In this important essay he takes on the comparison of Mies's work with traditional Japanese architecture, which emerged in descriptions of the Barcelona Pavilion early on (see text by Hans Bernoulli, p. 95–96) and later became more firmly established through writings by Ludwig Glaeser (p. 197) and Werner Blaser.[4] Yatsuka makes the important point that the ambiguity of structure at the Barcelona Pavilion, thanks to the late addition of the columns, makes it an unsuitable comparison, while his North American work, for instance the Farnsworth House, does indeed share a "common essence."

1   Editors' note: The imperial villa in Kyoto from the seventeenth century.
2   Editors' note: These drawings were made by Ruegenberg long after the fact, probably in the 1970s.
3   Editors' note: See text on page 129
4   Werner Blaser, *West Meets East: Mies van der Rohe* (Basel: Birkhäuser, 1996), 13–14.

2008

FUMIHIKO MAKI
Stillness and Plenitude: The Architecture of Yoshio Taniguchi

I happened to visit the reconstructed Barcelona Pavilion late in the fall of 1994. It was early afternoon on a clear day, and the strong sunlight endowed the elegant structure with a particularly crisp, sharp-edged quality. From the east, the pavilion was more extended longitudinally–perhaps I ought to say more imposing–than I had imagined. What was most impressive, however, was the materiality of the travertine that covered the plinth and the external walls. As the document concerning the reconstruction explains in detail, the matter over which Mies took the greatest pains in designing this building was the selection of the three varieties of marble, including the travertine, and the technical problems of their construction. It goes without saying that those who were in charge of the reconstruction were fully aware of the care Mies had taken, and took ample time and care in searching for and assembling marble that was close to the original. As a result, the structure, though a reconstruction, provides the same rich visual and tactile experience as the original pavilion. On closer examination, it becomes apparent that the impression of richness is not simply the effect of the color or texture of the travertine. For example, travertine is lavishly used in Lincoln

Center in New York, but the stone there has none of the sensuous quality of the stone in the Barcelona Pavilion. In Barcelona, the large units of marble, each measuring 2.2 meters wide and 3.1 meter high, and the geometrical rigor with which the units were treated, revealed to the world of the time an entirely new modernity. More than half a century later, even in a reconstructed state, the pavilion still creates in us a powerful impression. The report describes how, in the construction of the original pavilion, endless adjustments were made, such as shifting the dimensions of the floor marble by a few millimeters so as to match the joints created by the 2.2 by 1.1 meter marble units on the walls. Such accounts show that Mies considered the large travertine panels to be the thing that was to breathe life into the pavilion.

Fumihiko Maki, "Stillness and Plenitude: The Architecture of Yoshio Taniguchi," *Japan Architect*, no. 21 (Spring 1996), reprinted in Fumihiko Maki, *Nurturing Dreams: Collected Essays on Architecture and the City* (Cambridge, MA: MIT Press, 2008), 216-29.

Fumihiko Maki (*1928) is a Japanese architect who trained at the University of Tokyo, Cranbrook Academy, and the Harvard Graduate School of Design. He taught at Washington University in St. Louis and Keio University in Fujisawa. Together with Kiyonori Kikutake, Kisho Kurokawa, and others, he founded the Metabolism group in 1960. After working for Skidmore, Owings, and Merrill and Josep Lluís Sert in the US, he established his own office in 1965. He has designed museums, university buildings (such as the MIT Media Lab) and an expansion of the United Nations building in New York. In 1993 he received the Pritzker Prize for his work.

2010

AI WEIWEI
With Milk___find something everybody can use

Mies van der Rohe's Barcelona Pavilion stood in sight beyond all doubt. Its concrete materials weightless, barely held down to the ground. Stone and glass are nothing new to architecture, but now they are lenses and mirrors to see an enlightened age. The pools, blank, along with other highly polished surfaces, a timeless gaze reflecting everything else around, the building, the sky and the trees. This is a place only gods dwell.

Perhaps this view misinterprets Mies's work, it left out the modern dream of equality, as well as architecture of living, the need of every ordinary person. Speaking about design Mies frequently used expressions such as "general solutions" and "common language."

I approach Mies van der Rohe's Barcelona Pavilion as ready-made, the activities it experienced and the way it's been seen. The building is in fact not still, my intervention taps into the metabolism of a living machine. Liquid is being replaced because it is a part of the building that has always been replaced. Content in the two pools has in fact been replaced all the time, invisible to visitors. A pump recirculates water in the large outdoor pool, while the smaller pool is drained every two weeks, the bottom dark glass cleaned and the pool re-filled.

Regular work is done so the monument appears unchanged, stood against time; not to mention the entire building in existence is a perfect reconstruction. In the *With Milk__find something everybody can use* intervention, the underlayer of this monument surfaces and persists in consciousness; it refuses to be flushed away. Upkeeping the condition of milk and coffee is the same as to preserve a body, a demanding effort against light, air, warmth […] anything encourages growth and change. What is vigor of geometry, clarity of assembly and enlightened optimism combined with ordinary everyday life? Modernism, in correcting mistakes of the past, it might have made new mistakes. Today's cultural attitude is not minding mistakes, it is to go out and [be] unafraid of making another one.

Ai Weiwei, preface to *With Milk__find something everyone can use* (Barcelona: Actar / Fundacio Mies van der Rohe, 2009), 4–5.

Ai Weiwei (*1957) is a Chinese contemporary artist and activist. His installations often use ready-mades and engage political and social questions. In collaboration with architects such as Herzog & de Meuron, he has worked on the Olympic Stadium (2008) in Beijing and the Serpentine Pavilion (2012) in London. For his installation piece at the Barcelona Pavilion, he replaced the water in the two pools with coffee and milk, in order to demonstrate the continuous process of decay, which is part of the challenges of the pavilion's upkeep faced daily by the Mies van der Rohe Foundation.

2010

MARCO DE MICHELIS
The Smells of History

It is strange: to photograph again, half a century later, a building that had survived only in a few photographs, and be unable to find the smallest trace of the time that has elapsed, the wear and tear wrought by the passing of the years, the footsteps of the visitors, dust gathering in out-of-the-way corners, rust eating away at the chrome surfaces. Indeed: the colors, having transcended dichromaticism, shine for the first time with an intensity that is probably–though it is impossible to prove this–similar to that of the original, merging in the reflections and transparencies.

The rules of restoration and conservation prohibit such reconstructions. That said, in this case the reconstruction project has been an instrument of knowledge and constituted a critical dilemma powerful enough to justify any betrayal of orthodoxy. Not only that: much more than the photographic representations of the original, it is the physical experience of the space–even of the false space of the almost perfect imitation–that alone can enable us to understand how Mies van der Rohe managed to configure in this masterpiece of his that idea of the modern space that, from Gottfried Semper on, had been the most complex and the most distinctive goal and aspiration of modernity. In this space, Mies's cruciform

columns serve as the figures deployed in the foreground against which the gaze stumbles, while the walls—now walls of glass and shining marble—constitute the background on which the eye strives to recapture precisely that lost balance. [...]
Time leaves traces of its passage, those traces that modern materials like steel and glass tend to render barely visible, as Walter Benjamin and Ernst Bloch remarked many years ago: in those modernist houses it was "difficult" to leave a trace, but not impossible.[1] The traces were barely visible, but they were there. In the Mies Pavilion, the interruption of time, the long interval in which the work itself in its physicality had vanished, surviving only as an image, had erased the traces to the extent that the reconstructed work seems more "real" than its true representation in the period photographs.

Marco De Michelis, "The Smells of History," in *MUNTADAS: On Translation: PAPER/BP MVDR*, ed. Xavier Costa (Barcelona: Fundació Mies van der Rohe, 2010), 28–31.

Marco De Michelis (*1945) is professor of the history of architecture at the Faculty of Arts and Design at the University in Venice. He has published books on Heinrich Tessenow (1991), Walter Gropius (1983), the Bauhaus (1996), Luis Barragán (2000), and Enric Miralles (2002). From 1999 to 2003 he held the Walter Gropius Professorship for the history of architecture at the Bauhaus University in Weimar.

1   Editors' note: Marco De Michelis refers here to Walter Benjamin's essays "Experience and Poverty" and "Short Shadows (II)" (first published 1933) quoted from *Walter Benjamin, Selected Writings*, vol. 2, 1927–34, ed. Michael W. Jennings (Cambridge, MA: Harvard University Press, 1999), 699–702 and 731–36. The "new architects, with their glass and steel," Benjamin declared, "have created rooms in which it is hard to leave traces."

2014

CLAIRE ZIMMERMAN
Photographic Architecture in the Twentieth Century

Visual experience at the Barcelona Pavilion was calibrated by bodily experience carefully choreographed in the building's design. The architectural photographs correlate to this choreography well—not only do they allow the viewer to "walk through" the building, but they also show how particular moments in the plan might be considered visual opportunities, or three-dimensional pictures. In a plan of the pavilion that includes the station points for each photograph imposed over the circulation pattern of the building, directional changes coincide with the locations from which photographs were also made, with just one exception. The photographs thus reflect the plan strategies of the building. Whether the architects suggested these particular station points for the camera is not definitely known; in any case, these points appear as likely places from which to take pictures. As one mounts the stairs to the podium, for example, and turns to enter the building, one tends to pause at the entry to survey the space ahead. Here in 1929 the cameraman set up his machine and took a picture. [...] A plan laid out so clearly around a coordinated sequence of changing visual tableaux indicates the importance of pictorial concerns within design itself. [...] By "visual tableaux" I mean a place in the building that is framed or set up as an image, a kind of staging area that might prompt a moment of visual reckoning, causing the mover to pause, look, turn, and move on. While the photographs of the pavilion capture these image tableaux, which confronted the visitor at strategic moments, they do so only in part, as the reconstruction has shown. In contrast, the ways of moving through Mies's buildings seem somewhat static or overdetermined from the building's plans. But we might simply consider the seemingly exaggerated simplification of the plans in relation to the complexity created by the materials, their visual mutability, and their montage qualities. If the spatial choreographies are hieratic, excessively ritualized, and rhythmic, this is offset by visual abundance or complexity. A wider context develops these points in relation to photographic and architectural abstraction.

Claire Zimmerman, *Photographic Architecture in the Twentieth Century* (Minneapolis: University of Minnesota Press, 2014), 55–56, 58.

Claire Zimmerman is an architectural historian and professor at the Taubman College of the University of Michigan. Among her publications are *Photographic Architecture in the Twentieth Century* (2014), *Neo-avant-garde and Postmodern: Postwar Architecture in Britain and Beyond* (2010, edited with Mark Crinson), and *Ludwig Mies van der Rohe* (2006).

2014

DETLEF MERTINS
Mies

As [Hans] Richter was making Surrealist films such as his *Vormittagsspuk* (*Ghosts Before Breakfast*) of 1928, exploiting cinematic techniques to make fantasies and epiphanies part of everyday experience, Mies designed the Barcelona Pavilion to stage a similar *poiesis*. In the pavilion visitors could participate in a performance of self-estrangement and rediscovery on a higher plane, whereby essences could be apprehended directly through intuition. Stepping up onto the podium, visitors found themselves removed from the surrounding city, from their everyday lives, selves, and narratives. Unburdened, they were free to wander aimlessly and effortlessly in a rich and dazzling milieu of almost pure materiality. Transcendental and concrete, timeless and of its time, finite and infinite, the pavilion provided an immersive, labyrinthine environment without hierarchy, center, or end, a catalyst for opening perception and consciousness of mind to itself and Other. If Tafuri was right that the pavilion is an analogue of the fragmented, disoriented, and empty metropolis, it differs from the Dadaists' collages in that its parts have been mathematically purified into signs of essence, drained of any representational content other than their evidently engineered modernity. Visitors may experience themselves in a heightened state of awareness and anticipation—open to discovery and wonder, suspended between consciousness and sleep, clarity and delirium, liquefaction and crystallization, reality and sur-reality. And yet, nothing actually happens in the pavilion; nor are any specific insights gained. The pavilion does not offer didactic lessons or a blueprint for the future. It places the visitor in a perpetual motion that serves to figure a search without end. Yet this search was crucial, even structural—to the pursuit of an ethically lived life. For such a life does not have a determined content. Nor, as Augustine cautioned, can communication with God be hastened by attempting to purify oneself through one's own intellectual and moral powers, for which he criticized the neo-Platonists, but only by adapting to eternal things through temporal means already at hand. [...] Francesco Dal Co once eloquently alluded to Mies and his architecture as waiting for the self-actualization of being. Citing Nietzsche's observation that "a thought comes when it wishes, not when I wish," he inflected Tafuri's interpretation of the pavilion in terms of absence toward the positive moment of the event, understood as the becoming of being.

In launching confidence in man's ability to know and reach God, Augustine ultimately fueled the Reformation, the birth of modern science, and the development of technologies for mastering nature. [...] Augustine launched the modern subject precisely in trying to think through the idea in Scripture that to know God requires that one love God, but to love God requires that one know God. He called this a vicious circle. [...] By making transcendence and knowledge mutually dependent upon each other, what might be called the dialectic of revelation precludes any possible resolution. In harboring this *aporia*, Augustine's trinity of mind annuls precisely the resolution that it appeared to offer. The pavilion too harbors this *aporia* and consigns its visitors to an endless wandering in emptiness, striving for the impossible. Whether this enacts a negation and withdrawal of spirit, as Tafuri and [Massimo] Cacciari suggested, or the reaffirmation of eternal spiritual order, as [Fritz] Neumeyer proposed, may be a moot point. For these are ultimately two sides of the same coin. The great achievement of the pavilion is not that it resolved this *aporia* but that it staged it in a tangible new world-image—one with a strange new beauty, at once uplifting, hopeful, and melancholic.

Detlef Mertins, *Mies* (London: Phaidon, 2014), 165.

Detlef Mertins's book on Mies van der Rohe was finished posthumously by several of his colleagues (Barry Bergdoll, Ed Dimendberg, Keller Easterling, and Felicity Scott). While the section on the Barcelona Pavilion overlaps somewhat with Mertins's 2001 essay "Architectures of Becoming," it also differs significantly. In the earlier piece, following Manfredo Tafuri, Mies's connections with the Dada movement had played an important role, coupled with Mertins's Bergsonian reading of the material presence of the pavilion. In this chapter, written shortly before Mertins's death, the pavilion assumes an even more urgently spiritual and religious dimension.

2018

LANCE HOSEY
The Ship of Theseus

One of the most confounding puzzles of philosophy concerns the ship of Theseus. During its long voyages, the legendary Greek hero's vessel requires extensive repairs, and eventually every board and plank is replaced so that not a scrap of the original material remains. With its constitution completely changed, is it the same ship? [...]

Modern architecture's ship of Theseus is the Barcelona Pavilion. Built in 1929 and demolished in 1930, the pavilion was rebuilt with exacting quality and detail on the original site in 1986. Is it the "same" building? When the second pavilion appeared, architects, historians, and critics were deeply ambivalent. Some hailed it as a revived masterpiece, some condemned it as an impostor, and others confessed to be dumbfounded. [...] The apprehension is not easily explained. The similarities between the two pavilions far outnumber the differences, and the construction quality of the reconstruction is far superior to the hastily erected original. Yet, without much elaboration, many critics have rejected the second pavilion as inauthentic, even while lauding its meticulous execution. [...] Why the pavilion has inspired such doubt is an important question because it relates to the very definitions of architecture. What determines a building's identity—form, function, context, material, technique, or something else? [...] Although the original pavilion had been celebrated for its "expert craftsmanship," research prior to the reconstruction revealed that it had been a flimsy patchwork. On some surfaces, faux-painted stucco substituted for stone, and the plaster finish throughout the ceiling was inconsistent and splotchy. The pavilion was a pasteboard illusion, and the viewpoints, cropping, and airbrushing of the famous photographs masked its flaws. Even the Kolbe sculpture was plaster. For years, the travertine podium was thought to be continuous at the perimeter, partly because floor plans approved by Mies illustrated it as such, but in reality it was sheared off abruptly at the northeast corner. The canonical images and texts preserve a version of the pavilion that never existed: it was a mirage, a phantom of itself. [...]

The pavilion's relationship to the path of the sun has not been discussed thoroughly in the most widely read texts on the pavilion, possibly because pre-reconstruction reviewers and critics seemed not to know the structure's orientation. [...]

The original structure lasted through three seasons, from May through January, so days drew progressively shorter and the sun fell lower in the sky: by autumn, the long backdrop was dark by mid-morning. As a public stage set, it received frontal light only a fraction of the time, so most visitors' experiences would have been markedly different than the photographs capture.

The original pavilion was a theatrical prop, evidently intended to be seen only at certain times of day and year. In reality, it is a place defined by darkness as much as light.

The reconstruction allowed viewers to experience a broad range of light for the first time since 1930. In 1986, some of the first published images rendered it in softer tones, later in the day. Color alone must have been a shock to many readers. Could unfamiliar qualities of light have influenced judgments about authenticity?

Lance Hosey, "The Ship of Theseus: Identity and the Barcelona Pavilion(s)," *Journal of Architectural Education* (October 9, 2018): 230–47.

Lance Hosey was trained as an architect at Columbia and Yale and is now a principal and design director with Gensler. Previously he worked with William McDonough, Rafael Viñoly, and with Gwathmey Siegel in New York. He has published extensively on sustainable architecture. The excerpts here are from a lengthy article exploring the reception of the Pavilion's reconstruction and its representation in the media.

Endnotes Introduction

1   The most recent among those monographs being our companion volume: Dietrich Neumann with David Caralt, *An Accidental Masterpiece: Mies van der Rohe's German Pavilion in Barcelona 1929* (Basel: Birkhäuser, 2020).

2   Juan Pablo Bonta, *Anatomía de la interpretación en arquitectura* (Barcelona: Editorial Gustavo Gili, 1975), 78.

3   Charles Jencks, "Review of Juan Pablo Bonta, 'An Anatomy of Architectural Interpretations': A Semiotic Review of the Criticism of Mies van der Rohe's Barcelona Pavilion," *Journal of the Society of Architectural Historians* 35, no. 3 (October 1976): 226-27. Jencks's own essay, "History as Myth," anticipated some of Bonta's arguments. See Charles Jencks, "History as Myth," in *Meaning in Architecture*, ed. Charles Jencks and George Baird (London: Barrie & Jenkins, 1969), 245-65. Four years later, Bonta published an expanded version of his text, in which he demonstrated his phases of canon formation on other examples and streamlined his own categories; see Juan Pablo Bonta, *Architecture and Its Interpretation* (London: Lund Humphries, 1979). Bonta's work was subsequently complemented by Ignasi de Solà-Morales (1993), George Dodds (2001), Sarah Williams Goldhagen (2005), Detlef Mertins (2014), Lance Hosey (2018; see note 97) and others (See p. 296, 303, 328, 332). See Ignasi de Solà-Morales, Cristian Cirici, and Fernando Ramos, *Mies van der Rohe: El Pabellón de Barcelona* (Barcelona: Gustavo Gili, 1993; reprint by Fundació Mies van der Rohe, 2019; translated as *Mies van der Rohe: Barcelona Pavilion* [Barcelona: Editorial Gustavo Gili, 2000]), 68-71; George Dodds, *Building Desire: On the Barcelona Pavilion* (London: Routledge, 2005); Sarah Williams Goldhagen, "Something to Talk About: Modernism, Discourse, Style," *Journal of the Society of Architectural Historians* 64, no. 2 (June 2005): 144-67; and Detlef Mertins, *Mies* (London: Phaidon, 2014), 146-49.

4   Bonta's claim that the pavilion was noticed by all but a handful of visitors at the fair is probably true, but, thanks to Sasha Stone's photographs, its critical reception in international magazines was much wider, diverse, and contradictory than Bonta assumed.

5   Rafael Moneo, introduction to *Fear of Glass: Mies van der Rohe's Pavilion in Barcelona*, by Josep Quetglas (Basel: Birkhäuser, 2001): 9-13. See also William J. R. Curtis, *Modern Architecture since 1900* (London: Phaidon, 1996), 271ff.

6   The Exposition administration published the *Diario Oficial de la Exposición Internacional Barcelona 1929*, a weekly forty-page journal about current activities. The first issue appeared on April 21, 1929, and the last (no. 45), on January 11, 1930. From no. 46 (January 18, 1930) on, the publication was renamed *Exposición de Barcelona 1930: Diario Oficial*. For early newspaper coverage, see, for example, "Solemne inauguración de los parbellones de Alemania," *ABC*, May 28, 1929 (morning edition), 24, which contained the complete text of von Schnitzler's speech and a detailed description of the royal visit in the different German sections; and "Los Reyes e Infantes en la Exposición: Inauguración del Pabellón de Alemania," *La Vanguardia*, May 28, 1929, 11.

7   The text of von Schnitzler's speech is confirmed by its reprint in the "official diary" of the exhibition: "Inauguración del Pabellón y Sección de Alemania," *Diario Oficial de la Exposición Internacional Barcelona 1929*, no. 12 (June 2, 1929). Similar accounts, only slightly shorter, had already appeared in Spanish newspapers, such as "Los Reyes e Infantes en la Exposición" (see note 6). (See p. 36).

8   Lengthy reviews of the pavilion appeared in most of these publications, such as *Baugilde*, *Baumeister*, *Deutsche Bauzeitung*, *Die Form*, *Kunst und Künstler*, *Stein Holz Eisen*, and *Zentralblatt der Bauverwaltung*. There were also a few glaring lacunae—the conservative publications *Wasmuths Monatshefte für Baukunst* and *Deutsches Bauwesen* ignored the events in Barcelona altogether. The popular weekly *Bauwelt* merely showed a photograph of Mies's

pavilion, but had no comments; see "Deutscher Pavillon in Barcelona," *Bauwelt* 20, no. 29 (July 18, 1929): 665.

9   Jeanne Bailhache, "Deutschland auf der Internationalen Ausstellung in Barcelona," *Frankfurter Nachrichten*, June 2, 1929.

10   Walther Genzmer, "Der Deutsche Reichspavillon auf der Internationalen Ausstellung in Barcelona," *Die Baugilde* 11, no. 20 (October 1929): 1654-55. (See p. 72, 75).

11   Justus Bier, "Mies van der Rohes Reichspavilion in Barcelona," *Die Form: Zeitschrift für gestaltende Arbeit* 16, no. 4 (August 15, 1929): 423-30. (See p. 66).

12   Vs., "Der Pavillon des Deutschen Reiches auf der Ausstellung in Barcelona: Architekt Ludwig Mies van der Rohe," *Stein Holz Eisen* (September 26, 1929): 609-13. See also Francisco Marroquin, "Hacia una nueva arquitectura: El Pabellón de Alemania en la Exposicion de Barcelona," *ABC*, January 26, 1930, 13-14. (See p. 104).

13   Nicolas M. Rubió i Tudurí, "Le Pavillon de l'Allemagne à l'Exposition de Barcelone par Mies van der Rohe," *Cahiers d'art*, nos. 8/9 (1929): 408-11. (See p. 78).

14   "Der deutsche Pavillon auf der Ausstellung in Barcelona," *Rheinisch-Westfälische Zeitung* (Essen), August 18, 1929.

15   Guido Harbers, "Deutscher Reichspavillon in Barcelona auf der Internationalen Ausstellung 1929," *Der Baumeister* 27, no. 11 (November 1929): 421-27. (See p. 127).

16   See Genzmer, "Der Deutsche Reichspavillon" (see note10). (See p. 72, 75).

17   L.S.M. (Lilly von Schnitzler), "Weltausstellung Barcelona," *Europäische Revue* 5, no. 4 (July 1929): 286-88. (See p. 63).

18   Bier, "Mies van der Rohes Reichspavilion in Barcelona," 423 (see note 11). (See p. 66).

19   See the observations of the Italian and French architects Rava and Rubió i Tudurí or the Spanish journalists Sanz Balza and Sagarra: Carlo Enrico Rava, "Necessitá di Selezione: Parte Prima," *Domus* (1931): 36-40, 84; Rubió i Tudurí, "Le Pavillon de l'Allemagne" (see note 13); Eliseo Sanz Balza, *Notas de un visitante: Exposición Internacional de Barcelona 1929* (Barcelona: Tip. Olympia, P. Yuste, 1930), 140, 145; and Josep Maria de Sagarra, "Mabre y cristall," *Mirador* 1, no. 20 (June 13, 1929): 2. (See p. 58, 78, 109, 122).

20   Ángel Marsà and Luis Marsillach, *La montaña Iluminada: Itinerario espiritual de la Exposición de Barcelona 1929-1930* (Barcelona: Ed. Horizonte, 1930), 11, 14. (See p. 107).

21   Heinrich Wölfflin, *Renaissance und Barock: Eine Untersuchung über Wesen und Entstehung des Barockstils in Italien* (Munich: Theodor Ackermann, 1888), 18, 40, 52.

22   August Schmarsow, *Empathy, Form, and Space: Problems in German Aesthetics, 1873-1893*, trans. and with an introduction by Harry Francis Mallgrave and Eleftherios Ikonomou (Santa Monica: Getty Center for the History of Art and the Humanities, 1994), 291, 292. Originally published as *Das Wesen der architektonischen Schöpfung* (Leipzig: Hiersemann, 1894).

23   Paul Frankl, *Principles of Architectural History*, trans. J. F. O'Gorman (Cambridge, MA: MIT Press, 1968), 148. Originally published as *Die Entwicklungsphasen der neueren Baukunst* (Leipzig: Teubner, 1914). While the English translation uses the term *flow*, the German text employs different, but similarly liquid notions of flooding, streaming, and heaving (*Fluten, umfluted, durchströmt, wogend*).

24   Ibid., 46.

25   J. J. P. Oud, "Architectural Observations Concerning Wright and the Robie House," *De Stijl* 1, no. 4 (1918): 39-41, reprinted in *Writings on Wright: Selected Comment on Frank Lloyd Wright*, ed. H. Allen Brooks (Cambridge, MA: MIT Press, 1983), 135-37. See also Adolf Behne, *The Modern Functional Building* (Santa Monica: Getty Research Institute, 1996), 99. Originally published as *Der Moderne Zweckbau* (Munich: Drei Masken, 1923).

26   Gustav Adolf Platz, *Die Baukunst der Neuesten Zeit*, 2nd ed. (Berlin: Propyläen Verlag, 1930), 80-81. (See p. 114).

27   Arthur Stanley Eddington, *Raum, Zeit und Schwere* (Braunschweig: Vieweg + Teubner, 1923), 114-25. Originally published as *Space, Time and Gravitation: An Outline of the General Relativity Theory* (Cambridge: Cambridge University Press, 1920).

28 The mathematician Hermann Minkowski had first published this idea in his 1908 lecture "Raum und Zeit" (Space and Time), which provided the basis for the general theory of relativity of his former pupil Albert Einstein in 1915. In an attempt to explain his complex model to the general public, Minkowski had written: "Henceforth space by itself, and time by itself, are doomed to fade away into mere shadows, and only a kind of union of the two will preserve an independent reality. […] No one has ever noticed a place unless at a certain time, neither a time without a distinct place." Hermann Minkowski, "Raum und Zeit," in Hendrik Anton Lorentz, Albert Einstein, and Hermann Minkowski, *Das Relativitätsprinzip 1913* (Leipzig: Teubner, 1915), 57.

29 Hamburg's chief planning director Fritz Schumacher wrote: "As a result of our movement the notion of space is joined by the notion of time. […] The essence of architectural impact reaches into the fourth dimension, now commonplace thanks to the theory of relativity, which draws its scientific conclusions from the fact that all observations and events are bound by time." Fritz Schumacher, "Die Zeitgebundenheit der Architektur," *Deutsches Bauwesen* 5, no. 16 (1929): 238-43. See also Paul Zucker, "Der Begriff der Zeit in der Architektur," *Repertorium für Kunstwissenschaft* 44 (1924), 237-45, reprinted in *Architektur, Raum, Theorie: Eine kommentierte Anthologie*, ed. Andreas Denk, Uwe Schröder, and Rainer Schützeichel (Tübingen: Ernst Wasmuth Verlag, 2016), 301-11. Dutch architect Theo van Doesburg similarly declared: "The new architecture calculates not only with space but also with time as an architectural value. The unity of space and time will give architectural form a new and completely plastic aspect, that is, a four-dimensional, plastic space-time aspect." Theo van Doesburg, "Towards Plastic Architecture" (1924), in Joost Baljeu, *Theo van Doesburg* (New York: Macmillan, 1974), 144. See also John G. Hatch, "Some Adaptations of Relativity in the 1920s and the Birth of Abstract Architecture," *Nexus Network Journal* 12 (2010): 131-47 (published online February 9, 2010); and Linda Dalrymple Henderson, *The Fourth Dimension and Non-Euclidean Geometry in Modern Art* (Cambridge, MA: MIT Press, 2013). Van Doesburg titled several of his colorful axonometrics "Space-Time Constructions." See Els Hoek, *Theo van Doesburg oeuvre catalogus* (Utrecht: Centraal Museum, 2000), 370.

30 Walter Riezler, "Das neue Raumgefühl in bildender Kunst und Musik (1930)," *Zeitschrift für Ästhetik und allgemeine Kunstwissenschaft*, no. 1 (1931): 179-216. See also George Howe, "Abstract Design in Modern Architecture," lecture at the Annual Meeting of the College Art Association, *Parnassus* 8, no. 5 (October 1936): 29-31. (See texts p. 119, 132).

31 See Harbers, "Deutscher Reichspavillon in Barcelona" (see note 15); and Bier, "Mies van der Rohes Reichspavilion in Barcelona" (see note 11). (See p. 66, 127).

32 See Marroquin, "Hacia una nueva arquitectura" (see note 12); and Rubió i Tudurí, "Le Pavillon de l'Allemagne" (see note 13). (See p. 78, 104).

33 Gustav Edmund Pazaurek, "Ist der Werkbund auf dem richtigen Wege?," *Münchner Neueste Nachrichten*, November 12, 1930, 1. (See p. 102).

34 Eduard Foertsch, "Die Weltausstellung in Barcelona," *Vossische Zeitung*, June 11, 1929, 4. (See p. 56).

35 Bonaventura Bassegoda, "En la Exposición: Más pabellones extranjeros," *La Vanguardia*, October 31, 1929, 5. Alfredo Baeschlin, a Swiss architect, painter, and poet who lived in Spain, similarly feared that a visitor would stand "perplexed" in front of it, wondering "if he is looking at a building that is still being assembled." Alfredo Baeschlin, "Barcelona und seine Weltausstellung," *Deutsche Bauzeitung* 63, no. 57 (1929): 497-504, no. 77, 657-62. (See p. 81, 89).

36 Leberecht Migge, "Warum die (Kultur) Welt den Deutschen Pavillon nicht frisst," private correspondence, 20 November 1929, Thomas Elsaesser Archive. (See p. 93).

37 Elisabeth Elsaesser, private correspondence, Martin Elsaesser Stiftung, Frankfurt. I would like to thank Professor Thomas Elsaesser, Amsterdam, for sharing this text with me.

38 Wilhelm Hack, "Das Wunder der Ausstellung," *Deutsche Tageszeitung*, June 11, 1929.

39 Lenore Kühn, "Deutsche Arbeit auf der Internationalen Ausstellung in Barcelona," *Der Auslandsdeutsche* (June 1929): 400-402. (See p. 66).

40 Bier, "Mies van der Rohes Reichspavilion in Barcelona," 423 (see note 11).

41 Ernst Runge, "Die Baukunst am Scheidewege?" *Deutsches Bauwesen* 6, no. 4 (April 1930): 80-81.

42 "Deutsche Kunstausstellungen im Ausland und Deutscher Werkbund," *Die Baukultur* 3, no. 2 (January 17, 1931): 1.

43 Karel Teige, *The Minimum Dwelling*, trans. and with an introduction by Eric Dluhosch (Cambridge, MA: MIT Press, 2002), 197. Originally published as *Nejmenši byt* (Prague: Václav Petr, 1932).

44 Adolf Behne, "Abteilung 'Die Wohnung unserer Zeit,'" *Zentralblatt der Bauverwaltung* 51, nos. 49/50 (1931): 733-35. Behne had previously been supportive of Mies and included his Concrete Office Building in his 1926 publication *Der moderne Zweckbau*. G. Wolf, *Zeitschrift für Wohnungswesen*, quoted in Friedrich Tamms, "Die Deutsche Bauaustellung 1931 im Spiegel der Presse," *Die Baugilde* 13, no. 18 (1931): 1442.

45 Justus Bier, "Kann man im Haus Tugendhat wohnen?" *Die Form* 6, no. 10 (October 1931): 392-93.

46 Elizabeth Gordon, "The Threat to the Next America," *House Beautiful* (April 1953), reprinted in Alice T. Friedman, *Women and the Making of the Modern House* (New York: Abrams,1998), 141.

47 Vincent J. Scully, Jr. "Wright vs. the International Style," *Art News* 53 (March 1954): 32-35, 64-66, reprinted in Scully, *Modern Architecture and Other Essays*, ed. Neil Levine (Princeton: Princeton University Press, 2003), 54; see also "The Wright-International Style Controversy," *Art News* 53 (September 1954): 48-49.

48 Vincent J. Scully, Jr., *The Shingle Style* (New Haven: Yale University Press, 1955), quoted in Scully, *The Shingle Style and the Stick Style: Architectural Theory and Design from Downing to the Origins of Wright*, rev. ed. (New Haven: Yale University Press, 1971), 99, 121, 123, 127, 133.

49 Henry-Russell Hitchcock, *Architecture: Nineteenth and Twentieth Centuries* (Harmondsworth: Penguin Books, 1958), 376.

50 Franz Schulze, *Mies van der Rohe: A Critical Biography* (Chicago: University of Chicago Press, 1985), 290-91. (See p. 224).

51 William H. Jordy, *American Buildings and Their Architects*, vol. 5 (Oxford: Oxford University Press, 1972), 148-49. (See p. 187).

52 Kenneth Frampton, "Modernism and Tradition in the Work of Mies van der Rohe, 1920-1968," in *Mies Reconsidered: His Career, Legacy, and Disciples*, ed. John Zukowsky (Chicago: Art Institute of Chicago; New York: Rizzoli International, 1986), 35-53. (See p. 264).

53 Vincent J. Scully, Jr., *Modern Architecture: The Architecture of Democracy* (New York: George Braziller, 1961), 27. (See p. 172).

54 There was one exception: conservative critic Guido Harbers acknowledged that while there were "no formal similarities, [...] the attitude to building and the respect for the material" could be compared to "that of classical antiquity." See Harbers, "Deutscher Reichspavillon in Barcelona" (see note 15). (See p. 127).

55 Colin Rowe, "Neo-Classicism and Modern Architecture" (1956-57), in Rowe, *The Mathematics of the Ideal Villa and Other Essays* (Cambridge, MA: MIT Press, 1976), 119-58.

56 Arthur Drexler, *Ludwig Mies van der Rohe* (New York: George Braziller, 1960), 19. (See p. 157).

57 Hitchcock, *Architecture*, 376 (see note 49). (See p. 153).

58 Ulrich Conrads, "Von ausgestellten Bauten zu Ausstellungsbauten," *Bauwelt* 48, no. 31 (August 5, 1957): 777. (See p. 146).

59 Hitchcock, *Architecture*, 376 (see note 49). (See p. 153).

60 Scully, *Modern Architecture*, 27 (see note 53). (See p. 172)

61 Drexler, *Ludwig Mies van der Rohe*, 19 (see note 56). (See p. 157).

62   James Marston Fitch, "Mies van der Rohe and the Platonic Verities," in *Four Great Makers of Modern Architecture: Gropius, Le Corbusier, Mies van der Rohe, Wright*, Architecture and Decorative Art 37 (New York: Da Capo Press, 1963), 154–63. (See p. 174).

63   Drexler, *Ludwig Mies van der Rohe*, 19–20(see note 56). (See p. 157).

64   Frank Lloyd Wright to Philip Johnson, 26 February 1932, fiche #M029B03, Frank Lloyd Wright Archive, Avery Library Columbia University, New York. (See p. 129).

65   Drexler, *Ludwig Mies van der Rohe*, 19–20 (see note 56). (See p. 157).

66   Peter Eisenman, "miMISes READING: does not mean A THING," in Zukowsky, *Mies Reconsidered*, 86–98 (see note 52). See also Mertins, *Mies*, 152 (see note 3). Mertins was (wrongly) convinced that "cruciform columns are prone to twisting under loads," proof in his eyes that they were not load-bearing. Cruciform columns, in particular the one employed here, namely four rolled iron posts in L-form bolted together, are an exceedingly strong structural element. They were frequently recommended in construction manuals at the time. See C. Kersten, *Der Eisenhochbau* (Berlin: Wilhelm Ernst & Sohn, 1920), 108. (See p. 259, 305).

67   Sandra Honey, "Mies in Germany," in Honey, *Mies van der Rohe: European Works* (London, New York: Academy Editions, St. Martin's Press, 1986), 11–25.

68   Robin Evans, "Mies van der Rohe's Paradoxical Symmetries," *AA Files* 19 (1990), 56–68, here 65. (See p. 289).

69   "Der Skelettbau ist keine Teigware: Sergius Ruegenberg berichtet von Mies van der Rohes Berliner Zeit," *Bauwelt* (1986): 346–51, here 350. In his notes, Ruegenberg stressed the fact that the columns were nickel-plated, not chrome, which was not yet available. Sergius Ruegenberg, "Worte: Mies van der Rohe zum Barcelona Pavilion," undated manuscript (ca. 1969), Ruegenberg Papers, Berlinische Galerie, Berlin. See also Bruno Reichlin, "Conjectures à propos des colonnes réfléchissantes de Mies van der Rohe," in *La Colonne Nouvelle histoire de la construction*, ed. Robert Gargiani (Lausanne: Presses polytechniques et universitaires romandes, 2008), 454–66. (See p. 248).

70   Reyner Banham, *Theory and Design in the First Machine Age* (London: Architectural Press, 1960), 321–23. (See p. 168).

71   Robert Rosenblum, "Castelli Group," *Arts Magazine* 3, no. 8 (May 1957): 33.

72   Robert Venturi, *Complexity and Contradiction in Architecture* (New York: Museum of Modern Art, 1966), 56. (See p. 177).

73   See Jencks and Baird, *Meaning in Architecture* (see note 3).

74   Geoffrey Broadbent, "On Reading Architectural Space," *Espaces et Sociétés* 47 (1985): 99–143. (See p. 221).

75   See Jencks, "History as Myth" (see note 3).

76   Charles Jencks, *Modern Movements in Architecture* (New York: Anchor Press, 1973), 95–96.

77   Charles Jencks, *The Language of Post-Modern Architecture* (London: Academy Editions, 1977), 14–17.

78   Giovanni Klaus Koenig, "Gropius or Mies," *Casabella* (November 1969): 34–39. (See p. 182).

79   Renato Nicolini, "Mies, l'epilogo," *Controspazio* 2, nos. 4–5 (April-May 1970): 92–95.

80   Manfredo Tafuri, *The Sphere and the Labyrinth: Avant-Gardes and Architecture from Piranesi to the 1970s* (Cambridge, MA: MIT Press, 1987), 111. Spanish writers Ángel Marsà and Luis Marsillach were the first to describe the pavilion as a "labyrinth" due to its countless reflections in 1929. See Marsà and Marsillach, *La montaña iluminada*, 11, 14 (see note 20). (See p. 107, 203).

81   Kurt W. Forster, "No Escape from History, No Reprieve from Utopia, No Nothing: An Addio to the Anxious Historian Manfredo Tafuri," *Any* 25/26 (2000): 62.

82   Massimo Cacciari, "Eupalinos or Architecture," *Oppositions* 21 (Summer 1980): 106–16. Marco de Michelis, another Venetian scholar, would present a similar argument in an essay about the pavilion's reconstruction in 2010 (see note 113). (See p. 287, 324).

83 Roberto Segre, *Historia de la Arquitectura y del Urbanismo: Paises Desarrollados, Siglos XIX y XX* (Madrid: Instituto de Estudios de Administracion Local, 1985), 185–86. The same text appeared in Roberto Segre, *Arquitectura y Urbanismo Modernos: Capitalismo y Socialismo* (Havana: Editorial Arte y Literatura, 1988), 184–85. (See p. 233).

84 Manfredo Tafuri and Francesco Dal Co, *Modern Architecture*, trans. Robert Erich Wolf (New York: Harry N. Abrams, 1979), 155. (See p. 193).

85 Josep Quetglas, "Fear of Glass: The Barcelona Pavilion," in *Architectureproduction*, ed. Beatriz Colomina (New York: Princeton Architectural Press, 1988), 123–51. (See p. 206, 241, 284).

86 K. Michael Hays, "Critical Architecture: Between Culture and Form," *Perspecta* 21 (1984): 24. (See p. 218).

87 Peter Carter, *Mies van der Rohe at Work* (New York: Praeger, 1974), 24.

88 Rosalind Krauss, "The Grid, the Cloud, and the Detail," in *The Presence of Mies*, ed. Detlef Mertins (New York: Princeton Architectural Press, 1994), 133–47. (See p. 298).

89 Christian Norberg-Schulz, *Casa Tugendhat*, Architettura/Documenti 5 (Rome: Officina, 1984), quoted in Christian Norberg-Schulz, *Architecture: Meaning and Place: Selected Essays* (New York: Electa/Rizzoli, 1988), 153.

90 Paul Gapp, "The Pavilion Overcomes Its Demise," *Chicago Tribune*, April 4, 1986, N1, 3.

91 Robert A. M. Stern, "New Directions in American Architecture," *Architectural Association Quarterly* 9, nos. 2 and 3 (1977): 66–71, reprinted in Kate Nesbitt, *Theorizing a New Agenda for Architecture: An Anthology of Architectural Theory 1965–1995* (New York: Princeton Architectural Press, 1996), 100–108.

92 Michael Graves, "A Case for Figurative Architecture," in *Michael Graves: Buildings and Projects 1966–1981*, ed. Karen Vogel Wheeler, Peter Arnell, and Ted Bickford (New York: Rizzoli, 1982), 11–13, reprinted in Nesbitt, *Theorizing a New Agenda*, 86–90 (see note 91). (See p. 213).

93 Hubert Damisch, "The Slightest Difference: Mies van der Rohe and the Reconstruction of the Barcelona Pavilion," in *Noah's Ark: Essays on Architecture*, ed. Anthony Vidler (Cambridge, MA: MIT Press, 2016), 212–28, here 226. This view of authenticity can be traced back to John Ruskin, who found it "impossible […] to restore anything that has ever been great or beautiful in architecture," as the spirit of the original workmen was missing. "And as for direct and simple copying, it is palpably impossible." John Ruskin, *The Seven Lamps of Architecture* (New York: Wiley & Halsted, 1857), 161. Austrian art historian Max Dvorak similarly declared in 1918 that "a reconstruction could never replace what was lost […] because an imitation simply can never replace the original." Max Dvorák, *Katechismus der Denkmalpflege* (Vienna: Anton Schroll, 1918), 29. (See p. 281).

94 Jonathan Hill, "Institutions of Architecture," in *Offramp* 1, no. 7, *Detours + Dialogues* (2000): 72ff.

95 Solà-Morales, Cirici, and Ramos, *Mies van der Rohe*, 39 (see note 3). (See p. 296).

96 Dodds, *Building Desire*, x (see note 3). (See p. 303).

97 Lance Hosey, "The Ship of Theseus: Identity and the Barcelona Pavilion(s)," *Journal of Architectural Education* 72, no. 2 (October 2018): 230–47.

98 The architects of the reconstruction had already used a similar metaphor when pointing out that their work was that of a "conductor […] interpreting the composition of another composer." Solà-Morales, Cirici, and Ramos, *Mies van der Rohe*, 45 (see note 3). See also Maurice Lagueux, "Nelson Goodman and Architecture," *Assemblage* 35 (1998): 18–35.

99 Dennis L. Dollens, "Less is More Again," *Sites* 15 (1986): 35.

100 Max Bächer, "Barcelona Pavilion, Sagrada Familia: Original, Kopie oder Nachahmung?" *Bauwelt* 19 (1989): 850–53.

101 Rem Koolhaas, "Miesverständnisse," *Arch+* 161 (June 2002): 78–83.

102 Walter Benjamin, "The Work of Art in the Age of its Reproducibility," in Benjamin, *Selected Writings*, vol. 3, *1935–1938*, ed. Howard Eiland and Michael W. Jennings (Cambridge, MA: Harvard University Press, 2002), 101–33.

103 Warren A. James, "Barcelona: Reconstruction of the Barcelona Pavilion," *Progressive Architecture* 67 (August 1986): 62.

104 Alison Smithson, *La Vanguardia*, November 15, 1985, 44.

105 Peter Smithson, "All That Travertine (April 1986)," in Alison and Peter Smithson, *Changing the Art of Inhabitation* (London: Artemis, 1994), 39.

106 Christine Conley, "Morning Cleaning: Jeff Wall and the Large Glass," *Art History* 32, no. 5 (December 2009): 996-1015.

107 See Josep Quetglas, "Del pabellón de Mies al Pabellón del Patronato," *Diseño*, no. 73 (1986), reprinted in *Artículos de ocasión* (Barcelona: Editorial Gustavo Gili, 2004), 71-76; and Quetglas, "Du Pavillon de Mies au Pavillon de la Fondation Mies," *Criticat*, no. 5 (March 2010): 84-91, https://issuu.com/criticat/docs/criticat05/93.

108 Benjamin, "The Work of Art in the Age of its Reproducibility" (see note 102).

109 Ita Heinze-Greenberg made exactly this point when she celebrated the liberation from the "internationally equalized conditioning" of the pavilion's reception via those photographs. Ita Heinze-Greenberg, "Barcelona Pavillon," in *Geschichte der Rekonstruktion, Rekonstruktion der Geschichte*, ed. Winfried Nerdinger (Munich: Prestel, 2010), 359-60.

110 Evans, "Mies van der Rohe's Paradoxical Symmetries," 67 (see note 68).

111 Jean-Louis Cohen, *Ludwig Mies van der Rohe* (Basel: Birkhäuser, 2007), 64.

112 Barry Bergdoll, in *Mies on Scene: Barcelona in Two Acts*, directed by Xavi Campreciós and Pep Martín (Barcelona: Fundació Mies van der Rohe and Nihao Films, 2018).

113 See, for example, Martin Filler, "Barcelona Reborn," *House & Garden* (December 1986): 150-52, 216-20; Fumihiko Maki, "Stillness and Plenitude: The Architecture of Yoshio Taniguchi," *Japan Architect*, no. 21 (Spring 1996), reprinted in Maki, *Nurturing Dreams: Collected Essays on Architecture and the City*, ed. Mark Mulligan (Cambridge, MA: MIT Press, 2008), 216-29; Donald Dunham, "Beyond the Red Curtain: Less is More Utopia," *Utopian Studies* 25, no. 1 (2014): 150-73, here 170; Derek Sayer, "The Unbearable Lightness of Building: A Cautionary Tale," *Grey Room* 16 (Summer 2004): 6-35; Damisch, "The Slightest Difference" (see note 93); and Marco de Michelis, "The Smells of History," in *MUNTADAS: On Translation: PAPER/BP MVDR*, ed. Xavier Costa (Barcelona: Fundació Mies van der Rohe, 2010), 28-31.

114 Alison Smithson, "'Mies's Barcelona Pavilion: Myth and Reality,' extracts from a lecture, Barcelona 1986," in Smithson and Smithson, *Changing the Art of Inhabitation*, 35n39 (see note 105).

115 Wolf Tegethoff, "From Obscurity to Maturity: Mies van der Rohe's Breakthrough to Modernism," in Zukowsky, *Mies Reconsidered*, 28-94, here 87 (see note 52).

116 Peter Blake, "Afterword: Conversation at 23 Beekman Place: Interview with Paul Rudolph" (1996), in *Paul Rudolph: The Late Work*, by Roberto de Alba (New York: Princeton Architectural Press, 2003): 203-17.

117 Hays, "Critical Architecture" (see note 86).

118 Evans, "Mies van der Rohe's Paradoxical Symmetries," 65 (see note 68).

119 Eisenman, "miMISes READING," 93 (see note 66).

120 Toyo Ito, "Tarzans in the Media Forest," *2G*, 2 (January 1997): 121-44.

121 Koolhaas, "Miesverständnisse" (see note 101).

122 Frank Gehry, in "Tectonic Arts: Frank Gehry Talks with Julian Rose," *Art Forum* (May 2018): 215. Of course, as pointed out, there are no surviving structural drawings of the pavilion, but in any event, the photographs of the building under construction show very clearly that the columns do carry the roof structure.

123 Paul Rudolph, a practicing architect, is one of the rare exceptions: "Mies really wasn't able to make up his mind about a lot of things," he said about the Barcelona Pavilion. See Blake, "Afterword" (see note 116).

124 Werner Hegemann, "Holland, Wright, Breslau," *Wasmuths Monatshefte für Baukunst* 9, no. 4 (1925): 165-67.

125 Tim Gough, "Reception Theory of Architecture: Its Pre-History and Afterlife," *Architectural Theory Review* 18, no. 3 (2013): 279–92.

126 Paul de Man, introduction to *Toward an Aesthetic of Reception*, by Hans Robert Jauss (Minneapolis: University of Minnesota Press, 1982), xx–xxii.

127 Naomi Stead and Cristina Garduño Freeman, "Architecture and the Act of Receiving, or the Fact of Being Received: Introduction to a Special Issue on Reception," *Architectural Theory Review* 18, no. 3 (2013): 267–71. The authors conceded, though, that thanks to the work of Beatriz Colomina, Kester Rattenbury, and others, at least architecture's "close, even dependent relationship with media […] throughout the modern period" has become widely accepted.

128 Goldhagen, "Something to Talk About" (see note 3).

129 Moneo, introduction to Quetglas, *Fear of Glass* (see note 5).

130 Elliott J. Gorn, "Professing History: Distinguishing between Memory and the Past," *The Chronicle of Higher Education*, April 28, 2000, http://www.history.ucsb.edu/faculty/ marcuse/projects/reception/ReceptHistGornCHE004.htm.

131 Henry James, *The American Scene* (London: Chapman & Hall, 1907), 182.

132 Nelson Goodman, "How Buildings Mean," *Critical Inquiry* 11, no. 4 (June 1985): 642–53.

Translation into English
Dietrich Neumann

Copy-editing
Keonaona Peterson

Project management
Annette Gref, Katharina Kulke

Production
Amelie Solbrig

Layout, cover design
Séverine Mailler

Typesetting
Miriam Bussmann

Paper
Amber Grapic, 120 g/m²

Printing
Beltz Grafische Betriebe GmbH, Bad Langensalza

Lithography
LVD Gesellschaft für Datenverarbeitung mbH, Berlin

Library of Congress Control Number: 2020949492

Bibliographic information published by the German National Library
The German National Library lists this publication in the Deutsche Nationalbibliografie;
detailed bibliographic data are available on the Internet at http://dnb.dnb.de.

ISBN 978-3-0356-1985-0
e-ISBN (PDF) 978-3-0356-1993-5

German Print-ISBN 978-3-0356-1980-5

© 2021 Birkhäuser Verlag GmbH, Basel
P.O. Box 44, 4009 Basel, Switzerland
Part of Walter de Gruyter GmbH, Berlin/Boston

9 8 7 6 5 4 3 2 1
www.birkhauser.com